MW01483511

With illustrations

Andrew Sav

Walking Home

2000 km in 80 days

The adventures of three Aussie friends
walking from Cairns to Stanthorpe

Published by
L & R Morgan

This first edition published 2016
by L&R Morgan, Melbourne, Australia

ISBN: 978-0-9875792-1-8

Printed by Lightning Source
at one of their global locations

Is this book for you?

How many of these boxes do you tick?

❑ Young

❑ Aussie

❑ Christian

❑ Guy

If you tick any **one** of these boxes, then welcome aboard – you'll enjoy the read.

If you tick **two** or **three** of them, then I wrote this book thinking of YOU.

And if you tick all **four**, drop everything and get into it. Walk with me!

Foreword

This book is my story.

It recounts the dream behind this crazy adventure of walking 2000 kilometres and the physical and psychological pain I went through as it became a reality. It also recounts the kaleidoscope of weird and wonderful people I met.

I didn't walk alone. Dave and Carnsey shared those kilometres with me. However, while they are a huge part of my story, this is not their story. Even though we shared the same set of experiences, their stories would be told quite differently.

Many hundreds of other people are also part of this story – those who were involved in organising aspects of The 2000 Walk. A few will actually find themselves in these pages. However, if I included everyone, this book would end up reading like a telephone directory. And nobody would want to read that.

All people, places, languages and events are real, of course, and most are represented by their real names. A few names and some other minor details have been changed for various reasons.

There is a smattering of lighthearted Aussie sarcasm and exaggeration throughout these pages. This is not at all the way people relate to each other in my adopted country of France, so when I return to Australia, I enjoy re-living it.

And 're-living' was partly what this whole Walk was about for me – being re-acquainted with the land of my birth. In some ways, I am surprised to find that I write about my country almost as if I was a foreigner. But I'm an Aussie through and through. At least, I thought I was. I'm not so sure anymore. Maybe you can decide as you read these pages.

I thoroughly enjoyed writing this story. That was only possible though because I was looking forward to the day when you would enjoy reading it. That day has come.

oh, and I really enjoyed doing all the little ink sketches too!

Contents

Part One
The dream

Dangerous connections

驚心動魄[1]

Thinking back, I believe I did hear the whistle. But by the time I *really* heard it, the train was almost on top of me. Reflexes are wonderful things, however. At that precise moment they triggered me simultaneously to look up, take in the fact that 90,000 kilograms of metal was rocketing directly at me, and to leap in the right direction, i.e. *off* the track. The train and the long whistle, still blasting, screamed past me.

During my years of exile in France, I had longed for a deeper *connection* with Australia, the country of my birth. I may have been a little less enthusiastic though if I'd realised this meant the possibility of *connecting* with an oncoming train, a sideways careening truck, crocodiles, taipans, death adders ... and a green tree frog!

whose idea was this anyway?

---

[1] This is one of the thousands of four-word idioms of the Chinese language, and is made up of four parts: frighten, heart, shake and soul. It describes something that has a deep impact on an individual or a group.

An idea is born

I believe that a lot of ideas are born in solitude. This was one of them.

SCRATCH & SMELL

The air was clean and the fragrance of lavender from the nearby fields wafted my way on the summer breeze. The mellow and wholesome mid-afternoon sun, unlike the harsh rays that penetrate our ozone layer Down Under, soaked gently into my skin. I drank it up. I love the south of France. Shirt off, I was walking a familiar path alongside my old friend, the canal. I was an Aussie, a long way from home.

Home is a difficult word to define. The elasticity of the word hit me years back when my daughters were young. We'd been to Australia and England and were on a ferry, crossing the English Channel, on our way back to France. My wife, Hélène, was settled comfortably in the lounge looking after our luggage while I was taking both our girls for a walk on deck. After a few minutes, little Yésica suddenly went very quiet and started to get teary.

'What's the matter sweetheart?' I asked.

'I want to go home,' was her simple five-word, five-year-old's reply.

I was confused. What did she mean by *home*? My brain cells went into overdrive to try to compute exactly where she was referring to.

'You mean back to Grandma's house in Australia?'

A shake of the head.

'Back to Papi and Mamie's place in France?'

A more vigorous shake.

'Um, do you mean back to the place in England where we've just come from?' Surely, I reasoned, a brief stay at our friends' place there didn't qualify it for the title of *home*.

'No!' my little girl sighed with exasperation. So, obviously frustrated by having what must be the world's dumbest Dad, she very kindly spelled it out for me.

'I want to go back to where we've left Mum with the suitcases!'

My heart sank. I was raising homeless children.

Walking alongside the canal, breathing in the zesty fragrances of southern France, I continued to reflect.

My children's growing-up experience has been so different to mine. Home for me has always been a granite-soil corner of south-east Queensland known for its apples and cold winters – Stanthorpe. But a few decades later, with a French wife and four bilingual children, France has also slowly become *home*, my second *home*, though one that will never truly usurp the land where my identity remains deeply rooted.

Or would it?

That question played on my mind as the sun played on the gently flowing waters beside me. I didn't like the answer. I knew, without a doubt, that over the years I was becoming less and less Australian. I had sprung a cultural leak and my *Australian-ness* was on the way out. In the early days, the idea of *becoming French* was very exciting, and every step I took in that direction, learning the language and understanding the culture, affirmed my devotion and attraction to my wife, Hélène, and brought us closer together. Furthermore, I must admit, success at learning French was also a little *plume* in my *chapeau*. However, as the years rolled by, I realised not only that I would never truly become French but also, that in the process of *becoming* French, I was *un-becoming*

Australian. The tide had turned, sucking my Aussie-ness out with it. But was it possible to turn it back?

We were already planning to spend a year in Australia to reconnect with family and friends, and to give our two pre-teen boys an Aussie school experience. But there was a deep yearning in me for more. I longed for a deeper connection with the land that gave me birth, something more than just a year-long *visit.*

As I walked by the sparkling canal, the thought came to me. I would *walk*! *Tout simplement.* I would take a backpack and walk. I had visions of tree-lined national park trails, the Australian bush with gum trees all around, camping and meeting folk along the way. I found myself singing *I love to go a-wandering* and my heart was a-beating fast.

The idea was born.

in case the scratch + smell didn't work on the previous page, do feel free to use your imagination...

He didn't slip it to me

If I had thought this Walk was just going to slip into place, I had another think coming.

The Taruuba people of the Sahara Desert have a proverb: *When God wants to give you something He just slips it to you.* The turbaned friend who explained the meaning to me demonstrated it by reaching over and tucking a little packet under my arm.

'You see?' he said, 'Easy. Just like that!'

And for several months, it *was* easy. I simply mulled over the idea, allowing it to quietly mature like a good French cheese. Once it had ripened enough, I brought it out and cautiously unwrapped it for Hélène to delight in. At that point it became patently obvious that this Walk was *not* going to be one of those Taruuba *slip-it-to-you* things.

SCRATCH † SMELL

Hélène did not like my *camembert*. She in no way shared my enthusiasm for a long separation, leaving her on the home front to contend with our two pre-teen, testosterone-charged males, while I went gallivanting all over the countryside. No, she did not at all see this as a wonderful opportunity for husband to re-connect with the country of his birth. She was no doubt thinking of other words to describe this scheme, such as *selfish* and *inconsiderate*. She was probably right. Wives usually are.

Nonetheless, and not to be deterred, I began a behind-the-scenes secret mission. In the privacy of my garden shed cum office, barricaded behind closed doors, I quietly gathered my classified information.

Sporadically, over a six-month period, I pored over my little collection of road maps and National Trail maps, measuring and calculating. I began to hone my field of vision.

North. I would go north. *Cairns.* My brother lives in Cairns and apart from having the excuse to start from a *home base,* it would be great to start off in a warm, lush, semi-tropical region, something totally different to France. 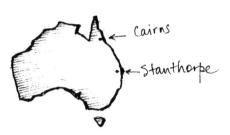 But where exactly would I walk? *South.* It was then that this outrageously absurd idea slipped uninvited into my brain – I could walk all the way back to my childhood home town, Stanthorpe. If I said it quickly enough, it didn't sound any more challenging than a stroll in the park and my heart would leap. Then I'd stare at my maps and reality would sink in, and my heart would sink along with it. Was I losing my mind? After all, seriously, who in their *right* mind would want to walk 2000 kilometres? Thus went my self-talk for days on end, backwards and forwards, like a dog constantly burying and digging up his bone for another chew. Over and over again.

I thought it best to keep this crazy idea to myself, having long since learned that Hélène doesn't *do* crazy ideas. It would take some skilful psychology on my part to successfully introduce this one, and a lot of patience while I waited for her to warm to it. But I had to tell someone. So when Carnsey, one of my mates from Stanthorpe, visited us during his stint in Europe, I spilled the beans. Mates are different. Mates will immediately jump on board, slap you on the back and raise a glass to an exciting plan. Right? *Wrong!* After enthusiastically sharing my idea with Carnsey, I had to wait until he picked himself up after ROFL. I decided not to tell anyone else.

That said, I did need to confide in someone – someone who had already done something similar, who would fill me with faith, tell me it was possible, and dispel the lurking fears and doubts I was unsuccessfully trying to suppress. The internet! I jumped on Google and typed: *Walking from Cairns to Stanthorpe.* Eureka! There was a man about my age, who had walked from Cairns almost to Brisbane, largely by the same route I would be taking. No! Wait! It wasn't someone who *had* walked but someone who *was* walking right there and then! I cautiously shared this news with Hélène. She cautiously said little.

A few brief emails with my new-found guru sped across cyberspace. I was due to return to Australia with my family at the end of that year, and Rod invited me to visit him and talk in detail face-to-face. As a result of my email communication with Rod, *The Walk*, as I was now calling it, became a glowing reality in my mind.

when I eventually met Rod,
that reality would lose
a little of its shine.

(image of a neutral face emoticon)

Reality check

By the time we arrived back in Australia, Hélène had started slowly coming around to my way of thinking. She hadn't said anything directly, but little by little she made comments indicating she was at least warming to her husband's crazy idea. I pushed ahead, believing that when the time came she would not just be warm, but actually supportive.

My family settled back into Stanthorpe when the fruit season was in full swing. Perfect timing! We moved into a cottage on the farm belonging to Carnsey's family, surrounded by fruit orchards and gum trees. Perfect location!

Not wasting any time, I soon found myself sitting in Rod's lounge. Guess who'd come with me? Carnsey himself. Call it curiosity, call it mateship, call it a change of heart ... he'd been tossing the idea around and thought it could be feasible after all. Then one day he announced he might join me on The Walk.

So now the two of us were meeting the man who would allay my fears and sketch out a foolproof plan of attack. However, if we were looking for encouraging stories to propel us towards our 2000 kilometre odyssey, we had come to the wrong place. As for *foolproof*, I didn't need any more proof that I was a fool, but there was no escaping and nothing to do but sit and listen.

And listen we did, as Rod recounted in detail the grind of daily trudging, the dangers of walking the highways, the sunburn and the foul moods that took over as day in day out he was forced to endure pain and utter exhaustion. He told of the rain that soaked him, the blisters that needed constant attention but never healed, and the unbearable groin chafe that had him walking down the highway, knees wide apart, John Wayne style. Looking over his shoulder he would see dark patches of his own

blood which had oozed out of his raw chafe and dripped down his thighs onto the road. He had no alternative but to keep walking. I shifted involuntarily in my seat, and realised I was holding my breath.

But the story that struck terror into my heart was *The Back*.

On the very first day, as Rod was stepping it out, he twisted his back and had to walk for a couple of days in excruciating pain, penguin-like, until it finally slipped back into place. This was too close to home. Having spent many weeks in recent years laid up in bed as a result of renegade vertebrae, I couldn't imagine myself continuing on if that happened to me.

As we stepped out of his home that sunny day, we didn't know whether to laugh or cry. It had been a jarring reality check for both of us.

More reality checks lay ahead.

Extreme Janine

Next came our visit with Janine, an Extreme Sports coach. Now convinced that this Walk idea fell fairly and squarely in the *extreme* category, we thought it would be wise to discuss the project with her. By this time, the *'we'* had grown from two to three. Carnsey had enlisted his young cousin, Dave, also from Stanthorpe. This should have been encouraging, and it was – safety in numbers and all that. But the worrying part was that both Carnsey and Dave are Physical Education teachers, and their combined ages about equalled mine. It was becoming glaringly obvious that I was the geriatric of the trio.

The two Phys Ed teachers and the geriatric listened intently to Extreme Janine while she dispensed screeds of useful advice, including the best way to treat blisters.

'Pop them, drain the liquid and pour methylated spirits on them, to dry them out.' *Right!*

'Yes, it hurts,' she added. *Right!*

'Of course, if you don't have metho, you can just pee on them.' *Right!*

She pointed out that as we were guys, logistically, this should be relatively easy. *Right!*

Why did I not find all this information reassuring?

'If one of you gets tired more easily than the other two, then it's possible to set up a simple tow rope system between you.'

I suddenly felt all eyes on me.

Her cherry on the cake was a personal story of running, trekking, paddling and mountain biking for a full, consecutive twenty-four hours with a broken ankle.

'You'll be amazed what your body can cope with,' she cheerfully concluded.

I decided I didn't want to be amazed. In fact, I didn't even want to know what my body was capable of. The term *couch potato* suddenly sounded really appealing.

A few weeks later I found out what my body was *not* capable of, when my lower back gave me grief again. After an  hour sitting around a table with a dozen supportive friends discussing The Walk, my back clamped up just as we stood to leave. Within minutes of actually fixing the dates for The Walk, I was unable to take a single step. I managed to half stand by leaning on the table, pretending all was well while I waited until everyone moved away. Then, hearing Carnsey laughing, I looked around to realise he'd seen the state I was in. My mind has since blocked out the smart comment he made.

Soon after that incident, my young cousin, Pessimistic Pete, announced with conviction that he was *sure* I wouldn't make it. Thanks buddy! By this time though, I didn't need any convincing. I knew he was probably right. An older friend also expressed doubt that I could do it. Nevertheless, *he* added a somewhat encouraging postscript, reminding me that failure is an acceptable part of life, and that failure isn't defined as *not achieving* but rather as *not attempting*.

However the real nudge to the starting blocks came when Hélène and I were watching the newly released movie *The Cross* featuring Arthur Blessitt. It recounted the amazing story of a man who, over a forty-year period, walked 60,000 kilometres carrying a four-metre wooden cross on his back through more than 300 nations.

21

I could hardly grasp these astounding figures: one man, forty years, 60,000 kilometres, 300 nations.

But there was one part that leapt off the screen into our living room. As a young man, before he started his incredible lifetime of walking, Arthur suffered from heart problems and his doctor had advised him not to attempt long walks. Believing, however, that if God had called then He would enable, Arthur did step out and continued to do so for forty years without further heart problems. He simply had to take that first step of faith.

Hélène and I both knew then that I needed to take that first step and God would pave the way for all the other steps that lay beyond.

Six months later I found myself at the airport, ready to fly to Cairns to begin The 2000 Walk.

But I was unprepared for the airport experience awaiting me ...

The knife

This was it! There was no turning back. I was just hours from boarding the plane for Cairns. And my mother was flying with me.

Having been my most faithful supporter in all endeavours of my life for forty-eight years, Mum was *not* going to pass up a golden opportunity like this. Wild brumbies couldn't keep her away – she *was* going to be at the starting blocks to cheer me off. So we were flying to Cairns together. She had a return ticket. Mine was one-way. I would be walking home.

By all accounts my mother is really a very average old lady – average height and weight. Well, now I come to think of it, in recent years she's become a little less than average in height and a little more than average in weight. She is quite a sharp dresser and always manages to find bargain clothing that matches either her sixty-year-old gold butterfly brooch with the mother-of-pearl worn off the wings or her equally ancient blue pendant – a reminder of the man she loved who left this world when I was only sixteen. His leaving broke all our hearts. Mum's never mended.

Now here we were together, going through the security check, Mum looking smarter than usual. I'm not sure how *I* looked – possibly comparatively scruffy. I do know how I *felt*: nervous – *very* nervous!

So you can imagine my reaction when, instead of picking up our cabin luggage from the X-ray machine and walking through *comme une lettre à la poste*, Mum and I were summoned by the menacing finger of one of the security agents.

'Do you have a knife in this bag?'

a 19th birthday gift, in 1947 —→

23

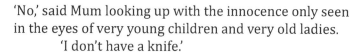

'No,' said Mum looking up with the innocence only seen in the eyes of very young children and very old ladies. 'I don't have a knife.'

'On the screen we can see a big knife in this bag.'

'No, there's no big knife in that bag,' said I, and turning to Mum, 'You *don't* have a big knife in your bag, do you Mum?'

'No, I don't have a big knife in my bag.'

'Do you mind if I have a look?' asked Mr Uniform.

Of course we didn't mind. But before I had time to say so, the uniformed man, obviously having been oh-so-efficiently trained in dealing rapidly with experienced terrorists, had deftly unzipped the bag and was holding aloft, with a barely disguised triumphant air of *I told you so!* – a knife. A *big* knife! A *very* big knife! No protective sheath, just a buck-naked, very big, carving knife. Images of Crocodile Dundee flashed through my mind.

Without missing a beat Mum said to me, 'Oh, that's just a present for your brother. He saw mine when he was home and he liked it so much I decided to get him one for his birthday.'

Fortunately, Mr Uniform didn't blow the whistle on us. Instead, he summed up the situation with as much

← this is the one
≈ life size

ease and professionalism as when he'd produced the concealed weapon. Most security officials don't make it their personal business to ensure little old ladies manage to smuggle extremely dangerous gifts for their sons on board aircrafts. We were lucky to strike the exception. He politely passed *said weapon* to me, handle first, and suggested I might like to check it in as a luggage item.

I began walking the 200 metres back to the check-in desk – slowly – in a crowded airport – carrying a very big naked knife.

Have you ever tried to look inconspicuous while carrying a huge carving knife through an airport? I hadn't gone very far when I realised this was probably not a good idea. There were only two choices – attempt to conceal it behind my back, which would look awfully suspicious to those behind, or simply step it out confidently, holding it in front of me as if this was the most natural thing in the world to be doing in an airport. I chose the latter.

I will never understand how the girl behind the check-in counter didn't faint or scream or both when she saw me making a bee-line towards her, brandishing my lethal weapon. The end of the story is that the knife *did* get checked in and it *did* make it to Cairns.

Mum proudly presented the knife to my brother who nonchalantly announced that he'd already bought an identical one for himself a few days before.

This incident only added to the sinking feeling that was growing in the pit of my stomach when I thought about the 2000 kilometres that now separated me from my home town of Stanthorpe. The flight to Cairns only took three hours. The walk home would take three months.

was I really ready for this?

Ready or not

The two questions I'd been most frequently asked during the days prior to The Walk were: 'Are you excited?' and 'Are you ready?' To be quite honest, now the day was almost upon me, I wasn't really either excited *or* ready because I had no idea what to expect. In fact, more than anything, I was worried about all the things that could go wrong.

In response to the *excited* and *ready* questions, Carnsey was coolness, calmness and collectedness personified. His typical reply to all and sundry was, 'Yeah, it's all good.'

And Dave? Dave was bouncing.

'Absolutely, I'm keen!' was his answer, with no attempt to hide the ingenuousness of youth. Dave was born with over-sprung inner suspension. Bouncing through life, his middle name should have been Tigger. We had each chosen a different coloured shirt to wear throughout The Walk to identify us in photos, on our website, and in meetings. However, even without his sky-blue shirt, Dave could have been picked out in a crowd simply by the energy that emanated from him.

'G'day, bloke' was his typical in-your-face greeting which he would inflict on me, not just every morning, but several times a day. How could I not warm to such candour? On reflection, from his perspective, he must have seen this old-timer as a crusty walking companion. In spite of our differences, we knew the three of us had better enjoy each other's company because we were sure going to have a lot of it over the following eighty days.

After several sleepless morning hours, I decided it was time to wake a friend. I extracted him from my backpack and caressed his pristine cover. I'd purchased *Longue marche* before I left France, saving it for this day.

The blurb invited me to join the author, Monsieur Bernard Ollivier, on his 1700 kilometre trek across Turkey. I accepted his invitation and embarked on the first steps of *his* adventure just hours before I embarked on *mine*. On the second page he described his beginning: *Les grands départs sont escortés d'une petite dépression.*

Yes, I have to admit that's where I was at too – a little depressed. It was comforting to know I was not alone and I felt a strange bond forming between myself and the author, ten years my senior and with an equally ambitious goal! I was already looking up to him and anticipating having him with me for those weeks on The Walk.

It was all due to start in just a few hours.

This is the book all tattered and torn with its paper back cover, crumpled and worn from which many an inspiration was drawn.

Part Two

The reality

Day 1
The starting line

Tuesday 24 August

Our starting line had been pre-arranged at Freshwater College, just outside Cairns. The entire student body turned out to farewell us, as did Mum, thankfully without the knife! Her bright red, broad-brimmed hat could be spotted from a satellite. Mum is big on hats and not just for aesthetic reasons. She should be an ambassador for skin cancer prevention in Australia. The year before, when I first told her about my plans to walk 2000 kilometres, she listened, twisting her aged lips from side to side, and said, 'Well, I hope you wear a hat!'

So, obediently, I was wearing a hat. With temperatures expected to hit the high thirties, a good hat was nearly as essential as good shoes. But my hat wasn't like Mum's. Her hat proudly said, 'Look at me!' My hat didn't say anything at all.

In contrast to my nondescript headwear, Dave's was a no-nonsense khaki colour. My brim tended to droop – Dave's was starchy-stiff. The stitches around mine were worn and faded – the stitches on Dave's stood crisply to attention. Yes, Dave's hat reflected the man.

G'day bloke

The big eyes of my six-month-old nephew followed the balloons the kids were diligently filling with helium gas and tying on strings – green, pale blue, yellow, orange. Not a red one in sight. Balloons must be like M&Ms – the red ones go first.

My faithful companion, until that fateful day when ...

It was surreal. There we were, about to step out, being joined for the first kilometre by hundreds of balloon-toting school kids – and Mum!

Noise and chaos subsided as the moment of the official launch arrived. The principal stood amidst the sea of bobbing balloons, said something I don't recall, and a moment later the rope was dropped. As a cheer went up, Carnsey and I stepped over the rope. Dave bounced over it.

0000 It was 9 am on the dot. A tidal wave of school kids surged out pushing us forward. I glanced back and caught sight of a bright red, broad-brimmed hat being swept along with the chattering children. The grass was lush and green. The bird song, like the sky, was clear and crisp. Clear blue sky may cheer the soul but when you know you'll be walking under it for the next eighty days it takes on a more sinister nature.

0001 The first kilometre over, we prepared to say goodbye to the school children and continue down the highway. On the signal, the balloons were released and like a burst of spermatozoa, tails a-swinging, they twisted their way in a frenzied race to the sun. The sudden rush of colour and energy seemed symbolic of us heading off and cheered me *up*. Then I watched as the last, pale blue balloon veered off course and became entangled in the fronds of a palm tree. It seemed somewhat of an omen and that cheered me *down*. The bright red, broad-brimmed hat made its way through the crowd to give me a farewell hug. Our hats got twisted up and Mum's tipped back.

'See you in another 2000 kilometres,' I shouted, trying to make myself heard over the hubbub of the kids. The last thing I remember as I turned away was seeing Mum's soft white arms reaching up to fit her hat back on. I didn't see a tear but I knew she was crying.

We broke from the pack, leaving in our wake the kids, the noise and the fanfare, and stepped onto the highway. This would be our place for seven or eight hours a day for the next couple of months. Our route would eventually take us onto smaller inland roads but, to start with, it was the Bruce Highway. The first quarter of an hour was an adrenalin rush – finally doing what I'd talked about, dreamt about and planned – now two kilometres down and only one thousand, nine hundred and ninety-eight to go.

0002

The magnitude of it all slowly seeped into my psyche with the *plod plod plod* of shoes on bitumen. It *was* exciting but, in other ways, a bit anti-climactic. All we were doing, after all, was walking. I enjoyed some silent minutes to think, pray and gather my thoughts. The rhythmic *plod plod plod* that would accompany us for the next eighty days was already becoming monotonous, and depressing thoughts were trickling in.

PLOD
PLOD
PLOD
PLOD
PLOD
PLOD
PLOD
PLOD
PLOD
PLOD

What have I got myself into?
Is my back going to hold out?
When will I stop feeling sick in the stomach with butterflies?
What's it going to be like to walk with blister upon blister?
Are the three of us going to get on each other's nerves?

After the first few kilometres I was already bringing up the rear while the cousins stepped it out ahead. Well, Carnsey stepped. But Dave, breaking in his new hat, continued to bounce. I wondered if *I'd* bought a new hat whether it would have put a bit more bounce into *my* step too.

It was good to have Carnsey out in front, his bright red shirt being the most visible to the oncoming traffic that was rocketing past us perilously close. Good visibility may well play an important part in our survival. Dave's shirt, on the other hand, merged perfectly with the pale blue sky. Carnsey shaded his eyes, scanning the heavens to no avail for any cloud that might provide temporary relief from the blistering sun. The long-range forecast indicated there would probably be none for the duration of The Walk. Better get used to it, or 'Suck it up!' as I would hear Dave say hundreds of times.

After two hours walking through the city, we unanimously agreed to a KFC distraction conveniently located en route on the southern side. We enthusiastically told the phenomenally unimpressed cashier that we'd just started a 2000 kilometre walk. She grunted and returned a blank stare. We headed out the door loaded with chips and cans of Solo, justifying our indulgence on advice we'd been given by Extreme Janine, to increase our calorie intake. We were obediently complying.

Heading away from Cairns, I spied a parallel road to the highway. At first chance, already irritated by the close proximity of the killing machines on wheels, I ran across to it, leaving Big Red and Sky Blue to face the traffic. The side road was an access for the sugar-cane vehicles, perfect for walking. Thus began my love affair with side roads.

After another hour of plodding, Maxine, from Cairns, waved us over and unloaded a box of *things* for us. I say *things* because, depending on your country of origin, they could be called iced lollies, lollipops, popsicles, ice-blocks, fruit lollies or icy-poles. We didn't care what they were called; they were cold and sweet, and a rest out of the sun made a welcome break. Maxine confessed she'd been a tad suspicious when she drove up and saw only Big Red and Sky Blue, wondering if I was already slacking off somewhere. She was relieved to see me appear, running back across the highway, dodging several lanes of traffic, magnetically drawn to the *things*. Thus began my appreciation for roadside special deliveries.

The rest of the day went by without incident, just the relentless searing rays of the sun. After only (!) twenty-seven kilometres we arrived at Gordonvale, our destination for Day One. 0027
This was one of our shortest planned walking days. We had decided to make it easy on ourselves the first day, to give a sense of accomplishment and success right from the start.

Dave celebrated our arrival by doing several chin-ups on the Gordonvale sign at the entry to the town. I just walked under it.

G'day Bloke

Soon afterwards, I was experiencing the sheer delight of taking off my shoes, a ritual that would be repeated with increasing satisfaction over the next seventy-nine days and 1,973 kilometres. It was probably *not* such an enjoyable experience for our different hosts, but they were too gracious to mention the subject and, on this occasion, I was too absorbed with my immediate needs – tending to sunburnt calves – to notice.

Note to self: apply more sunscreen tomorrow!

North Queensland is a matchless little corner of the world which I was both re-discovering and discovering all at once. Our hosts for the night, Tarzan and Jane, lived in what was affectionately known by some as *The Tree House*. After driving up the winding road, we found ourselves sitting out on a deck no less than twenty metres long. A sheer drop gaped below us as we looked out over a canopy of mango trees, gums, milky pines and strangler fig trees knitted together with vines and creepers. The multiple hues of green, tinged by the orange tones of the dying sun had the effect of a Mozart symphony. I sighed deeply. Contentedly. Several times.

Having released my toes from their sweaty prison

cells, and enjoying the sensation of cool air on hot skin, I was congratulating myself on my choice of shoe. It hadn't been an easy one but, over the months, dozens of helpful people provided lots of advice that gave me the confidence to make my choice.

That's when Tarzan, our host, a legendary character in this part of North Queensland, announced that he *never* wears shoes. I cast my eyes downward. *No shoes!* It was obvious he was telling the truth – those tough, calloused feet had clearly not been in shoes for a very, very long time. Alongside *his* feet, mine were pathetically pink, soft, and puffy. I felt a little exposed and vulnerable, as if this was a part of my body that shouldn't be on public display. He then proceeded to inform me that if he'd had time he would have joined us on The Walk and that he wouldn't have worn shoes, even when walking on bitumen.
He had my total attention. I know bitumen can reach temperatures of 70°C.

I looked at Tarzan's amazing feet again and believed him. If I'd had any sense of pride in my accomplishment that day, it vanished immediately upon comparing feet.

Jane appeared bearing a tray laden with gloriously sizzling fish fingers. I have wondered since if we were actually meant to leave any for them. Then came the mango ice-cream and I don't think we left any of that either. You can't go to North Queensland without indulging in mangoes. Some people think the fruit that Eve ate in the Garden of Eden was an apple but I'm sure it was a mango. No other fruit evokes quite the same passion as the marvellous mango, though Carnsey was decidedly less passionate about it a few hours later when, in the middle of the night, he brought all his up again. Sunstroke!

Note to self: drink lots of water.

Carnsey's seedy face was a reminder that we had *not* embarked on a Sunday afternoon stroll in the park, and

 that it really *was* on the extreme side of the scale. I was more convinced than ever that my sceptical young cousin, Pessimistic Pete, *was* right – I *wasn't* going to make it. If a young robust Phys Ed teacher could come down with sunstroke and be reduced to a vomiting mess, missing most of an all-important night's sleep, what chance was there for me?

With my thoughts focussing on my own uncertainties, I forgot that on the other side of the world a different set of uncertainties of much greater proportions had captured the eyes of the world. Thirty-three Chilean miners, trapped underground for three weeks, had just been found, still alive. Would they survive until a rescue plan was implemented?

Evening passed and morning came, and this was only Day One.

los 33 mineros chilenos

Day 2
Clouds and crocodiles

Wednesday 25 August

The day dawned bright and clear, which would have sounded romantic if you were going to be sitting in the shade all day, sipping ice-cold lemonade. However, that definitely wasn't on our agenda and it was shaping up to be another scorcher!

By 6 am we were on the road, the *side road* parallel to the highway passing by the cane fields, accompanied by the peewees' cheerful morning ring tone. The sun's rays were still soft and pleasantly warm. Our long shadows flickered across the tall stalks of sugar cane beside us. There wasn't a wisp of wind and the leaves hung limp and silent. Some of the cane seemed to be leaning over to greet us, and every now and then one would high-five us as we passed. Friendly chaps.

We knew, however, that there were less-than-friendly chaps slithering among the cane. Thousands of them! Sugar-cane fields are the perfect breeding ground for small rodents, which, in turn, are favourite snacks for snakes. So the fields are home to many varieties of the latter, including the infamous Mr Taipan. Even the name strikes fear in the heart, and not without reason. The Australian taipan is claimed to have the most toxic venom of any snake on the planet, sixty times more toxic than the Indian cobra. I read that a single drop from one particular species of taipan is enough to kill 50,000 mice or a dozen men. While I warmed quite quickly to the idea of the instant demise of a very large number of rodents, the second half of the equation brought little cheer. It occurred to me that I was walking a fine line between the legless ankle biters on one side and the killing machines on wheels, on the other.

Note to self: don't walk too close to the cane fields.

With more than thirty kilometres ahead of us, and no KFC en route, we were well prepared with food and water, and our calves and arms were plastered with white sunscreen – we'd learned from our mistakes. I, for one, wanted to keep down every last spoonful of mango ice-cream that we might meet along the way!

The kilometres slipped by, often in silence. It would be totally bizarre not to talk to a friend for even a few minutes at a time if you were, for example, sitting in a lounge. However, walking seemed to be activity enough in itself to happily allow for quite long periods of silence.

The previous night, my new-found paperback friend, Monsieur Bernard Ollivier, had shared with me his discovery of this solitary reverie. His words, *La marche est porteuse de rêves*, now struck a chord with me. *Walking lends itself to dreaming,* he wrote, *not to constructive thinking. Walking is action, momentum, movement, and with this constant exertion the mind is reluctant to apply itself.*

The poet's pen continued: *I simply sip and harvest the images, sensations and odours around me, storing them up, until later when the time comes to rearrange them and reflect on them.*

Mum always used to say that she was never closer to God than in her garden. This wasn't exactly a garden, but I *was* feeling a special nearness to the One who had put it all in place – the balmy morning light, the touch of the sun, the birds, the stillness and the purple mountains beyond the endless fields of cane. It was breathtaking, and I thought of my yearning, back in France, to reconnect with the land that gave me birth. I breathed a prayer of thankfulness for these special moments.

A few hours happily passed this way, until I was slowly drawn out of my reverie by the realisation that our weather prediction had been *wrong* – the sun *wasn't* burning down on me. A glance upward was sufficient to reveal the sky veiled, as far as the eye could see, behind a perfect, natural shade cover – clouds! We hadn't been aware of them moving in and were taken by a very pleasant surprise. A soft breeze had picked up too. Perfect! A welcome contrast to our first day.

'If only,' I commented, 'we could have even one day a week like this!'

We knew this was exceptional, and we took it as a gift, literally, from above.

As we crossed several bridges, we looked down at the inviting water below, but pressed on. A very large and lethal-looking cane knife lying on the ground brought back recent airport memories.

We'd been on the road for six hours. I was tired, my feet were sore and I could feel they were hot and blistering. I wanted to let them out. Carnsey was all for pressing on but, when the next river came in sight, I convinced him to let me take a break, just time enough to cool off my feet. Neither of us stopped to consider the possible consequences of such a move in tropical North Queensland, where danger lurks in rivers, and floating logs have teeth.

We clambered down the embankment. Carnsey didn't want to go to the bother of taking his shoes off, so instead he flipped open my little video camera and filmed me taking great delight in removing my shoes and dipping my burning feet into the water. Ahhh, nice!

Video evidence shows the water sizzling and steam rising when my feet made contact. I stepped out a little further where the coolness of the water around my ankles was bliss. Then deeper, up to my calves – sheer bliss. And then up to my knees – pure bliss! I waded around in circles, feeling the small pebbles under my soles but not being able to see them through the murky water. Carnsey continued filming – a nice little memory of one of our stop-to-smell-the-roses moments.

Feet dry, shoes and hat on, I was ready to roll. I would remain blissfully ignorant of my folly until later that evening.

Carnsey is a cricketer from way back – even playing for the State's under-nineteen team – so we were sometimes privy to advice he'd gleaned from those cricketing days. At one point, after sucking vigorously on his Camelbak tube he recalled the words of wisdom of one of his coaches: 'The night before a match you should drink and keep drinking water until your urine is clear. Then you'll be right.'

As he talked of the importance of keeping the liquids going in, I realised I hadn't had to water the horse for hours. The cloud cover was deceptive, lulling me into thinking I didn't need to drink, when all the time I was drying out. If I wanted to avoid being another candidate for dehydration or sunstroke, I would need to learn to suck more regularly on my tube. It did occur to me though, that it was a shame Carnsey hadn't remembered his cricket coach's advice the first day – he might have been able to keep his mango ice-cream.

Arriving at our destination, Babinda, in the early afternoon, we stepped just a few metres off the highway into the waiting hospitality of our host, Curly. When he was younger and had more hair, I guess it *was* curly. Now it was just wavy, silver and respectfully receding. We loved our stay with Curly and his wife, starting with the roast dinner waiting for us as soon as we were able to rip off our shoes and put our feet under the table. They possibly still remember the foot odour but all I remember is the smell and the taste of the beef and vegies.

The total population of Babinda is only around a thousand but we had an impressive 5% turnout in the small public venue for our evening meeting. This was more than we'd had in Gordonvale the night before, or even Cairns just prior to our launch. The population of Cairns is 150,000 but we'd only managed to draw a total *crowd* of twelve to our meeting, about 0.01% of the population. It had been a little disheartening. Proportionally speaking, Babinda's turnout was 500 times more than Cairns. When I reported this to my wife on the phone, she replied in a typically candid French way, 'Shame on Cairns.' And we laughed.

Not really concerned about the numbers that came to our meetings, we were happy to get our message out to the few ready to hear. We wanted to talk to people about God's Word and the many, many languages in the world that don't have any part of it translated. Most people live their entire lives without thinking too much about other languages, or without thinking too much about where the Bible came from, as if it had already been given to Adam and Eve in the English language.

Those enthusiastic kids and adults in Babinda were astonished to learn that there were 6900 languages, not counting dialects, currently spoken on our planet. One brown-skinned girl shot her hand up and asked if it could take even as long as two years to complete a Bible translation into a new language. Her almond eyes grew wide when she heard the answer: The shortest translation of a New Testament would be five years, and the longest might be fifty.

I explained that young people are sometimes called by

God to dedicate their entire lives to the task of helping an isolated group of people receive God's Word in their own special language.

I looked around and wondered if this meeting might be God's call for one of those kids – perhaps even that girl? There might be a seed planted in a heart – just as the idea for The 2000 Walk had been planted in mine – that would one day grow into something big.

'Please Lord,' I prayed, 'for the sake of a hidden people group, so that another people and another language can be added to the God-worshippers around the world.'

Another hand went up. This time it was a young mum, eyes sparkling through small spectacles, who wanted to know what type of Bibles we translate. She had trouble finding the words to explain what she meant. 'You know, in English we have lots of different Bibles: NIV, Living Bible, King James, Good News. What type of Bible do you translate? Are they like the recent slangy ones?'

I explained that in English we have over one hundred different translations, as well as many different formats and presentations of each. Again the eyes across the room opened wide. The message was simple. How could we stand back when *we* have so much choice, while there are still *millions* of people in the world who haven't even had the chance to hear a *single* verse of God's Word in a language they can understand?

It was then Curly's turn to have a say. He was presiding over the gathering like the benevolent grandfather, reclining in his chair and observing proceedings with obvious relish. He explained how he'd come in contact with us.

'When we heard about you guys attempting to do this walk – 2000 kilometres – it was really *exciting* and we floated it by our Youth Group kids and got them fairly *excited*. Then it was even more *exciting* when we got in

Exciting
exciting
Exciting
Exciting
Exciting
Exciting
EXCITING

touch with you guys about having you stay in our little town. *Everybody got excited.'*

Is it any wonder that the Babinda group was *excited*? They'd caught it off Curly and his family. Dave, Carnsey and I talked about them for months afterwards.

There was something else we talked about for months afterwards which was anything *but* exciting and caused me nightmares on more than one occasion.

Following our presentation and in the course of chit-chat over brightly iced cake and equally bright cordial in plastic cups, the grim reality of my midday folly was exposed. There was every chance that the river where I'd splashed around was home to unfriendly residents. That local knowledge had come too late for me to avoid making the mistake, but perhaps just in time to prevent me making it again, with possibly more dire consequences.

Now, when I think how I peered into the murky water, trying to make out my happy toes twisting in cool delight, two beady eyes surface in front of me and a jaw full of crooked teeth gapes. I imagine the appalled cameraman capturing the gory last seconds before the geriatric walker disappears beneath the surface in a froth of blood and bubbles, never to be seen again. In my nightmare I see my children, now grown, and their children, and their children's children, watching wide-eyed for the hundredth time, the footage of their foolish forefather's flailing feet.

And I wake in a cold sweat.

Day 3
Andre

Thursday 26 August

It was another short night followed by a 6 am start.

To our right, the sky was painted in shades of pastel greys and blues, offering a perfect background to a milky-white full moon that would soon slip behind the mountains, seeking refuge from the soon-to-rise sun. In a few hours *we* would be seeking refuge from it, too. To our left, the pre-sunrise colours were soft pinks and pastels. Equally worthy of my early morning admiration, my eyes scanned from one side to the other – like a spectator at Wimbledon.

We were decked out with blinking headlamps and reflective safety vests to warn oncoming motorists of our presence on their turf – well, *very* close to their turf. Too close really. If they didn't see us, it would be because they had their eyes shut, which was actually not such a happy thought, since motorists *do* sometimes shut their eyes and when they do, they normally drive off the side of the road – which was exactly where we were walking.

This would become our daily routine: up well before the sun to avoid the heat. It didn't take a rocket scientist to calculate that to get our requirement of sleep – which was increasing by the day – we'd have to get to bed very early. Conducting a meeting almost every night and then returning to our very friendly and oh-so-expectant hosts was going to make that essential early night more difficult than I cared to think about. In fact, to get a decent night's sleep, I'd have to be in bed hours before

our meetings ended. Hmm. Somewhere along the line
I had clearly miscalculated the scheduling.

Dave looked like he could have used a bit more sleep
too, but it would take more than that to knock the
bounce out of him. He was up and at it. A cane train
chugged past at quite a pace, pulling a long line of
empty cages behind it. Like a whippet after a rabbit, Dave
was off. I sometimes wondered why he couldn't just walk
through life. I mean, that's what we were supposed to be
doing – walking. He leapt at the side of one of the cages
and clung on, being happily carried along, free of charge.
I think he must have watched too many prison camp
escape movies in his short life. However, when the siren
didn't sound and the prison guards and dogs didn't come
running, he soon gave up, dropped to the ground and
returned to the road. Later we would learn of the danger
(not to mention, illegality) of jumping cane trains.

It was then we witnessed a simultaneous sunrise on
one side and moonset on the other. It'd be a little while
longer before I realised it was impossible to have such
a gorgeous multi-coloured sunrise without ... *clouds*!
Once more, against all hope, the sky was wall to wall with
wonderful, fabulous, awesome clouds. My heart leapt for
joy – we'd once again be walking thirty kilometres under
nature's shadecloth.

The sunrise and clouds lifted my spirits and once more
I got to thinking about all those kids, enthralled at our
meeting, with all its colour and lights, videos and stories.
Yes! Perhaps several of them would be Bible translators
in a few years.

Suddenly, as if my excitement had willed him to appear,
one of these budding young translators materialised a
little way ahead waving at us from the side of the road.
And even from that distance, I recognised Andre with his
cowlick forehead. As it turned out, he lived in this small
township called Mirriwinni – Aboriginal for *here's your*

46

chance to get off the main highway. And that's exactly what we intended to do. On a map, I'd seen an alternative road which, while actually adding a few kilometres to our tally, would be a welcome change and get us away from the highway for an hour. However, I wasn't sure which road it was and we didn't want to take the wrong one. Little Andre appeared at the perfect time and was able to point us in the right direction – bless him! Making the most of the opportunity before we said goodbye, and wanting to buoy myself up with a little more encouragement about the effectiveness of our interaction with the children the night before, I asked him what he remembered about our presentation.

I leaned forward in anticipation. Andre, hands in his pockets, screwed up first one eye and then the other. He twisted his freckly face to the side and bit his top lip. This kid was made for Hollywood. The answer was coming, I could tell. Yes, he was going to make us proud. He scratched his chin, pulled at the skin of his neck, looked up at the sky and then did all of the above simultaneously. Finally, he tapped his fingers on his chin and said, 'I've got to get going. My Dad's waiting for me.'

And just like that, he was gone! He hadn't remembered anything.

The clouds continued all day.

'You've really got good weather,' said a lady at a petrol bowser as we walked past. We agreed. Two consecutive days of cloud and mild weather was more than we could have expected. What's more, we then found ourselves on a quiet back road, keeping an eye out for movement as we walked cautiously past Crocodile Swamp. The name did nothing to entice me after my earlier episode, but the lure of a quiet back road was strong. I'm told crocodiles can only run on land at about twenty kilometres per hour. Under normal conditions I couldn't top ten kilometres per hour, but with a croc on my heels I could easily accelerate to sixty! I knew as long as I saw him coming, I'd be right.

We survived Crocodile Swamp and I was actually disappointed not to see one.

Note to self: try to see a crocodile before leaving North Queensland.

A car pulled up. It was Curly's son, who'd wondered why he couldn't find us on the highway but tracked us down in the end.

'Thought I'd come along to make sure you're not slackin' off,' he said in true Aussie style, and added, 'Good meetin' last night.'

However, with the wisdom acquired from my recent encounter with Andre, I chose *not* to ask him if he actually remembered anything about it.

Three days down.

0096

Day 4
Jurassic Park

Friday 27 August

After we had walked twenty-six kilometres
south, our host for the night picked us up   0122
and drove us to the local beach.

Etty Bay opened out in front of us in all its quaint beauty.
Apart from a few barefoot nature lovers at a picnic table,
we were alone in this idyllic deserted little corner of
creation with the sea quietly licking the shore. Dave and
Carnsey happily set about playing games in the sand
with our host's offspring, releasing additional energy
from their still-not-depleted reserves. I chose instead to
stroll along the waveless beach, enjoying the sensation
of *softness* underfoot instead of *hardness*, and *padding*
instead of *plodding*. I was tired – very tired. My back
had been feeling a bit ordinary throughout the day and
somehow, when things are not right in that department,
I feel overwhelmed with fatigue. I was grateful, however,
that so far I had not lived the horrors of Rod's penguin-
walk experience.

As I padded, digging my toes into the sand with every
step, I reflected on the previous night's meeting in
Innisfail. It had been a small gathering of just eight
people, but seemed significant. Carnsey had once more
produced our *Real Estate signs* – small white rectangles
made from lightweight corflute material. No, we weren't
selling anything, only *telling* – about languages. The
signs displayed numbers – statistics. We wanted to
communicate the message regarding the number of
languages that still had no part of the Bible translated.
The actual figure was 2252 but we had rounded it down

49

to 2000 to make it easier to remember. In fact, that was the figure that jumped out when we first started calculating the distance from Cairns to Stanthorpe, and seemed to confirm this crazy Walk project. We were walking 2000 *kilometres* and talking about the 2000 *languages* still with *nothing* of God's Word translated. The correlation between kilometres and languages inspired the name The 2000 Walk.

Yep, Carnsey did a great job presenting the statistics, and gave a heartfelt call for people to get behind this Bible translation movement.

His message was simple: 'Translating the Bible into 2000 languages sounds a lot. Then again, so does walking 2000 kilometres. But it's just one kilometre at a time. To date we have walked 120 kilometres. It sounds a lot, but really it's just one kilometre after another. It's do-able.'

My reverie was interrupted by a dark shape emerging from the scrub just metres away and heading towards me as if out of the set of Jurassic Park. Dinosaur-like crest on its head, striding confidently on two powerful legs and leaving unusually large, three-toed footprints in the sand, a cassowary stepped right out of the pages of a pre-history book. These huge, heavy-set, flightless birds are usually shy and solitary, preferring the cover of rainforest. But the promise of scraps left by visitors lured this one out. Judging by her confident air, she was a regular around these picnic tables. I enjoyed a close-up view of the almost fluorescent blue and rich red colourings around her head and neck, and recalled the last time I'd admired one of these magnificent creatures through the protective wire of a fence in a zoo in Sanary-sur-Mer on the southern coast of France. That one had looked miserable locked in his enclosure, a long way from his native land. In a moment of melancholy he had reminded me of myself,

also a long way from *my* native land, and I felt a certain affinity with him. By contrast, this colourful female was dignity personified. She positively swaggered through life, majestically placing her massive feet on the beach as if every square metre belonged exclusively to her.

Cassowaries have had a bad rap over the years, largely because of their long razor-sharp middle toes that look like lethal daggers (though they don't hold a candle to Mum's carving knife!). They have been known to attack and even disembowel their victims with their toes – prime candidates for Jurassic Park! The picnickers nearby were taking no chances with this one. As she approached they climbed onto the table until she had walked past and melted back into the forest.

Sitting on the sand, I breathed in the salt air. In spite of the fact we were supposedly following the coast, beach stops would unfortunately be a rarity. The Bruce Highway runs, for the most part, a good way inland from the coast and our schedule wouldn't allow us to be going off the beaten track. But at last we had free time. After four consecutive nights of meetings, this was our first night off. I felt the stress and fatigue drain out of me as the light drained from the sky.

I lay on my back and allowed my eyes to follow the fluid, hypnotic movements of white across a mostly-veiled backdrop of blue. I didn't formulate words, spoken or unspoken, but I was praying and grateful to God for a third cool, consecutive, overcast day.

My journal entry for the day: *Cloudy.*

Day 5
Tree ferns

Saturday 28 August

The day dawned dull and damp. With not a single scratch of blue sky visible, it was immediately obvious that the friendly clouds of the previous few days were drawing ominously closer, no longer content with providing shade from a distance.

The sky began to descend and, at about the same time, the trees closed in. In France, a highway of this importance would be endowed with a broad emergency stopping lane. By contrast, the Bruce Highway allowed barely room enough for one person to walk, so we covered our kilometres in single file, trees and tropical vegetation close on one side and speeding vehicles much too close on the other.

The drone of each approaching vehicle, the sudden roar for the split second we – almost – shared the same space, and then the disappearing drone, were becoming only too predictable, and far too frequent for my liking. To pass the time, I calculated their frequency. On average there was one every eleven seconds. The constant road noise, combined with the fact that we had to walk in single file, made any hope of conversation impossible.

I invented activities to pass the time. I pitted myself against the stream of cars, imagining them the *enemy* to be defeated. In order to *win*, I needed to clock a period of sixty seconds when not a single vehicle passed. I would wait till there was a lull in the traffic, start the stopwatch on my phone and watch excitedly as the car-less seconds slipped by – ten, twenty, thirty – only to have to re-set it again as a car roared past. More than an hour went by, re-setting the stopwatch a hundred times. Once I was certain I had won, but the stopwatch registered fifty-eight seconds. By persevering, I finally defeated the enemy. But they apparently didn't know they'd been defeated because they still kept coming.

During the course of the morning, an ambulance raced past, lights flashing and sirens wailing. I wondered if one day soon that same ambulance might be speeding down the highway to pick up pieces of *me*. I thought of Arthur Blessitt and his epic 60,000 kilometre walk over forty years. Arthur's testimony of God's protection rang in my ears: 'I still can't believe that I wasn't taken out by a truck.'

Already, after just five days, I too was beginning to consider it a miracle that I hadn't met my demise. I don't believe for a minute that God had any obligation whatsoever to protect me, or that I had any guarantee He actually *would*, but I knew He *could*, and that was more than enough. The outcome was in His hands.

While my thoughts were sometimes less than optimistic, they were far from faithless. And while I devised silly games to pass the time, I was far from bored.

In fact, I spent most of my time not worrying about the metallic monsters roaring *past* me, but rather revelling in nature's beauty pageant *around* me. I was particularly drawn to the myriad shades of green. Each species of plant and vine and tree seemed to be painted a different hue – leaves and stems, fronds and foliage, a breathtaking *mélange* of hundreds of shades of green: lime, olive, emerald, pea, mint, moss.

Interestingly, the Taruuba language of the Sahara Desert makes no distinction between different shades of green. That's not surprising given the under-abundance of plants that grow there.

What's more, in Taruuba there is only a single word – *kashaa* – for what we would classify separately as plant, bush, vegetation, shrub, creeper, vine, grass, tree, weed, pasture, lawn and so on. That makes for quite a challenge to translate Genesis 1:11 that talks about God creating vegetation, plants, grass and trees. The Taruuba translation reads simply: *God created all the kashaa – all the big kashaa and all the little kashaa.*

Of all the *kashaa* around me as I walked, the species that charmed me most was the elegant tree fern which, like the cassowary, appeared strangely pre-historic. With their broad, bright, feathery fronds rocking soothingly with the air movement from passing cars, they took on a life of their own. A file of happy spectators, strategically positioned to cheer us on, they waved gracefully and bowed respectfully before us. I don't think there was a single tree fern along that stretch of highway that didn't catch my eye and cheer my heart.

Several hours later, the landscape opened out and we could see the low-lying clouds hovering around the mountaintops, threatening to unleash their load. I was enjoying the perfect walking conditions but I wasn't enjoying the prospect of getting drenched. Walking in wet boots is a recipe for blisters and once more Rod's indelibly etched horror stories sprang to mind.

Note to self: apply more Elastoplast, *just in case.*

At the first available opportunity, I was happy to get away from the highway and I convinced Dave to join me. I'd had enough of cars and bitumen. This time, we found ourselves on the railway track, running parallel to the highway and quite a do-able alternative. Nice!

'A change is as good as a holiday,' I said to Dave as we crunched over the rocks and competed to see who could walk the furthest along one of the rails before losing balance. It was Dave – of course. He seemed to grow in stature by a centimetre or two with this win.

We arrived in Tully after an awesome day's walk. It was too good to be true, almost perfect! After our initial hot day, we had just clocked up *four* consecutive cool, overcast days.

No sooner were we settled into a cabin at Green Way Caravan Park when down came the rain. Residents of Tully are not surprised by the rain, since they live with 4000 millimetres of it per year, making this the town with the highest recorded rainfall in Australia. It is little wonder the *kashaa* are so green.

A young shopkeeper made a comment about sunless days and, rolling his eyes sarcastically, added, 'Another perfect day in paradise!'

Little did he know, I actually thought it *was*.

56

Day 6
The big boot

Sunday 29 August

I had taken no convincing to curl up in my bunk and, after catching up with Monsieur Bernard for a few minutes, the regular rhythm of the rain on the roof soothed me to sleep. But I woke early with a start, worried. The rain had obviously not let up all night, and was still falling.

What would happen, I wondered, if we had to walk in the rain for days on end? It'd be slow going. Rod's blisters would set in. We'd fall behind on our schedule, tight with meetings already lined up in thirty-five towns. We couldn't afford delays, especially at this early stage. It was to be the first of our weekly rest days and, though I desperately *needed* rest, I suddenly felt even more desperate to get a few more kilometres under my belt. That could mean the difference between keeping to our schedule and dropping out of the race.

For Carnsey and Dave it wasn't such a big deal. For one thing, given their age and fitness, it was far less likely they would drop out. On top of that, they were there to accompany me and, when no-one else was available, take turns driving the support vehicle. Neither of them would be walking the full 2000 kilometres. For me however, it was an important personal challenge. I had planned and trained for it for three years. I intended, as far as it was within my ability, to walk every last one of the remaining 1851 kilometres.

STUBBORNNESS ? PRIDE ?
COMMITMENT ? TENACITY ?
SOMETHING TO PROVE ?

57

It was probably a mix of all of these.

I extracted myself from the bed and it creaked painfully. I dressed and the unsteady cabin rocked. I flushed the toilet and it sounded like Niagara had broken through. The cousins were not impressed at having been woken up so early and were even less impressed when their eyes opened enough to see me ready for action. *But I was determined.* They moaned that this was meant to be a day off. *I was still determined.* They let me know in no uncertain terms that *they* had plans for the day and wouldn't be walking with me. *I was more determined.* They reminded me that we'd agreed to always walk together – either all three of us, or at least two of us. *I was even more determined still.*

The cabin, up until that point warm and cosy, suddenly became cold. We avoided eye contact. Our sentences were reduced to monosyllabic grunts. Conversation was punctuated by long silences. We'd gone five days without a run-in. This was the first.

I went to great pains to invent a way to keep my feet dry, slipping a plastic shopping bag between two layers of socks like a waterproof middle sock. I then spread the bag out, like a collar, over my boots, tying an elastic band around it at the top of my socks. I called them my *clodhoppers*. Both the name and the resulting arrangement were rather inelegant, but all I wanted was dry, blisterless feet.

I was glad to be away from the cabin and away from the icy stares. I was also, I realised, very happy to be walking on my own.

I found out it was actually helpful to wear my hat under the too-small raincoat hood, since the brim kept the rain from dripping onto my face – until, that is, it could

*I think you get the message, right?
I was determined... :)*

no longer hold up under the weight of the water and drooped like the ears of an Irish setter. That's when I discovered it was helpful to wear my sunglasses too – they held up the sagging brim allowing me to actually see where I was walking. So there I was in the pouring rain, still wearing my hat and sunnies. No-one had thought to attach mirrors to any of the gum trees along the Bruce Highway, so I didn't have any idea what I looked like, which was no doubt a good thing.

Walking alone gave me plenty of time to think – and to drink.

Since that first fateful day when Carnsey succumbed to dehydration, I had been dutifully carrying and imbibing copious amounts of water. It took a few hours for me to realise, however, that on a rainy day, almost everything that goes in also has to come out. My stops behind gum trees became frequent.

I didn't drink as much after that, but I did continue to think – about rain.

My brother told me a rain rhyme once and I smiled as I remembered it:

> The rain falls on the just
> and the unjust fella,
> mostly on the just,
> 'cause the unjust stole
> the just's umbrella.

Smiling when you're on your own is quite a treat. You don't have to wonder whether it's appropriate or who's watching. You just smile as often or as little as you like.

The rhyme was adapted from the passage in the Bible where Jesus says: God *sends rain on the righteous and the unrighteous* (see Matthew 5:45).

I mulled over the significance of *rain* in this Bible passage. For some of us, a fall of rain brightens our day. For a rural community like Stanthorpe that prides itself on its apples, stone fruit and grapes, rain is needed and welcomed. I have fond memories as a small boy of standing beside Mum and Dad, peering up happily at the gathering rain clouds. As a result, I've always equated rain with *good*. For others, like Hélène, brought up in Normandy on the English Channel (not to mention my shopkeeper friend from the day before), the word rain is a very close synonym for *bad*, little more than a necessary evil and perhaps even an unnecessary one.

But in that verse, the key is the last part – *on the righteous and the unrighteous*. The conclusion of my solitary pondering on that rainy day was that God doesn't have favourites.

When Mr Shopkeeper wearily surveys the rain, he sees it falling on *every* house. There is no such thing as *Sunshine Street* in Tully. *Every* street gets the rain, all four metres of it every year, and some years considerably more. The record from 1950 stands at 7.5 metres, more than ten times the average precipitation in London! There is even a 7.5 metre tall gumboot erected in the centre of the town commemorating that amazing year. My shopkeeper buddy would have done a lot of sighing and eye-rolling that year. No, God has no favourites in Tully, and He has no favourites in all the world.

Yet another gum tree stop!

Note to self: drink less!

I was still thinking about favouritism and the words of the best-known Bible verse which says, God loved the world so much that He gave His only son, so that whoever believes in Him would not die but have eternal life - see John 3:16. No, God has no favourites. His love is a *whoever* type of love.

That one single verse has been translated into more than

half of the world's 6900 languages. But what about those that still don't even have that one verse? Does God love the people who speak those languages *less* than He loves us? Doesn't that show that He *does* have favourites? No, rather it shows that *we* have favourites – that is, *us*. We are our own favourites.

It's not because God loves them *less* that they don't have His Word – it's because we don't love them *enough*. It's not because the job of translation *can't* be done – it must be because we don't *want* to do it.

While pondering all this, I had walked nineteen kilometres and, thanks to my clodhoppers, I still had dry feet. That left only 1832 kilometres to go. I phoned my now less-grumpy fellow walkers to come and pick me up and we returned together to our cabin in Tully.

0168

After the bad start in the morning, I decided they were right – we should walk together.

That would be the last day I'd walk alone.

Day 7
Magoo and Blackbird

Monday 30 August

Leaving Tully wasn't just leaving a town, or a caravan park, or even a giant gumboot. It was leaving the people we'd met at our meeting the evening before. On yet another *perfect day in paradise*, we got a hearty send-off from a few of our new friends and heard some of *their* stories while I prepared my clodhoppers.

The silver-haired pastor told about his experience living with the Aboriginal people. 'When we were in Arnhem Land, the translation of the New Testament was completed after twenty-two years,' he marvelled. 'It was about four times as thick as ours. The people were just thrilled to get it in their own language.'

A young father, Pete, was amazed at the time commitment necessary to complete a Bible translation, saying, 'That's a picture of the cross for the disciple.' He added, shaking his head ruefully, 'And some people think they're doing God a favour by just going to church on Sunday!'

An enthusiastic woman, Jennifer, recounted, 'When I was young my Dad wouldn't let us read the Bible. It was hidden away in Mum's cupboard.' Then shocked, thinking about all the bibleless people from these 2000 language groups she exclaimed:

" they don't even have a Bible to hide in a cupboard..."

As I donned sunglasses, raincoat and hat, those words resonated in my mind: *they don't even have a Bible to hide in a cupboard.* Even if they wanted to read the Bible, there isn't one for them to read. I started to pull out the bottle of sunscreen, then glanced up at the heavy cloud cover, and slipped it straight back.

Our friends gave us the latest news on the Chilean miners. Having lived in Chile for over a year and visited on several occasions, I was keenly following the progress of the rescue efforts. Work had begun on drilling a mine shaft that would hopefully enable their evacuation. It would take many weeks to complete, and opinions differed as to whether it would be successful or not. In reality their situation, like the sky above me, looked bleak.

Chile

SOUTH AMERICA.

We settled into our now-familiar, single-file walking routine. Big Red was walking ahead so I got an eyeful of his special, you-beaut, expensive, top-of-the-range, circulation-stimulating sports socks. To me they looked more like French stockings from the Renaissance period. Since there hadn't been any white ones in stock, they sent him *skin-coloured* instead. They may well have been the colour of somebody's skin, but certainly not his. Stretched over his sizeable calf muscles, they looked uncannily like artificial legs or knee-high Granny socks. However, Carnsey was so happy with his Granny socks that we didn't want to pay him out too much. Besides, with my clodhoppers and flaccid hat I didn't feel I was in the best position to be making smart comments about inelegant walking attire.

It had only been one hour since breakfast, but it already seemed like several. Over the week I had begun to make acquaintance with a largely ignored part of my body – my stomach. It had come alive, whining at me in quite a demanding manner. By 9 am I was already devouring the Vegemite sandwiches *(see over page)* which were supposed to tide me over till lunch time. Extreme Janine was right – my body was clamouring for carbohydrates. I was constantly thinking of food but there were no KFCs in sight. We carried some carbs on our back, though mostly we took advantage of stores and service stations en route. A few hours later we had seen neither, but the promise of food came in the form of a too-fast-approaching vehicle.

There was something about the car that caught my eye. Even from a distance I could see it was intruding into *my* space over the white line, and I had a very personal vested interest in that space between the white line and the ditch – my life. With the car heading towards us, I was on full alert. The headlights flashed. I was on fuller alert. Just metres away it lurched to a halt, and that's when I recognised Keith.

I call him Magoo, because he reminds me of the charming elderly cartoon character of the same name from my childhood days. Standing before me, beaming from ear to ear, he was such a pleasant-faced gentleman that I couldn't help the comparison. Out of the passenger side stepped a silver-haired member of the fairer sex, his lovely lady, Merle.

I call her Blackbird which is what her name means in French, but also because she reminds me of those energetic and cheeky little birds that bring cheer to many a French garden. I wouldn't have been surprised if the pair of them had broken into a dance right there on the highway. Everything about them defied their eighty years.

Magoo commented with a smile, 'I thought you might be in a motorised wheelchair by now.' And Blackbird laughed. The cheek of them! They were old enough to be chair-bound themselves, and yet it could well be their fun and laughter that kept the wheelchairs at bay.

Then something wonderful happened – the promise of food. Just an hour ahead, in Cardwell, Magoo and Blackbird had spotted a seafood shop and wanted to buy us fish and chips. Instantly, that's what I wanted too.

As they drove on ahead, something else wonderful happened. I fell in love. Passionately! It was another gorgeous side road. With unashamed infidelity (and the promise of fish and chips luring me on), I stepped off the Bruce Highway and threw myself into this new affair. It was close to ecstasy feeling the earth beneath my shoes and walking under silent trees that didn't fling themselves towards me at a hundred kilometres an hour.

The orange compacted track, layered with gum leaves from the past who-knows-how-many years, reminded me of many relaxing bushwalks in national parks. That was what I'd dreamed of. Not black asphalt. Away from the clamour of the highway, I could whistle, sing, talk to myself and sometimes all three simultaneously.

With the fish and chips getting nearer by the minute, we walked the last stretch along a mangrove beach under a charcoal watercolour sky with smudges of pastel blue.

I noted the warning sign:

> Crocodiles inhabit this area.
> Attacks may cause injury or death.
> Keep away from the water's edge
> and do not enter the water.

Feelings of foolishness resurfaced as I recalled my cool-off in the river a few days earlier.

Dave's energy level was still set on *high*. He bounded ahead and tiggered up a coconut tree – just because he could. As for me, I was running on *low* and so walked in an energy-conserving straight line until finally Magoo came into sight,

beckoning us to take our places at a picnic table.

Blackbird hopped around the table cheerfully feeding us generous portions of plump chips and melt-in-your-mouth chunks of white fish.

'How good is it, Sav?' Dave asked.

'It doesn't get much better than this,' I replied between mouthfuls.

0192   We finished the day with a rather last-minute meeting in the hall at the Catholic Church. With our 2000 Walk banner strung out the front, we stood back to watch the crowds pour in. The place was packed to capacity – all twelve chairs were filled. Magoo and Blackbird were there beaming from the back row, and in the front was a lovely South African lady with an equally lovely name, Hannelie.

Meeting over, we bunked down in the priest's vacant apartment at the back of the church. Before turning the lights out, I walked a few more paperback kilometres in Turkey with Bernard – we were now on first-name terms – and then slept soundly.

VEGEMITE FOR FOREIGNERS

VEGEMITE FOR AUSSIES

AS FOR ME, I JUST SPREAD IT ON WITH A TROWEL

Day 8
Meals on wheels

Tuesday 31 August

Bright and early in the morning, at our appointed spot on the Bruce Highway, Magoo and Blackbird turned up to see us off. Magoo was wearing an in-your-face blue T-shirt emblazoned with the slogan: *This is what a really cool eighty-year-old looks like.* We parted ways with the really cool eighty-year-olds. They continued their journey north, we continued south.

The novelty of the day would be another highway encounter – my uncle and aunt. A text message had confirmed they were heading up The Bruce and would be looking out for us. I figured we'd be pretty hard to miss – this was now our eighth day on the road and we hadn't seen *any* other walkers. Three guys travelling at five kilometres an hour would stand out in stark contrast to all the others travelling at a hundred kilometres an hour.

We hadn't gone far when I was once more seduced by the sight of an irresistible parallel path fifty metres away. I plunged off the highway in that direction, not wasting a moment in distancing myself from the incessant fizzle and swish of rubber on wet asphalt. Big Red and Sky Blue chose to stay on the highway. They said:

They nailed it on both accounts.

Weaving my way through a myriad of sparse bushes, I disturbed a plover that took to the wing, its shrill cry cutting the air. As I moved my way between saplings and slender gum trees, it was like stepping into a Frederick McCubbin canvas. The brighter greens of the tropical north had given way to the more familiar subdued olive and grey tones that most people associate with Australia – and with McCubbin. However, there was no teary-eyed lost child standing among the trees. Instead, the frogs croaked their welcome, the birds chirped cheerfully and the ground sponged beneath my clodhoppers. It was intoxicatingly beautiful.

That quiet hour went by quickly, and I was all too soon back on The Bruce with the boys, waiting for my rellies to appear.

'They'll come bearing food,' I assured my hungry companions. 'They'll pull up, open the hamper and produce a thermos of hot soup. There'll be bread, coffee, tea, Mars bars. They're great like that.' Conversation turned easily around the anticipation of such delights and my salivary glands joined my stomach in singing discordant harmonies of their latest rendition of *Carbohydrate Cravings*.

We walked in single file, in step, like a mini army parade of three. As we marched on, shadowless in the dull light, hour after boring hour crawled by, broken only by intermittent drizzle and the headlights and swish of cars that sprayed us with water. These unsolicited showers finally got the better of Carnsey. After extracting a very large garbage bag, he proceeded to fight with it until he got his head and arms in the appropriate holes of this makeshift raincoat. As he flapped his way down the highway, the combo garbage bag and Granny socks must have startled many a driver. I hadn't thought to bring a garbage bag, but it did occur to me that if I'd had the foresight to bring some shower gel, I could have taken advantage of the road spray to soap up and startle some drivers myself. These thoughts provided a momentary distraction from the fact that there was still no sign of our much-anticipated roadside picnic. By then my salivary glands had almost salivated themselves dry.

Without fanfare and according to our best possible estimate, we crossed the 200 kilometre mark to complete ten per cent of our walk. Carnsey said, 'Very do-able, just like the task of translation – one step at a time.'   0200

Dave added, '*Only* 1800 kilometres to go.' We all laughed. We were in good spirits, probably due to the combination of the kilometres completed, the wonderful walking weather and the promise of a picnic.

Minutes later, the promise materialised. Meals on wheels! Not wanting to appear overly eager, and feeling it would be inconsiderate to pounce immediately on the spoils, we engaged in a good deal of polite and friendly banter with my aunt and uncle. We were oh-so-polite but oh-so-hungry, and the picnic was taking oh-so-long to appear. It took so long in fact, that we were finally forced to face the sad fact that there *was* no picnic. Like a mirage that evaporates into the hot desert air as you approach, so our soup, Mars bars and drinks disappeared into the drizzle. When I could no longer avoid Carnsey's eye, his glance told me that I would never live this one down. At last though, the situation took a turn for the better when my aunt reached into the glove box. But it took a turn for the worse when all she produced was a packet of chewing gum.

As we said our goodbyes, three sets of jaws working on our gum, Carnsey made a great show of gratitude, entirely for my benefit, explaining how much he enjoyed electrolyte gum and how it would provide us with the energy needed for the last leg of the day. My uncle hadn't even changed into second gear before the cousins started paying me out. They got a lot of mileage out of that chewing gum incident, which at least helped pass the next couple of hungry hours, until we'd clocked up our thirty kilometres for the day.

0222

While Dave and Carnsey enjoyed a wonderful South African meal with Hannelie and her family, I enjoyed the evening alone, reading how Bernard was faring under the scorching Turkish sun.

And in the meantime, unbeknown to us, 1778 kilometres to the south our home town of Stanthorpe was enjoying its brand new status as winner of the *Tidy Towns of Queensland* competition.

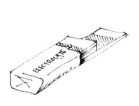

Day 9
8 kms 2 many

Wednesday 1 September

The new day dawned – once again – cloudy. We hadn't seen the sun for a full week. I was staggered. We were prepared for a lot of things, but never for a week of refreshingly cool, cloudy days.

Speaking of refreshing, Hannelie was there to see us off with three individually wrapped aluminium foil bundles containing our lunches. We popped them gratefully into our backpacks, knowing full well that we would be popping them right out again long before lunchtime.

Hannelie's English was wonderful really, close to faultless apart from some minor word order issues. However, I suspected that while giving an appearance of confidence, there lurked a different story. I couldn't help gently plying her with questions. Her mother tongue? Afrikaans. Where had she learned English? She knew quite a bit before coming to Australia, and had huge exposure to it growing up, including in the South African education system.

'But I still pray in Afrikaans,' she added. 'If I have to, I can pray in English but it doesn't come so easy. I have to think more and I sort of lose a bit of the emotion behind it. I'm more confident in my own language. I take even to church my Afrikaans Bible. The verses much more stick in my head than actually the English verses.'

This short conversation stuck in *my* head because, like Hannelie, I can pray in another language too: French. Even though I am fluent, it doesn't come easily. I too have to think, and can lose the sincerity and emotion.

But that isn't the main reason her words stayed with me. You see, there is one question that I am frequently asked regarding people groups that don't have the Bible translated in their language:

"Since we already have English Bibles, why don't we just teach them all English?"

That question is understandable in this third millennium when Speed and Economy are spelt with capital letters. Hitting on a solution that bypasses 2000 languages seems to be a logical winning plan, until, that is, you meet someone like Hannelie who in the course of a five-minute conversation shatters that logic. Even as a *very* fluent speaker of English, she is not a model for the *teach-them-English* approach. Quite the contrary – praying in English takes effort, Bible verses don't stick and she doesn't use her English Bible in church. Basically, even after all these years, English is *still* a poor second for Hannelie.

How then to respond to the *Why don't you teach them English* question? I needed more than words to do that. I needed a story or maybe an illustration, something visual to use in our meetings to help people remember – but while nothing came immediately to mind, eventually I would be inspired. I knew that unless people were convinced that the Bible *had* to be translated in the different languages, nobody would move from their lounge chairs *(as per page 21)*.

In fact, I could have used a lounge chair right at that moment, but they were few and far between along The Bruce. Over the previous few days my feet had begun to get sore. I managed to keep the blister damage to a minimum though, with layers of plaster strips, regular popping and ... ouch ... methylated spirits. However, I stopped complaining because for a change we were walking on soft grass, away from The Bruce, alongside cane fields.

The grass soon came to an end, however, and so too did Hannelie's chunky chicken and mayo sandwiches. A Taruuba proverb advises: *Wait till you're hungry if you want to eat great food.* Well, I was hungry and those sandwiches were truly great.

On that stretch of road, for the first time and for some unknown reason, several cars stopped to offer us lifts. I checked to see if I had a sign on my back: *Pick me up.* We had to explain each time, of course, that we were walking home – to Stanthorpe – which inevitably caused the drivers' eyebrows to raise a full centimetre. Everyone knew that Stanthorpe was a very long way away.

Carnsey came very close to having his elbow *shaved* by a car coming from behind. We didn't usually worry about vehicles from behind, because they were in the far lane, unless of course, they were overtaking, which is what this one was doing. I stepped back with a yell and Carnsey instinctively drew back as if hit, clutching his elbow. We will never know just how close that shave really was.

A few kilometres further, a police car slowed down to our pace and rolled along beside us. The window eventually slid down and from behind dark sunglasses Mr Cool Cop asked in his Mr Cool Cop voice:

WHERE ARE you BOYS WALKING TO?

STANTHORPE.

He ungraciously retorted under his breath, before gunning his car out of sight, 'Bloody idiots!' I had to concede, after our elbow experience, that he was probably right.

0245 Stepping into Ingham brought back a flood of childhood memories, as that is home to another uncle and aunt. As a boy, along with my brothers, I suffered – on more than one occasion – the interminable drive to visit the Ingham rellies. Not only was the suffering of the car trip itself something akin to torture but, on arrival, the heat added insult to injury. The local swimming pool was hot, the sheets on the bed were hot, and even the cold showers were hot. But now it was different. It was *cool*!

My heart leapt as I turned into my uncle and aunt's street, Sir Arthur Fadden Parade, named after the Australian Prime Minister who was born in Ingham. Sir Arthur Fadden held the position of Prime Minister for all of six weeks – he used to tell people that he *reigned for forty days and forty nights*. I'm not sure what happened to *Artie* (as he was affectionately known) for his stay at the top to be so short-lived, but the thought occurred to me that he spent less time as Prime Minister than I was spending walking along the Bruce Highway.

My initial concern that this uncle and aunt might have been in cahoots with the others – and would only serve us chewing gum – proved unfounded. We settled down to tuck into a hearty cold meat and salad lunch.

My uncle offered to show me the sights. Instead, as fate would have it, he'd have the indubitable delight of driving up and down the Bruce Highway in his Mitsubishi Magna for half the afternoon, searching for his lost nephew.

It happened like this:

After lunch I'd had another one of my last-minute panic attacks. We *were* on schedule, but I was painfully aware that a simple blister or a dose of mango ice-cream –

not to mention floating logs or overtaking cars – could throw a serious spanner in my carefully planned works. Having arrived in Ingham early, and still revelling in the inexplicably ideal walking weather, I made the executive decision to forego the sightseeing and much-needed rest, and instead, clock up some more kilometres for good measure.

As we strode down the main street and out of town heading south, we window-shopped at a brisk pace of five kilometres an hour – pharmacy, newsagent, Bossi Boots shoe shop, JK's delicatessen – just time enough to notice the names but not enough to be enticed to any retail therapy. Perfect! The main street, like many in North Queensland, is so wide that you have to take a packed lunch when attempting to cross it. But we didn't have to cross it; we just walked on, facing the oncoming traffic and headed out of town. Deep in conversation, we realised that walking had become more pleasant, quieter. I could now easily clock a minute, or even two, between passing vehicles.

It was curious how few cars there were *south* of Ingham as opposed to the *north*. If we had been more observant we would also have noticed that the road was somewhat narrower and that the sinking sun, visible behind thin cloud cover, had now swung around ahead of us, instead of being on our right. So thoroughly were we enjoying the unexpected quiet and the ensuing conversation that was possible as a result, we were oblivious to the obvious. A full two hours later, wondering why Uncle hadn't arrived to pick us up as planned, we passed a street sign:

ABERGOWRIE RD.

It all became painfully clear. The unthinkable had happened. We had taken the wrong road and walked eight kilometres in the wrong direction. The next day we'd have to start all over again, on the right road.

Dave asked, 'How are you feelin', Sav?'

It took me a while to reply. I ran my fingers through my hair, sat down wearily on the lush green grass, removed my shoes, massaged my toes and looked up at the first patches of cobalt blue showing through the clouds.
'To be really honest,' I replied quietly, 'I don't feel so discouraged.' After another long pause, recalling Mr Cool Cop's words, I added, 'I just feel like an idiot.'

There was no way to contact my uncle while he was scouring the Bruce Highway making repeated trips back and forth – for over an hour – which we would hear about in detail when we finally got a lift back to Ingham.

The folk who turned out to meet us at the Uniting Church got a good laugh hearing how we ended up on Abergowrie Road.

All except Uncle, of course.

Next time I eat at his place, I'm only expecting chewing gum.

Day 10
Magpie geese

Thursday 2 September

As we set off south, this time on the *right* road, it was shaping up to be a hot one – the first cloudless sky for over a week, and it was already very warm. My thoughts, however, were not on the blue of the sky overhead but on the green of the grass underfoot. The Bruce Highway spread out before us so ridiculously wide and with enough green edging to set up a cricket field. How *could* we have mistaken Abergowrie Road for The Bruce!

My thoughts tumbled over each other and gelled into a sort of metaphor. Our *wrong road* had begun as a great experience until we realised we weren't actually *on track*, at which point it immediately lost its lustre. You see, even though we were having a good time, *that* road was no use to us. We needed to be on the *right* road because we had a destination and an arrival date to stick to. Walking on that comfortable road was an epic waste of time and energy, no matter how *good* it felt.

In the same way, as God's people, we are on a journey with a destination and an arrival date as well, even though no-one knows the details. That journey comes with the mandate to preach the gospel *to all nations, and then the end will come* (Matthew 24:14).

We have not yet come to the end! But how easy it is to become side-tracked and waste our resources. How difficult to stay on the right road and get behind the great task of seeing the gospel message translated and preached in every language.

Dave bounced into the lead while I fell to the back,

enjoying my own company and my own thoughts. A small shadow in the blue canvas above caught my eye. A hawk was circling on outstretched wings, a lone ice-skater on its private, immaculate, celestial rink. I paused a moment, and my spirit soared. Further on, I paused again before a magnificent python, four metres long and as thick as a man's arm, lying perfectly still. Unlike the dreaded taipan, and despite its impressive size, the python is harmless. This one was even more harmless than most as its head had been crushed by a passing vehicle. Most of the road kill up to this point had been snakes – dozens of them – but none to match the size of this beauty. I removed my sunglasses to admire its opulent checkerboard cloak, shimmering in the sunlight.

The phone vibrated in my pocket. Hélène was phoning from Stanthorpe to tell me the weather forecast predicted blue skies and sunshine. She wished me well for what was looking like being a very hot walking day.

Little by little over the next hours, the skies and trees came alive, teeming with happy chirping, trilling and whistling. My ears tuned in and my heart overflowed with praise to the Mastermind behind it all. All these feathered friends who had been snugly tucked away during the long, cool, drizzly days, were now celebrating big time – and I was privileged to witness it. The sunshine made everything seem more animated. Even my hat, crispy dry again, was celebrating by flaunting a firm brim. I'd forgotten what it was like not to have it flopping over my ears and eyes.

A snow-white heron stepped elegantly through the long grass beside me, and some way ahead a family of ibis, in a Monet-like pond of croaking frogs and pink and white water lilies, turned their heads in my direction. Ibis are among my all-time favourite birds. The curve of beak and back, and the contrast of white and black have often been the subject of my pen and ink sketches. As I came nearer however, I realised I was wrong – these were birds I'd never seen before, except that is, on one of Mum's ancient biscuit tins. Now here before me, the scene depicted on the lid of that tin was unfolding magically. A hundred gaggling magpie geese were happily congregating in this wetland. I recalled the name, thanks to the biscuit tin, but for some strange reason had never realised the magpie goose was an Australian bird, found here in my own state of Queensland.

Perhaps being inspired by the geese in their happy water world, four hours later, the cousins and I – at my insistence – took a detour to Jourama Falls for a dip in the creek. A creek guaranteed, so they say, to be crocodile-free. Framed by a large rock face on one side and a line of trees dipping low on the other, our naked torsos were mirrored perfectly on the surface of the refreshing, still water, while the echoes of a hundred tiny birds sparkled incessantly and joyfully all around.

'It doesn't get much better than this,' I commented to Dave.

We agreed that it certainly beat walking. We wondered why, instead of walking 2000 kilometres, we hadn't come up with something like visiting the world's top 2000 tourist destinations to raise awareness for the 2000

Bibleless languages. But somehow that didn't *quite* have the same ring to it.

Carnsey wanted to Twitpic me in my wet jocks and send the photo instantly to our millions of followers who were spending sleepless nights waiting for tasty morsels from the walking trio. Thankfully, common sense prevailed. He no doubt weighed up the amusement the photo would provide for one brief moment (no pun intended) against the likelihood of a vindictive walking companion for the next two months.

0262   When my mother phoned from Cairns a couple of hours later, I told her about the biscuit-tin birds. She said she was thinking of me in the *withering heat* – one of her well-worn phrases. Withering heat? Apparently in Cairns it was. However by that time we were happily 262 kilometres south of Cairns, walking once more, as cool as the proverbial salad vegetable, under heavy cloud cover and, once more, with a pleasant breeze.

And the clouds hung around – again – for the rest of the day.

Day 11
Disorganised

Friday 3 September

In the years leading up to The Walk I had often daydreamed about this adventure, smiling as I imagined myself meandering through the silent Aussie bush along dapple-shaded paths, whistling *The Happy Wanderer*. In those self-indulgent moments I would see myself a-wandering lazily, with numerous tranquil detours and enjoying chance meetings along the way. Now, however, I had to face the hard truth – the reality was something different altogether. We'd set ourselves a schedule and mostly had to keep up a cracking pace. And even when not *a-cracking*, we were certainly far from *a-wandering*. And the Bruce Highway was far from silent *or* dapple-shaded. Nor was any of the adventure left to chance. It was all organisation, schedule and deadlines. I was often up until after midnight, burning valuable sleep time writing up the daily blog, sometimes with tears of fatigue and resentment filling my bloodshot eyes. Yes, my dream had turned pear-shaped. We'd tied ourselves up in a straitjacket.

I say *we*, but in my gloom – which I tried admirably to keep to myself – I have to admit that what I meant was *them*. Well, what I really meant was *him*. In his typical fervour and zeal (read: *obsessive workaholism*) Carnsey couldn't conceive of investing a block of eighty days of his life – without *filling* it. One by one the ideas had surfaced: website, blog, meetings, interviews, mailings and posters. The list had grown ad infinitum. His enthusiasm had been contagious and, one by one, I had nodded my agreement to each idea. In all fairness, perhaps one or two of those ideas *may* have originated with me. But fairness wasn't an invited guest at my private pity party.

The days were full and, like clumsy circus clowns, we were constantly juggling all the different aspects of The Walk. Thanks to Dave, though, we generally did remarkably well since he took on a huge part of the logistics, including accommodation, meeting venues, finance and food. No, we'd never have done it without Tigger! In the public eye I believe we mostly gave the appearance of being highly organised, though behind the scenes it was often a very different story. For example, if today had been a baseball game, we would have been completely struck out.

We were on the road by 7.30 am, accompanied once more by what we were now affectionately referring to as our *2000 Walk clouds*. Nice. Not only that, but within the hour we discovered a side road parallel to The Bruce. After a few kilometres, however, it turned into a dead end. Through the trees we could see the highway, with fifty metres of very long grass and as many taipans separating us. I knew the taipans were there, I could see each and every one of them with my super-Sav, infra-red vision.

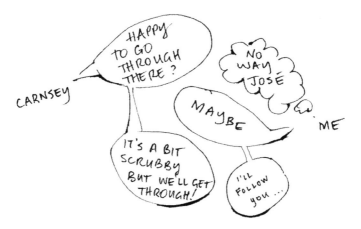

Carnsey, not mentioning the unthinkable, was keen to push through.

Needing no more encouragement than my feeble reply, Carnsey plunged noisily towards his certain death, up to his shoulders in grass. I tiptoed after him. A decayed log split in half as he stepped onto it and a dozen *somethings* slithered out from under it. Every blade of grass that brushed against my leg had fangs. Halfway across, at the point of no return, he bellowed loudly (and I *would* eventually forgive him for it), 'Good thing there are no taipans in North Queensland.' As in the cartoons, at the

mention of the T word, my feet touched my ears and didn't come near the ground until I was safely over on the Bruce Highway.

STRIKE ONE

Note to self: don't do that again.

A long-awaited live radio interview from Townsville was scheduled for 9 am. I should say it had been *re-scheduled*, since previous attempts – while we were out of phone-coverage area – had been unsuccessful. It was surprising they hadn't given up on us. As Carnsey addressed the region live on air, his enthusiasm turned to horror when his phone battery died. Snatching up our other phone, he dialled the station's number, remembering as he did that there was almost no credit left on that one. Totally embarrassed, he quickly gave the number to the DJ and asked him to phone back, which he did. The first question asked was, 'What day did you guys set out on your Walk?' Now this question was really not rocket science. For months now we had been living, eating and breathing the launch date: 24th of August. Without a moment's hesitation though, and for some bizarre reason unknown even to himself, Carnsey gave the wrong answer, declaring, 'The 14th of August.' I stared at him in disbelief. He screwed up his face, mortified. The rest of the interview went by in a blur. I don't think those people ever phoned us again.

Strike Two

A call came through from Ingham to remind us to pick up the shirts – a whole batch of specially printed 2000 Walk T-shirts we'd be selling in our meetings. We'd totally forgotten. That was one more thing for Dave to fit into his schedule – drive back almost one hundred kilometres to collect them.

Strike Three

There is really no word in the English language to describe how we felt following our three strikes. That's why we had to borrow one from our German friends: *klutz.*

The phone buzzed to indicate a text message. It was from Hannelie: *Thinking of you three today. You guys are so organised!!*

Little did she know.

Day 12
Scars

Saturday 4 September

I cut wide strips of plaster and carefully positioned them over my blisters. Some blisters were old – little more than scars, hard and calloused. Others were fresh, recently jabbed and drained, and already drying out nicely thanks to the ever-present bottle of metho. Satisfied with my handiwork, I pulled on a fresh pair of socks and laced up my shoes ready for the kilometres that lay ahead. It was my twelfth consecutive day treading bitumen. Twelve days without a break! Starting out both tired and with very sore feet, I was slowly wearing down. Glancing up, however, I smiled at our 2000 Walk clouds that were faithfully mustering for duty once more. I knew without a doubt that I wouldn't have made it that far without them.

Like my battered feet, the first stretch of highway also bore scars. The tree trunks were charred and blackened, testimony to one of the greatest natural dangers and takers-of-life in this huge country – bushfire. The worst in our nation's history, known as Black Saturday, was

in Victoria in 2009. It took 173 lives. The grisly scenes of destruction wrought in those few short, nightmarish hours will be forever engraved in our collective memory. I paused to look up into one of the trees where someone had nailed a small white sign *(see previous page)* with hand-painted red lettering: *The Lord's Return is Near.*

It somehow seemed a fitting place for an apocalyptic message. Given the size of the sign and the speed of passing traffic, however, I doubt whether one person in a thousand would even be aware of its presence. That too seemed fitting – a small voice crying in the wilderness.

My thoughts turned to the Bible, which tells us that our planet has a limited shelf life. The end will come, it says, when the good news of the Kingdom of God is preached throughout all the world, so that all nations will hear it (Matthew 24:14). This doesn't refer to countries as we know them, with boundaries established as a result of war or treaties, but rather to groups of people, each one bound by a common culture and language. While *political nations* only number around 200, the *ethnic nations*, each with a distinct language, number almost 7000.

The hours wore on.

G'day bloke

Dave walked along the top of a segment of the twenty-seven kilometre water pipeline running parallel to the highway – just because he could.

0300

Somewhere we crossed the 300 kilometre mark. The distance separating me from Hélène and the boys seemed huge. They were 1700 kilometres away and a wave of homesickness overtook me, brought on largely by sleep deprivation.

0315

The day's quota of kilometres completed, we ended up at lovely Balgal Beach, at a wonderful takeaway – *Fisherman's Landing.* The proprietor had heard of these three crazy walkers and lunch was on the house.

86

Sitting is an extremely pleasant activity after seven
or eight hours on your feet, and even more so when it
happens on a shaded deck overlooking the estuary with a
very full plate of fish, chips, battered prawns and scallops.
As I washed it all down with a Bundaberg *Lemon, Lime
and Bitters*, the radio played one of my favourite songs by
Bryan Adams:

Homesickness kicked in again. Until, that is, a voice called
'Crocodile!' and all three of us stood in unison, straining
to catch a glimpse of the resident reptile. Alas, to no avail.

In the evening we found ourselves in Townsville,
eating again, this time barbecued sausages. A couple of
hundred people were gathered, keen to hear our story
and our message. The sausages came in very handy, the
obligatory jaw movement helping keep my eyes open.
In my state of fatigue, I thought I was hallucinating
when I saw Maxine, our roadside *things* delivery lady
from Cairns, suddenly appear looking twenty-five years
younger. I rubbed my eyes, but when she didn't go away,
I began to suspect the sausages were spiked. It turned out
that it was Miss Maxinette, Maxine's daughter, who has
inherited more than her Mum's charm. What a delight
to meet Miss Maxinette and her equally affable brother,
Mr Mediterranean who, with his complexion, looked like
he'd just stepped off a beach in southern France.

After the meeting, I trundled home to bed and it
wasn't long before Mr Sandman came knocking. Before
opening the door to him, however, I opened Bernard to
discover that he *too* was on the twelfth day of *his* walk.

He was going at a cracking pace and had completed 360 kilometres, forty-five ahead of us! Inspiring! I was also inspired by the questions he asked himself and *his* questions became *mine*:

Vais-je tenir moralement, physiquement? Will I hold out psychologically, physically?

Irai-je jusqu'au bout? Will I make it to the end?

Bernard was pessimistic. I felt the same way. This was hard going. I was wearing down and wasn't a very cheerful walking partner. I had no idea if I *would* make it to the end or not.

However, if we only attempt challenges where success is guaranteed, life would be superlatively boring!

One of my favourite books is "The Road Less Travelled" – but the funny part is that I've never read it – haha. I just find the title really challenging!!

Day 13
Father's Day

Sunday 5 September

Waking up gently, unhurriedly, leisurely – nothing less than *ecstasy*!

There was no raucous alarm clock screaming into my auditory canal, and no light burning into the recesses of my eye sockets. Just silence. It was my day off – my first. Dave and Carnsey had slipped out to their church meetings, leaving me alone in our beach cabin. I turned over, slowly and deliberately, savouring the contact of clean skin with clean sheets. I plumped up my pillow and slept again.

This afforded me the joy, two hours later, of waking up gently and leisurely for a second time. A deep yawn surfaced like a slow bubble and I stretched, long and hard. Automatically, I slid my foot sideways reaching for one who might have been beside me, but wasn't. She was nearly 1700 kilometres away.

It was the first Sunday in September – Father's Day. For the first time since we welcomed our daughter, Estelle, into our family, twenty years earlier – and subsequently our second daughter, Yésica, and our two sons – I was childless on this of all days. A phone call with the boys back in Stanthorpe was a cheer up, but there was no call from my girls in France. They wouldn't have known it was Father's Day. In France it's celebrated on the third Sunday in June, as it is in many other countries where I have also celebrated Father's Day, including Chile.

Speaking of Chile, it was exactly thirty days since the miners had been trapped. Most of them were fathers too, also separated from their families.

I spent the day reading, snacking, snoozing, writing emails and sitting on the beach watching the tide come in. With every passing hour, like the incoming tide, my sanity returned. When Dave and Carnsey showed up at the end of the day, they found a much more agreeable Sav.

G'day bloke

Two stately retirees, Bruce and Elaine, hosted us for the evening meal and told the story of their work in Bible translation among the Aboriginal people. It was an opportunity for us to learn a little about the language situation in our own country. When Australia was colonised in the late eighteenth century there may have been more than 500 distinct indigenous languages. Now there are fewer than 150 in daily use, and it is estimated that perhaps only twenty of them will survive to the next generation.

This cloud represents the aboriginal languages from Queensland only. At first glance how many names do you think are listed here? Then count them and see how close you get — I'll bet you're way off! I was!

90

What about Bible translation? A major landmark was reached in 2007 when, for the first time, an entire Bible was completed in one of the indigenous languages, Kriol, which has 30,000 speakers. That project took thirty years and involved the work of a hundred committed people.

Then it was my turn to tell a story – about my shirt. I was celebrating Father's Day by wearing my favourite T-shirt – a light blue $9.99 special from Crazy Clark's. That shirt held incredible sentimental value for me. Bruce and Elaine wanted to know the story behind it. It happened the previous year when I went shopping with my sons:

Ten minutes later...

Lining up at the check-out, and in spite of my severity,

I noticed Flynn surreptitiously drop something among the other items. I saw red, and in no uncertain terms instructed him to take it back immediately.

To my shame, I made a scene in front of the check-out girl who wasn't fazed. She'd no doubt seen a lot worse.

I raised my voice and made point-blank eye contact, which my boys know to mean the end of all negotiation. My father's heart was not totally insensitive, though, to the shiny tears welling up in Flynn's big blue eyes. I managed to swallow my pride and picked up the object.

As I lifted the shirt high and in utter embarrassment read the words emblazoned across the chest, I couldn't bring myself to look the check-out girl in the eye. Even then, I could feel the smirk on her face. I'm sure she's got a lot of mileage out of that incident. I certainly hope so, because it was priceless. In my Alzheimer years I hope it will be one of the very last memories to leave me.

I was proudly wearing that T-shirt, not because I am the world's greatest Dad, but because I have the world's greatest kids.

Can you believe it .?
I think I've lost this shirt.
Very sad! I wanted to
keep it forever!! ☹

Day 14
Erastus

Monday 6 September

My alarm went off at 5.30 am and, with sincere apologies to Willie Nelson, I was *not* singing *Just can't wait to get on the road again*. Quite frankly, I could have easily waited another day or two. My version was: *Just can't wait to get a day off again*. After just a few kilometres, my day off already seemed light years away and my feet didn't really feel any the better for it.

Once more, we encountered thousands of cars, hundreds of trucks and scores of road kill. The road kill, apart from snakes of different colours and sizes, also included kangaroos, owls, hawks, bandicoots, bats, echidnas and – saddest of all – the lovely ibis, dignity crippled and bleached plumage stained crimson. Some of the road kill we smelt long before we saw it, which provided us with a wonderful opportunity to practise both holding our breath *and* sprinting as fast as we could.

At one point, I was re-united with my shadow. For just half an hour, our 2000 Walk clouds parted, revealing a sizzling sun, a reminder of the affliction they had been protecting us from. My trusty hat and sunglasses momentarily served their intended purposes. At that stage, however, I was less concerned about the sun and increasingly concerned about my feet. After several hours walking on bitumen, my soles were rasped tender and burning hot. As a result I was beginning to limp. Not

0334 only that, a splitting headache kicked in and my neck was out – both of which often accompanied back trouble. It had been my hardest day so far. I mentioned that to Dave and Carnsey.

'Pain is just weakness leaving the body,' chirped Dave. Carnsey said nothing. I was staggered and not a little downhearted.

Nevertheless, Bernard had already prepared me for this: *L'insouciance des jeunes en bonne santé ne tient pas compte des plaintes des moins jeunes et leurs petites douleurs.* He confirmed from his experience that the 'carefree attitude of young people in good health doesn't give heed to the complaints of the not-so-young and their aches and pains.' The word he uses to describe the attitude of young people is *insouciance.* According to my dictionary there are many synonyms for this word including: flippant attitude, lack of commitment, carelessness, disregard and neglect. Some of these came to mind regarding the apparent lack of concern of my fellow walkers.

I mostly decided not to say anything – not wanting to be known as a whinger – but, at the same time, they had to know I needed them to cut me some slack to be able to pull through.

0352 Our kilometres over for the day, we walked into Weir Primary School and achieved instant hero status from a thousand screaming, arm-waving children at a special assembly arranged in our honour. There was a television crew from Channel Seven and journalists from the *Townsville Bulletin*, known locally as *The Bully*. We were filmed and photographed while a jumble of hands – brown and white – reached out to touch the intrepid heroes as we passed nobly through their midst – courageous and fearless knights worthy of veneration. I silently contemplated the title for a book: *Hero or Hypocrite.*

We had fifteen minutes to address this swarm of hyperactive kids and say something of consequence. Languages! I'd begin with languages.

'How many of you speak English?'

A roar went up and so did every hand in the room.

'How many of you speak two languages?'

Another roar and most of the hands still waved madly. I was impressed and slightly dumbstruck.

'How many of you speak three languages?'

no, this is not the charred remains of a bush fire !! sigh...

A louder roar and still the hands were waving furiously. Now I knew they were taking the mickey out of me. I felt just a tad peeved, not to mention embarrassed, as several members of the teaching staff tried every trick in the book to bring back some semblance of order, including roaring and waving *their* hands in the air too.

Carnsey did a better job than me and soon calm replaced chaos. He talked about the Harry Potter books, which have been translated into 68 different languages. By way of comparison, he then talked about the Book of Books, the world number-one bestseller of all time which has been translated into a massive 500 languages, and the New Testament into a further 1000. Those stats make young Harry pale into insignificance.

I did wonder, though, why the kids listened quietly and calmly to Carnsey and not to me. Another of life's little mysteries.

My highlight for the day, however, was not the arm-waving, primary-school kids but meeting Miss Maxinette's pet baby python, Erastus. I instantly recognised the same abstract diamond markings as the one that lay across our path a few days earlier. Erastus was a miniature version, a Coastal Carpet Python. I was spellbound as my new friend flowed across my hand, slipped effortlessly around my wrist and coiled, cold, around my forearm. He was a spectacular piece of workmanship, awesome in every aspect from flicking tongue and angular head, all the way down his one hundred centimetres of sensual spirals to the tapering tip of his tail.

How my sons would *love* to have a pet Erastus.

Day 15
Radio interview

Tuesday 7 September

Radio announcers the world over, regardless of the language they speak, have rich and well-oiled voices. Looking up at us over the microphone, Dan was no exception.

'Well, we've got the boys here with me this morning at 99.9 Live FM,' he broadcast to the early risers of Townsville, with enviable clarity and confidence. 'It's great to have Dave, Carnsey and Sav as they're about to embark on the next stage of their journey. It's fantastic to have your company this morning, boys.'

We responded in chorus with appropriate grunts and greetings. I smiled at the word *boys* – it had been a long time since anyone had called me a boy. Dan's first question, however, quickly wiped the smile off my face.

'So you've really just started out on this epic journey, haven't you?'

I spluttered. Just started out? We'd been trudging along for a full two weeks, clocking up 352 kilometres, and he said, 'Just started out?' I *wasn't* impressed! My strong reaction to Dan's choice of words was probably only *partly* due to feeling that this had already been a mammoth achievement. Perhaps it was *more* due to the sudden shocking realisation that his throwaway comment was *true*. Yes, we *were* still in the early stages, with less than twenty per cent of The Walk completed.

The interview continued. Dan chuckled at our megastar status at Weir Primary School – he'd seen the clip on our blog that morning. I recounted how The Walk had started as a personal dream. He confessed to being shocked when he heard about the number of languages in the world, and said that when he tried to name as many as possible he couldn't get past twenty. The interview was drawing to a close and when Dan asked if there was any last comment, Carnsey finished by expressing our thanks to Live FM, 'on behalf of the 350 million Bibleless people.' Dan had already turned away, finger poised to hit the button that would put us off air, but at Carnsey's words he turned back, stammering, '... can we ... go back ... just going back, because we haven't heard that number before.'

'The number of people represented by the 2000 languages without the Bible,' Carnsey explained, 'is 350 million. That's how many people can't read or hear God's Word because it hasn't yet been translated into a language they understand.'

Dan was almost – just almost – lost for words.

We stepped out of the studio into the sunshine.

Mr Mediterranean and two other uni students were waiting to walk with us. All three were about to embark on the longest walk – by far – they'd ever done; our goal was forty kilometres. Even though there was a veil of cloud, the sun's rays were already biting through. In preparation for what was ahead, all six of us liberally splashed on sunscreen, looking like we'd come off second-best in a war against low-bombing seagulls. Dave led off. He walked along a wall. He walked along a narrow handrail. Sometimes he even walked along the path with the rest of us. Carnsey challenged, 'Now we want to see you walk on water, Dave.'

0392 Late in the afternoon a car pulled up beside us. It was our pick-up, Miss Maxinette. She said she'd nearly turned back, thinking she must have missed us. She couldn't believe we'd actually walked that far. My feet certainly believed it.

A wonderful shower later, sitting bare foot at the meal table and tucking into our plates of carbs, we witnessed our faces and feet appear on the Channel Seven news. *The Three Wise Men*, they called us, before proceeding to broadcast to the world about our wrong turn which cost us eight additional kilometres. The sweetly smiling young newsreader quipped, 'They needed more than spiritual guidance.'

our support vehicle

Day 16
Slump

Wednesday 8 September

One skill we developed very quickly, and to a high level of proficiency, was texting while walking. There are no laws governing this, in the way there are laws governing mobile phone use while driving, though both are equally dangerous. Whether you drive off the road into a tree, or step onto the road in front of an oncoming vehicle, the speed at the time of impact is identical. But we had it down to a fine art since text messaging can be a lifeline in a time of crisis. It was crisis time for me.

In spite of almost perfect walking conditions – heavy cloud cover (yet again!) *and* cane-field service roads – every kilometre, even early in the day, was a struggle. My back was feeling somewhat ordinary and my feet were hard and sore. As I walked I could feel myself going under, slumping, both physically and psychologically. Through tears of utter fatigue and bitter disappointment I tapped out a message to Hélène.

So hard to keep going. So different to what I'd hoped. This is not my dream. That dream is dead. Hard pretending to be excited. Just trudging and getting more and more exhausted. Another conflict with Carnsey. He wants to fit something else in. Caught up in a big machine, a treadmill going faster than I wanted. My heart is not in it. Hard to come to terms. Will it be like this for 66 more days??? Hope your day is better. Miss u all. Can't wait for this to be over.

But it wasn't over. Far from it. We still had exactly 1600 kilometres to go. However, the upside was that we reached the invisible 400 kilometre landmark.

To commemorate that milestone in some visual way, we looked around to see what we had on hand. Behind us were the ever-present sugarcane fields and we contemplated twisting some cane into the shape of a four and two zeros, but gave that up as a bad idea. Several handfuls of mown grass sufficed and, *voilà*, there we had it! Those few minutes were a welcome reprieve before we were off again. But I was still feeling down.

Later in the day things brightened up a little, thanks to some people from Giru who blew winds of encouragement into my sagging sail through a deed, a word, some timely advice and a personal story.

While some of our other hosts lived a long way from our scheduled route, requiring us to be picked up and driven to their homes, in Giru we simply stepped off the highway and into a warm welcome.

Our host, Mr Mango Farmer, on learning that we weren't representing a particular denomination, launched into a convivial conversation about John Flynn, an Australian pioneer and personal hero of mine, who had also worked with various church denominations. I had been so moved, years before, from reading about the selfless, long-term commitment of this man, that I named my first son, Flynn, after him. Just talking about this amazing visionary and recalling the sacrifices he'd made to bring medical care and the gospel to the Australian Outback, was a boost to my faith.

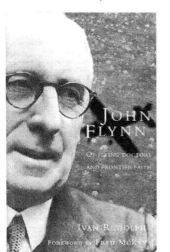

This book is a great read. I strongly recommend it!

101

Mrs Mango Farmer had an amazing roast beef and vegetable dinner waiting. It was a welcome feast for a hungry, footsore walker that went some way to dispelling my blues, reminding me how much my physical wellbeing was intrinsically linked to other areas of my life.

Note to self: sleep and eat well.

With people like Mrs Mango Farmer along the way, at least the *eating* didn't look like being a problem.

A lady at our meeting, not even knowing about my back and feet issues, offered her advice as a nurse. The conversation with her was a boost, and the next morning I discovered a reminder note from her about walking posture:

> *Just imagine you have a wire attached to the centre of your skull pulling you upwards, a heavenly wire, lifting you and keeping your chin up and shoulders back.*

I would think of that heavenly wire many times during the following weeks, lifting my head as I did so.

However, the biggest encouragement in this little Catholic community came from an older woman. 'I had seven children and a brain-injured boy – very brain damaged,' she said. 'He couldn't talk or feed himself and he lived for twenty-one years. But he was a gift and because of him we learned how to live by speaking the Word.' She explained that when she was overwhelmed she would walk down the road and speak out God's Word. 'When I'd turn to come home,' she added, 'I'd be just so happy that I'd sing all the way, and be able to go back and live the rest of the day.'

The lines in people's faces tell stories. Some tell the story of substance abuse – alcohol or cigarettes. Others tell the story of pain – physical or psychological. The lines on this woman's face told the story of love – sacrificial love for her children, love for God and love for His Word. She was particularly moved to hear that there were 350 million people in the world who didn't have God's Word in their language. 'I don't know how they live,' she said shaking her head, 'when they haven't got the Word to depend on, to help them do everything they need to do.'

And, of course, there was Hélène. Her email reply to my text came through before I hit the sack:

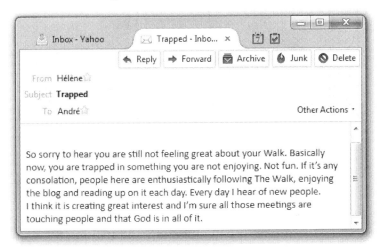

Inbox - Yahoo   Trapped - Inbo...   x

Reply   Forward   Archive   Junk   Delete

From Hélène
Subject **Trapped**
To André

Other Actions ·

So sorry to hear you are still not feeling great about your Walk. Basically now, you are trapped in something you are not enjoying. Not fun. If it's any consolation, people here are enthusiastically following The Walk, enjoying the blog and reading up on it each day. Every day I hear of new people. I think it is creating great interest and I'm sure all those meetings are touching people and that God is in all of it.

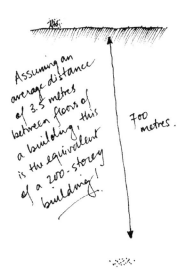

Assuming an average distance of 3.5 metres between floors of a building, this is the equivalent of a 200-storey building!

700 metres.

The one word that jumped out at me from Hélène's email was *trapped*. Perhaps her choice of word was subconsciously inspired by the continuing ordeal of the Chilean miners still waiting to be rescued, trapped 700 metres below ground.

Like those miners, I too felt trapped.

Day 17
Pogo-sticking

Thursday 9 September

We didn't have time to visit our hosts' mango farm – I was becoming resigned to this relentless pace – but we did at least get to take some dried mango with us. Mrs Mango Farmer loaded us up with fistfuls of neat plastic bags bulging with rich orange slices of the delectable fruit. While we were walking and intermittently munching on our spoils, further down the road thousands of people were reading all about us.

No matter where you go these days someone or some group is walking or riding or skipping or pogo-sticking or roller-blading for charity, began Anderson's article in *The Bully*, right alongside a big colour photo of our smiling faces at Weir Primary School. Anderson was only warming up. *If there is a disease, a sickness, a starving nation, a cause anywhere that hasn't got a money-raising walk or ride or something attached to it, then whoever is in charge should sack their PR person and start afresh.* I smiled at his frankness.

We are, as a population, suffering walk-for-charity fatigue, he quipped, *but just when you think there is no cause left ... along come three good Christian lads.* There it was again – he'd written *lads*! I loved it, and smiled broadly. It had been a long time since I'd been called a *boy* or a *lad*. It was nearly worth going through all that to enjoy again the fleeting status of youth.

Surprisingly though he went on to give us a pretty good wrap, saying *These blokes are walking for a cause that is right out of left field.* He got all the information right with details about the number of languages which is more than we can say for another local paper which reported that we were *Walking for the last 2000 Bibleless countries.* Whoever wrote that article needed a quick trip back to their high school geography class, and to chop a zero off the figure to get the total number of *countries* in the world. Oh well, accuracy has always been somewhat arbitrary in media reporting. *The Observer* in Home Hill, however, got it spot on: *Each kilometre represents a distinct language that doesn't have a single verse of the Bible.*

But regardless of sarcasm or inaccuracy, any publicity can be good publicity, and we saw the effects of the media coverage immediately. We discovered that a lot of the cars – which up till then had been simply zooming past – now had horns and we found ourselves regularly waving in response. This gave us the opportunity to exercise our arms a little too. Some of the cars even had brakes.

The first to use her brakes was a French lady who pulled over and walked back to meet us, discovering to her amazement that one of these Aussie lads could speak to her in her language. She immediately invited us to her home, just up the road, for a drink. Alas, tide, time and treadmills wait for no man.

Next came Red Lips, who spied us on a side road beside a cane field. She swung off the highway, sending a pair of ibis into the air with a flurry of white wings, and came speeding straight towards us. I was left with the choice of either braving the impact of her little green Toyota or throwing myself at the taipans waiting for me with open arms in the cane field. I chose to stand my ground. She swung to the side, thrust a hand through the open window waving a bank note and said, 'You're the kids doing God's work, aren't you?' (Okay, I confess, she really said *guys*.) She'd read our story in the *Townsville Bully* and, with a lovely lipstick smile and from behind dark glasses, cooed, 'I just think you're awesome.' I *did* begin to feel a tad awesome at that point too.

By late morning, our 2000 Walk clouds had deserted us. Midday saw us hiding from the heat, resting our feet, sprawled out on some soft lush grass under a little grove of too-good-to-pass-up shady gum trees. Love those gums. It is almost worth a trip across the globe just for a few minutes under a gum tree.

0451   Our host from Ayr found us several hours later, three hillbilly hicks, splashing in the town fountain with steam rising from our feet. Possibly to ensure that none of his friends saw him with us, he bundled us into his car and hurried us off home for a very late lunch. His purpose for the lunch invitation was obviously to see if he could kill us from overeating. Seeing we survived round one, he then lined us up with another would-be assassin only three hours later who provided our evening meal – Fijian-Indian chicken, curry and roti with local mango chutney.

The next morning we would cross the famous Burdekin Bridge, but that night it was all I could do to cross the bedroom floor and crash out on my mattress.

Day 18
Burdekin Bridge

Friday 10 September

The Burdekin Bridge is, not without reason, one of the most important landmarks in North Queensland – and the pride of locals. Known as *The Silver Link*, it joins the towns of Ayr and Home Hill with its impressive span of more than one kilometre, making it one of the longest multi-span bridges in Australia, practically the same length, in fact, as the Sydney Harbour Bridge. Without it we would have had to walk 355 extra kilometres on the alternative inland route via Charters Towers.

Behind the building of this bridge is an incredible story and you don't have to be an engineer – which I'm not – to appreciate this one. You see, there was no rock foundation in the Burdekin River to build on – it's all sand as far as you can dig. Consequently, in the 1940s, two engineers travelled to India to inspect a number of bridges that had been successfully built on sand foundations. With the knowledge they gleaned, they ended up creating eleven huge (read *ginormous*) concrete blocks, or stumps, for the bridge to rest on. Each block weighed in at 4000 tonnes and measured seven by seventeen metres at the base, and fifty metres high, thirty metres of which was sunk into the river bed. The entire bridge took almost a decade to build.

In less than a minute you can hop in your car and pop across to the other side. On foot, it took us twenty minutes and I enjoyed every one of them. I wondered how many of the 7000 drivers who cross daily actually realise the expertise, time, effort and expense that went into this incredible construction.

0458

Probably few. Something there is that loves a bridge.[1]
I may not pass this way again, thought I, in a melancholic moment.

Barely off the bridge, a car pulled up and a pretty young girl stepped out, introducing herself as a reporter from *The Advocate*. I wondered if *The Advocate* didn't pay very well; we could tell she was struggling to make ends meet because she could only afford a very short skirt. Miss Mini was visibly disappointed to find us already on the *south side* of The Silver Link, and clicked both her tongue and her fingers as if to say, *'Rats!'* explaining that she'd hoped to photograph us *before* we stepped onto the bridge. A silence followed.

Hesitantly I ventured, 'You're not suggesting we walk back across just for you to take a photo of us, are you?'

She smiled. 'I could drive you?'

Two minutes later we were in her car, driving back across the bridge. It's a strange phenomenon how one can easily, and without a guilty conscience, refuse a simple and even quite reasonable request from almost anyone – except when the person in question is a young impoverished and sweetly smiling female. Nigh on impossible.

Our photo shoot over, the three of us having been pathetically keen to comply with all manner of poses, we piled into Miss Mini's car again to return to the spot where she'd picked us up. So, for the third time in half an hour, we crossed The Silver Link. I didn't bother to have another melancholic moment though, the previous one having proved an epic waste of time.

South of the Burdekin, as if we'd walked through an invisible curtain (or perhaps the back of a wardrobe) three things happened, and all at once – it got really hot, people started giving us lots of things and I began

---

[1] Inspired by a line in Robert Frost's poem, *Mending Wall:*
'Something there is that doesn't love a wall.'

to feel ill. I put the latter down partly to the heat, and so made sure I was keeping up the fluid intake and carefully monitoring the colour of the output. Small things take on disproportionate importance when all you do for eight hours is put one foot in front of the other – approximately 40,000 times a day.

As we walked through the quiet main street of Home Hill, with me feeling increasingly seedy, a lady tumbled over herself, rushing out of her fruit shop, urging us to come in and take any fruit we wanted, free of charge! She'd read about us in *The Advocate* and wanted to do something to help. Coincidentally, I had just read how people had also offered gifts of food to Bernard. *Ils m'offrent des pommes, des cerises, des boîtes de coca ou de jus de fruits, des barres chocolatées.* As for us, Dave scored a Gala apple, Carnsey grabbed a handful of beans (go figure!) and I chose a plump tamarillo, which was about all we could carry.

Note to self: next time bring a wheelbarrow.

Then there was a roadside delivery. Mr Bushy Beard and his teenage daughter pulled up beside us and produced drinks, including a very cold chocolate milk for yours truly – *inasmuch as ye have done it unto one of the least of these* (Matthew 25:40 KJV). Was it bad manners, I wondered, to down an entire chocolate milk without drawing breath before first greeting and thanking Bushy? Unfortunately that question came to mind a little too late.

Next, another familiar face pulled up alongside us. It was a guy who'd been in our meeting the previous evening. He said he hadn't been able to sleep all night, thinking about the thousands of Bibleless peoples. Our presentation had got him all stirred up, and he quoted the verse that kept coming to mind: *this gospel of the kingdom will be preached in the whole world*

tamarillo – a South American fruit also known as the "tree tomato".

109

as a testimony to all nations, and then the end will come (Matthew 24:14). He gave us a gift of money before driving off.

A bloke from Babinda stopped on his way past. Babinda seemed light years away already, which was instantly a *wonderful* thought. It meant that, in spite of seemingly slow progress, we actually *were* putting some distance between us and the starting line. Our Babinda friend produced a packet of humbugs – those little black and white striped boiled lollies (or *sweets* or *candy* to the non-Aussies). I hadn't seen one of them for decades, and, since the French don't do humbugs, I sucked mine slowly, suspecting I may not see another one for a long time. Learning from the bridge experience, however, I decided not to make a melancholic moment of it.

My head continued to fuzz up with each passing hour, and I became more and more exhausted as the early signs of flu set in. The day dragged on, and the end of our allotted kilometres was a long time coming. No sooner had I walked through the doorway of our hosts place, than I pulled off my shirt and fell back in a heap on my bed, staring at the ceiling and groaning. This was *not* a good sign! How many days would this set us back? Dave and Carnsey kept buzzing around me. I caught snippets of their hushed conversation: *carry – stretcher – wheelbarrow – bridge – push – burden – rock – rope – river*. In my delirium however, I didn't manage to piece any of it together. Suddenly, out of the blue and with a spine-chilling war cry worthy of a role in *Braveheart*, Dave pounced on me. Scrutinising my armpit, he triumphantly proclaimed I had a *tick* – a bush tick! And maybe even a typhus tick! One of those nasties that dig under your skin and make you really sick! No doubt I'd picked it up off the grass the day before where we'd enjoyed a shady break under the gums.

'Did you know,' Dave asked, not missing an opportunity

to instruct, 'that ticks are not really insects, but part of the spider family, and as such they have eight legs and not six?' Quite frankly I didn't care how many dirty little legs the blighter had, as long as we could get him to extract them from my body. Dave deftly removed the offender with Boy Scout prowess, advising me to check all the potential tick-harbouring body regions – the armpits and legpits being their favourite haunts.

Not enjoying the prospect of having beasties sucking my blood, I took his advice to heart and immediately went on the warpath. Behind closed doors, a close inspection of the nether regions revealed to my horror yet another dastardly uninvited hitchhiker tucked away, sucking on my sunless flesh, and stuck fast. Not to be outdone by Dave's deft extraction procedure – and feeling distinctly *monkey-like* in both poise and purpose – I proceeded to tug with determination on what turned out to be a particularly stubborn individual until I suddenly realised, with simultaneous embarrassment and relief, that it was the legless variety that goes by the name *mole*. I made the instant decision not to extract it after all.

Thus ended my close encounter of the tick kind. If eagle-eyes Dave hadn't intervened, it would almost certainly have led to a worsening of my condition and a serious setback in our schedule. It did strike me, however, just how *inglorious* it was to survive a mere tick bite. I mean, in comparison, surviving a bite from a croc or a taipan would have been singularly *glorious!*

Little did I know that a close encounter of an even *much* larger kind was awaiting me just down the highway.

Day 19
Close encounters

Saturday 11 September

After an early morning check for further stowaways on
my soft body parts and being sure not to remove any
permanently attached ones, I raised anchor and set sail
for another day on the open highway.

With a certain macabre curiosity, I had recently read
a list of dozens of torture methods administered in
different countries and at different times in history.
This list included such exotic names as *strappado*,
abacination, scaphism, picquet and *ta'liq* and of course
the more readily recognised *thumbscrews, keelhauling,
denailing* and the *rack*. The list did not include, however,
highway. A letter to the editor was in order to correct that
oversight. As once more we encountered the dizzying,
never-ending onslaught of vehicles, it occurred to me that
it was close to self-inflicted torture, from which I was
continually trying to escape. For a short time, escape
I did, on my own.

A train line offered respite a hundred metres from the
highway where I had left Dave. Blissful! That feeling
when the neighbour finally turns his mower off, when all
the kids go home after a rowdy party, when the wind that
has howled all night dies down at last and the shutters
stop rattling. Immediately my disposition changed.
I loved the sky, the birds, the grass and even the rocks
that crunched under my feet as I tramped between the
train lines. My sighs of happiness were punctuated by
my phone vibrating. It was our *Blog Babe* responsible for
updating our website – blogs, stats, kilometres walked
etc. We were in contact with her daily, which was a real

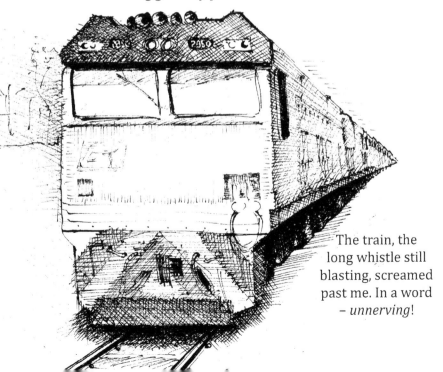

treat because she had a sense of humour that could brighten the dullest of days. She'd been accusing us of secretly riding Vespas and dumping them in the bushes when we had photo shoots or media interviews, and had been building this up to be a daily in-joke. Talking to Blog Babe while walking on the train track, far from the madding crowd who were all playing follow the leader at breakneck speeds along The Bruce, was, quite simply, enjoyable.

Thinking back, I believe I did hear the whistle – in that far off way you hear things that you don't *need* to hear or perhaps don't *want* to hear. In fact, I'm not sure that I didn't actually hear it *twice*. But by the time I *really* heard it, in a *this-is-for-me* kind of way, the train was almost on top of me.

Reflexes are wonderful things. At that precise moment in time, they triggered me to simultaneously look up, take in the fact that 90,000 kilograms of metal was rocketing directly towards me, and leap in the right direction – *off* the track. And all of that in a heartbeat. *Without* letting go of my phone.

The train, the long whistle still blasting, screamed past me. In a word – *unnerving*!

I thought of the copper's words, but the ones I heard were Babe's, coming from the phone still clenched in my hand. When we resumed conversation, and having understood exactly what she was witness to, albeit almost 1500 kilometres away, she simply said in a very quiet, subdued voice, 'That was close!' And then, '*Please* don't walk on train tracks anymore. You won't, will you?' I shook my head. But I knew I would anyway.

0500   A few kilometres further, I found myself reporting this close encounter with the locomotive to The Nutters. When Dave and I first spied The Nutters, or at least their old Chevy truck, laden with fruit for sale, it appeared like a desert mirage on this desolate stretch of highway – a mobile fruit and vegie stall, complete with fridge propped up on a wooden pallet and stocked with cold rockmelons – so said the handwritten sign. Faces buried unashamedly in the sweet cold flesh of the melons, and slurping noisily, we struck up conversation.

'What do you think of a few guys walking 2000 kilometres?'

'Bloody idiots,' retorted the buxom lady without a blink of a hesitation.

We were starting to get the message. And then she threw back her head and laughed. That was when I knew we were going to like these people. The four of them were like a group of silly teenagers who, decades later, still hadn't grown up. They called themselves the Gumlu Nutters, Gumlu being the name of this spot on the highway.

We liked them so much, we told them all about ourselves and they liked us so much, they listened with rapt attention. They thought we were awesome, and in direct proportion, we thought they were. When I recounted my close shave with the train, they were horrified and asked if I planned to continue on the train line. For the second time in an hour, I shook my head hypocritically. We also told them we had just crossed the 500 kilometre mark and wanted to celebrate by taking a photo of the number 500, composed of – and we looked around us – *fruit!* And because we were now lifelong buddies, all four sprang obediently into a flurry of action, transferring avocadoes, mandarins, apples, pears and passionfruit from their neatly displayed cases, to a picnic table where they were moved, shuffled, shifted, rearranged and repositioned amid squeals of merriment, while I gave instructions.

'Don't worry about us,' bawled the buxom Nutter sarcastically in typical Aussie style. 'We're just here all day to accommodate you!'

I filmed it all as they chortled and hollered. One of the Nutters noticed and crowed, 'Look at him, thinks he's Baz Luhrmann.' That's when we discovered that the 1942 Chevy in front of us, still in full-working order, had played a role in *Australia,* the movie, carrying the troops on the back. *Australia* had been filmed in Bowen, only two days' walk away, and The Nutters made us promise to visit the set when we got there. Amidst loud farewells, hugs, exchanging of phone numbers and more laughter, we parted company. Feeling buoyed up, we pushed out onto the highway once more.

Half an hour later, I got a phone call from one of The Nutters squealing at me that there was a train approaching. She knew I'd be back on the track. I stepped off and several minutes later I was waving to the passing train driver.

Back on the highway, a car pulled up – though there was precious little room to do so – and out stepped a rather buff young man with a Hollywood smile who introduced himself as Joel, my cousin's son. I hadn't seen him since he was knee-high to a mango, and a mini family reunion took place amidst trucks thundering past.

'How did you know I was here?' I yelled, over the road noise.

'We just stopped at this fruit stall back there,' he said. 'And they started spruiking on about these awesome guys who were walking down the highway. They told us all about you and that's when I realised that one of those guys was you!'

Across the road I noticed Joel's wife and kids waiting in the car, and at the same time another car pulled up and out stepped the buxom Nutter waving a bag of drinks and bananas. I knew then that we'd been officially adopted by the Gumlu Nutters!

Then it happened: screeching tyres – locked-up brakes – smoke – a semitrailer veering sideways – reeling – coming towards us – fast.

With a blast of wind as it rocketed past, filling our nostrils with the stench of burning rubber, the mass of metal and tyres somehow managed to right itself and navigate back onto the road, slipping miraculously between pedestrians on one side, and passengers on the other. I climbed back up the embankment. My reflexes were getting plenty of practice that day. The white smoke and stench hung heavily in the air. Joel, smile gone, had turned ashen. 'I saw it going straight for my family,' he said.

Turning back we saw what was left of our close encounter of the apocalyptic kind – heavy black scrawl marks snaking over the white line and back again, thirty metres long. Even the buxom one was subdued and said in a hushed tone, 'I thought it was going to clean us up.'

The words of Arthur Blessitt, the 60,000 kilometre man, came to mind, 'I still can't believe that I wasn't taken out by a truck.' His words and his miracle became mine.

No, God had no obligation to protect me but He *did*. It somehow seemed appropriate that I should be reflecting on God's protection that day, the anniversary of the terrorist attack on the Twin Towers.

Talking to Hélène on the phone later in the day, she reminded me that in just one week we'd be reunited. She'd be flying in to Mackay from the south with our two lively lads and, in a somewhat less lively manner I'd be walking in from the north.

If, that is, I survived the next seven days on The Bruce.

Day 20
Mr and Mrs Banjo

Sunday 12 September

During my years of voluntary exile in France, I had longed for a deeper *connection* with the country of my birth. I may have been a little less enthusiastic though if I'd realised this meant the possibility of connecting with an oncoming train or a sideways-careening truck.

The dawning of a new day, however, found me alone, and connecting in a new way – with the beach.

The term *absolute beach frontage* certainly applies to the little community of Wunjunga where the houses are built with their yards leading right down to the sand. However, a fifteen-minute walk up the beach reveals a type of *frontage* that redefines the term *absolute*. A tract of boulders along the cliff base has provided a solid foundation for a series of very small and rudimentary brick, block and cement dwellings right *on* the beach, all vacant and waiting for the owners to return and take up their sporadic weekend and holiday getaways. The absence of square angles in these constructions is more than amply compensated by huge doses of resourcefulness and colour. Salvador Dali would have approved. A staircase hugs the curve of a boulder, a footbridge spans two rock ledges, a vertical wall emerges creatively from a round rock base. I climbed the thirty steps to one of the highest houses and sat on the tiny balcony looking out to sea, conjuring up narratives of those who come with the keys to these locks and what they do behind closed doors. A writer's haven? A lovers' hideaway? A businessman's retreat? A fisherman's shelter? It was all, in a word, charming.

Perhaps the charm of Wunjunga actually had more to do with me and the fact that it was my day off – a whole day to soak up the solitude and the peacefulness. By association, this would forever make Wunjunga a wonderful place in my memory. However, more important than the peacefulness would be the association with people, in particular our hosts Mr and Mrs Banjo, who had recently retired there.

I soon discovered that one of Mr Banjo's specialties was barbecues, and what he produced from a you-beaut converted forty-four gallon drum was nothing short of spectacular. The smell and taste drew quite a little crowd, including Bushy – this time *minus* the chocolate milk – as

well as a horde of blood-hungry mosquitoes kept at bay by the smoke produced from burning coconut husks.

It turned out that Mr Banjo was a poet, or at least he recited other people's poems, including those of the famous Australian, A.B. (Banjo) Paterson. Having produced all manner of primitive groans and pleasurable sighs from us as we munched happily on the fare from The Drum, he now drew out all-round laughter and mirth from his oh-so-Aussie renditions of *A Bush Christening* and, a favourite of my sons, *Mulga Bill's Bicycle*. With gusto, and the inimitable Aussie vowels gliding easily all over the place, he recounted the misfortune of the cocky Mulga Bill:

> *He turned the cycle down the hill*
> *and mounted for the fray,*
> *but 'ere he'd gone a dozen yards*
> *it bolted clean away.*
>
> *It left the track, and through the trees,*
> *just like a silver streak,*
> *it whistled down the awful slope*
> *towards the Dead Man's Creek.*

I can't remember the last time someone read an Aussie poem to me, though I have often read them to my boys, and I smiled all the way through this one, feeling embraced by the heritage of my homeland. In just six days' time I would be seeing my boys and I determined to read them more of Paterson's poetry.

Mr Banjo then pulled out the Aussie Bible, an innovative rendition by Kel Richards, and the familiar words of Psalm 23 took on new meaning when seen through eyes from Down Under:

> *Even when the droughts are bad*
> *and I cross the Desert of Death,*
> *God is close beside me,*
> *so close I can feel his breath.*
>
> *God is the One who holds the map*
> *that gives me my direction,*
> *And God is the one who guarantees*
> *provision for my protection.*
>
> *Although there are dingoes in the hills*
> *and the paddocks are full of snakes,*
> *God serves up a barbecue*
> *of beautiful T-bone steaks!*
>
> *His patience and compassion*
> *and forgiveness fail me never;*
> *And I'll live with him in the homestead,*
> *beyond the end of forever.*

We talked together about the different versions of the Bible available in English, about the remaining task of Bible translation, and the 350 million people who didn't have God's Word in their language. At that point Mr Banjo added his name to the long list of those who have asked *the* question:

" why don't you just teach them all English ? "

I had a chance to respond to his question with a demonstration that Dave and I had cooked up for the occasion.

Dave produced a tray with an empty teacup and asked Mrs Banjo simply to pick up the cup and imagine she was enjoying sipping the tea, which she did, with dramatic flair to the amusement of everyone gathered. Dave repeated the exercise, with Mrs Banjo repeating her Hollywood performance. And then, to the bewilderment of all, he did it a third time. Had anyone noticed anything interesting about the way she drank the tea? A few hazarded a guess – great acting abilities, she was pretending because there was not really any tea, and so forth. Finally someone got it! She'd picked up the cup every single time with her right hand! The question was, could she pick it up with her left hand? She demonstrated that this was indeed possible albeit with a little less confidence, and put it to her lips.

'Well,' Dave asked her, 'Why did you pick it up each time with your right hand?' She replied, 'Because I'm right-handed. I'm used to doing it with my right hand and it's easier.'

'It *is* possible,' I explained, 'for a *very* small number of people in *some* of these language groups to learn English. However, even if they do, and even if they become very fluent in English, they will always still have a strong preference for their own language, in the same way most of us have a strong preference for using our right hand. If we want people to read God's Word for the first time, do we want them to read it in a language that is their second-best?' The point came across but I knew the illustration needed more work.

In the meantime Bushy had been mulling over the statistics we'd shared and had been quietly doing his sums. Being sparing with words, when he does speak, he's worth listening to. He excitedly declared that

350 million Bibleless people came to a total of five per cent of the world's population.

'A whole five per cent,' he repeated, while we all waited for him to get to the point.

He went on, 'In the parable of the Lost Sheep the figure is just *one* per cent. A shepherd had one hundred sheep and lost one so he left the ninety-nine to go looking for it. If the moral behind that parable is to make sure that the one per cent is not excluded and left out in the cold, then how much more should we be investing time, effort and money in making sure that the five per cent are included and able to hear the Word of God?'

Yes, it was definitely a day of 'connecting' with my country – with the beach, with a hearty barbecue, with the works of Banjo Paterson, but above all, with people like our new friends Mr and Mrs Banjo.

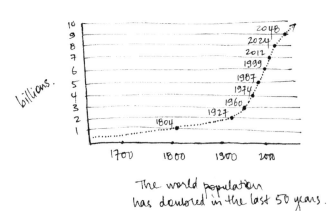

POPULATION OF THE EARTH

The world population has doubled in the last 50 years.

Day 21
Malayalam

Monday 13 September

Trading the beach for The Bruce felt like trading a Tim Tam for a poke in the eye with a sharp stick. But the show must go on. Besides, I had a hankering to inspect the famous set of the film *Australia*.

When it came out, the film was a hit with my family. Following my youngest son's idea, we had enthusiastically dragged mattresses off our beds (Hélène less enthusiastically than the rest of us) and laid them out in the lounge room where we stretched out in the dark on comfy pillows, side by side like French *baguettes*, watching the film projected onto the ceiling. Got to give it to him, Joseph's idea was brilliant – a cross between a home cinema and a drive-in theatre, only better than both. And now I was going to be able to step into the place where it was filmed. Woo-hoo!

Recalling such warm memories, and knowing I was just five days away from my boys, should have cheered me up, but those five *days* might as well have been five *months* given my current state of heart and mind.

The day was a drag – almost literally as far as my feet were concerned. The only reprieve from monotony was some of Mrs Mango Farmer's rationed dried offerings and a young couple who offered us a lift, delighting us no end by proclaiming authoritatively:

YOUSE ARE IDIOTS !!!

Apart from that, the day was a long, drawn-out, boring blur of sore feet, 30,000 tyres and rising temperatures. Oh, and did I mention the sore feet?

Dave delighted us – not – with his pain declaration for the umpteenth time.

Pain is just weakness leaving the body!!

During the first weeks on the road, the expression *a spring in your step* could possibly have applied at a pinch, but not any longer. Like an old discarded mattress, I had lost my spring. Carnsey still stepped it out without missing a beat (complete with Granny socks) and Dave still bounced, but I was happy just to be able to plod.

One of my first lino-prints done way back in 17 BG

As we neared Bowen, a lone, friendly ibis, in her immaculate formal dinner dress, strode across the road in our direction – a stately welcoming committee of one. It was easy to see why ancient civilisations like Egypt attributed nobility to these lovely creatures. Mrs Ibis lost all her nobility, however, along with the spring in her step, when to my horror she was instantly reduced to a stain on the road and an impressive snow storm of feathers by a passing vehicle. A violent death at such close range was disconcerting to say the least – just a little too close for comfort.

മലയാളം

Arriving at our host's home, we discovered it strewn with all manner of illegible literature bearing squiggles resembling a cross between the Wing Dings font and the Hebrew script. It was neither. It was the Malayalam language, just one of the twenty-two official languages of the Indian subcontinent. Our host, the local priest, a mother-tongue speaker, proudly introduced us to his language. He explained that the name of his language - Malayalam - is a palindrome, a word that can be read the same way in either direction – left to right, or right to left.

We learned that this language is spoken by thirty-six million people, more than the entire population of Australia, and that its amazing script is made up of 578 characters. Our host produced his Bible and enthralled me by reading a few verses with a flourish of exotic retroflexed consonants and crystal-clear vowels that fell from his lips with ease and effortless grace. It was with obvious relish and delight that he speaks his language, but who does he speak it with in Bowen? No-one! He watches films in his language on-line, and reads Malayalam newspapers instead. What about his Bible? Of course he can speak and read English but, he stated categorically with his unmistakeable Indian accent, 'There is no comparison between reading God's Word in my own mother tongue and reading it in English.' I decided there and then that I wanted Mr Malayalam to accompany us for our remaining 1435 kilometres and thirty meetings as living evidence that *teaching them English* is a very poor second-best. Instead I came up with an improvement to my picking-up-the-teacup demonstration and I was looking forward to putting it into practice in our next meeting.

That night, however, there was no meeting. Just eating! Local deep-sea fish – caught and cooked by another of Dave and Carnsey's cousins. With our tummies full, and while the three cousins did the family talk, I assumed the horizontal position on the lounge-room carpet. Cousin number three suggested, 'If you like, we can take the boat out one night and bring in a few more big ones.' Yes, we liked. Definitely! And therein lay our dilemma – how to make time to fit in *both* the deep-sea fishing *and* the visit to the *Australia* movie set.

I needn't have worried, however, because our tight schedule meant we would leave Bowen without having had time for either.

Part Three
The middle mile

Day 22
The middle mile

Tuesday 14 September

I knew the day was going to be a hard one. I could feel it in my bones. The bones of my feet that is, and there sure are a lot of them down there – 26 in each foot to be precise – making up one quarter of the bones in my entire body. Apart from bones, in that marvellous, unattractive member called a *foot*, there are 33 joints, 107 ligaments and 19 muscles. And if you add all that up and multiply it by two (for those of us who are indeed fortunate enough to have *two* feet) that comes to 370 important *bits* that were all working together just for me to be able to put one foot in front of the other. Overnight, all 370 of them had signed a petition pleading to give them a break. Sorry guys, duty calls.

$$\left(26 + 33 + 107 + 19\right) \times 2 = 370$$

My feet were almost the entire focus of my thoughts. I carried a *foot kit* with me at all times – dry socks, a needle to drain the blisters, metho to dry them out and toughen the skin, *Elastoplast* to bind the sensitive hot spots and scissors to trim any protruding nail. I needed my feet to be in good condition. Everything depended on them. A wiser man than me once wrote: *The head can't say to the feet 'I don't need you.' On the contrary, those parts of the body that seem to be weaker are indispensable.* Never a truer word was writ. *God has combined the members of your body so that there should be no division, but so that all the parts should look after each other.* It was the apostle Paul writing (adapted from 1 Corinthians 12:21-27), referring to people. *You are the body of Christ, and each one of you is a part of it.* I amused myself imagining a group of 370 people, all as different as the bones, joints, ligaments and muscles in my feet, working together in such amazing unity and harmony, all operating selflessly for the good of the body rather than the individual. It was difficult to imagine.

I glanced down glumly at my boots as they appeared one after the other in front of me with dizzying regularity.

I was struggling and knew something was wrong, but I couldn't put my finger on it. In hindsight, I would realise that I was approaching *the middle mile*, a term coined by the late Vance Havner in a sermon by the same name which has become quite famous:

please, feet... let me don't down today...

> To most of us the most important parts of a journey are the start and finish. But the part of a trip that really tests the traveller is neither the beginning nor the end, but the middle mile. Anybody can be enthusiastic at the start. The long road invites you; you are fresh and ready to go. It is easy to sing then. And it is easy to be exuberant at the finish. You may be footsore and weary but you have arrived, the goal is reached, the crown is won. It is not difficult to be happy then. But on the dreary middle mile when the glory of the start has died away and you are too far from the goal to be inspired by it – on the tedious middle mile when life has settled down to a regular routine and monotony – there is the stretch that tires out the traveller. If you can sing along the middle mile, you've learned one of life's most difficult lessons.

Yes, though still a way from the middle of The Walk, I was coming up to my *middle mile*. However, with apologies to Vance, I certainly wasn't singing. I wondered whether the Chilean miners were singing down in the bowels of the earth, where they had been now for forty days, while work on the evacuation shaft continued above them.

As the sun rose higher and began to bite, we came upon a Mobil Roadhouse – a great excuse for a short air-conditioned break and to stock up on carbohydrates.

The man behind the counter grinned a toothy smile as I plonked down my G-force drink and chicken sandwiches in front of him, 'You guys are with some charity or something, aren't you?' A little annoyed, I wondered if there was such a thing as a *charitable look* that made us identifiable even to a total stranger. I was immediately ashamed of my reaction, not only because we actually *wanted* to be identified (which was, after all, the purpose of our Wiggles shirts) but also because he added with an even broader smile, 'It's on the house, no charge!' explaining that he'd seen us on TV. What's more, he was able to direct us to a cross-country short cut away from the Bruce Highway, following the railway line, which would slice five kilometres off our walk.

But the free food, the smiley man and even the prospect of an alternate route did little to cheer my flagging spirits. We crossed the Don River, turned off The Bruce at an unusual little grove of palm trees and found ourselves following, just as Mr Smiley had predicted, a quiet little road parallel to the railway.

Deep inside, I was still struggling to accept what this Walk had become. My dream had died. Yes, *that* was it. I felt like the kid who'd dreamed of owning a horse. He asked his parents and they said yes, so he really got his hopes up. Then they asked whether he'd mind if the horse didn't have a full tail that stood proud and blew in the wind. No, he supposed not. Later they asked if he minded if his horse didn't whinny. Nope, he could cope with a horse that didn't whinny or neigh. They asked if it would be a problem if the horse wasn't too fast. Not at all, such was his excitement to have his own horse. Even when they said that his horse mightn't have a mane, his excitement didn't wane. When the great day came, and with a new saddle he'd bought and beating heart, he

opened the stable door, to find, not a *horse*, but a *cow!*
True, it was a big domestic animal. It was the colour he
wanted, the size he wanted and it *was* all his, but it *wasn't*
a horse. He didn't want a cow.

Here I was on The Walk, but it *wasn't* what I had hoped
and dreamed of – and it wasn't *doing* for me what I so
badly wanted and needed. Instead of riding a horse, being
energised and feeling the wind in my hair, I was dragging
a cow by a rope. The bitumen, the noise, the many
meetings – it was all so wearying. I had agreed to all of
the above, but now that reality had set in I was paying
the price. Instead of returning to my family recharged to
begin a new, big step forward in our translation project,
I'd be arriving home depleted of energy and with little
motivation to even think of the next step, let alone be
able to lead my family into it.

As these thoughts swilled in the weary recesses of my
mind, my phone vibrated. It was Hélène. Perfect timing
– perfectly bad! The combination of days of aching
feet, my dark thoughts, the quiet road, the sound of my
wife's voice and the fact that I was out of earshot of the
cousins a few hundred metres ahead, caused me to lose
it. Welling up from somewhere inside my chest and
without warning came an unidentifiable emotion – an
ache, a pain, a grief – erupting in deep sobs. Tears and
words spewed out, '*J'en peux plus. J'en ai marre.*' Over and
over into the phone I spat the words out, 'I can't take it
anymore. I'm sick of it. *J'en peux plus. J'en ai marre.*'

Yes, I had reached the middle mile – *the dreary middle mile, the tedious middle mile, the stretch that tires out the traveller.* The starting line with its bright balloons and cheering children was long forgotten, and the finish line was still an inconceivable 1420 kilometres away.

The remainder of my exchange with Hélène was a blur but I do remember, as a result, feeling a burden lifted. While there was still no spring in my step, at least my feet were dragging somewhat less.

The peaceful road became a track and then a trail, a crooked trail winding its way through open bush. The cawing of crows pierced the still, crisp air while, for more than an hour, we crunched along this *calf path*, dodging cow pats.

I recited aloud to myself the first verse of one of my favourite poems, *The Calf Path* by Sam Walter Foss:

> *One day, through the primeval wood,*
> *a calf walked home, as good calves should;*
> *But made a trail all bent askew,*
> *a crooked trail, as all calves do.*

The vault above us was a deeper blue than I'd seen since we left Cairns exactly three weeks before – a rich blue, almost the colour of my shirt, with only a few sailboat clouds dotting the horizon. In the silence, I could hear myself breathing, which was quite a novelty. A kookaburra, sitting in an old gum tree, threw his head back and laughed loud and hard as we passed. There are days in France when I'd love to look out our kitchen window and see a kookaburra in our walnut tree. His harsh call would be a welcome interlude to my day, as it was then.

It was there that it occurred to me – insight brought on by the abundance of inviting gum trees – that in spite of regular intake of liquid during our five hours of walking, I hadn't had to drain all morning. This was clearly due to the sudden change of weather conditions. It was drier and considerably hotter. Even though the breeze was deceptive, cooling us just enough to lull us into a false sense of security, I knew I wasn't hydrated enough and my water supply was depleted. During the damp weeks, water hadn't been a problem, but we'd need to be careful from now on as it looked like our 2000 Walk clouds had abandoned us.

When the calf path bent away we were left with no choice but to cross into the railway corridor, a broad strip of land fenced on either side to keep cattle out. Carnsey crunched along the stones, stepping over the sleepers; Dave bounced along the railway lines, improving his balancing skills; I plodded along the grass at the side.

After an hour of stepping, bouncing and plodding, the corridor still stretched as far as the eye could see. It reminded me of my old friend, the canal, back in France – the silence, the perfect blue sky, the heat, the open space and the straight flat walkway. I was becoming quite attached to the railway line in much the same way I was attached to the canal and it all brought on a pang of homesickness for my *other* country. That's when I heard the rattle of an approaching train.

We stepped back from the track and waited till it approached, greeting the long, hard blast of the whistle with a friendly wave. Then we realised that the train was actually stopping. Friendly bunch these train drivers. Maybe this one had seen us on TV and wanted our autograph or a photo. We hurried along the track to the QR NATIONAL 2846 locomotive to come up level with the window. Alas Mr Train Driver was not the jovial 2000 Walk friendly fellow we had imagined him to be.

He announced, to our utter astonishment, that we had

broken the law by entering the corridor zone. 'Highly illegal,' he sternly remonstrated. He further announced that he'd just phoned through our location and direction to the Bowen Police who, he informed us, would be waiting to pick us up at the other end. Stopping short of leaping out and snapping handcuffs on us three felons, and satisfied with the delivery of his accusation, verdict and sentence all rolled into one, he set his machine in motion and slowly and noisily pulled away.

Rooted to the spot, we watched the train disappear. There was an unspoken agreement among us that, being so close to the end of our allotted kilometres for the day, we were *not* backtracking. However, would we be able to continue forwards? The prospect of stepping out into the waiting clutches of Mr Bowen Policeman was not a happy one. We imagined a follow-up national television news story, the eyes of the entire country watching on as the Three Wise Men, handcuffed and wearing silly Wiggles shirts were pushed into the paddy wagon, driven off amidst a thousand scrambling microphone-wielding reporters and camera-toting paparazzi and humiliatingly cast into the clink. What would my wife say? What would my boys say? In just four days they were due to arrive and they would be visiting me behind bars. The shame of it all would be too heavy to bear. When I got out – *if* I got out – I would have to change my identity, take on a new name, undergo plastic surgery, settle in Antigua or Belize and start a new life.

It's interesting how the advent of a common enemy can instantly increase team spirit. I'm not sure we would have been able to identify exactly *who* the common enemy actually was – the train driver? Queensland Rail? the Bowen Police? But suddenly there was a sense of *them* and *us*.

No police were waiting when we stepped out of the corridor and we concluded that Mr Train Driver was full of sham. We got on with our Walk, taking care to avoid the sacred corridor. Over the next few days, however, we would hold our breath at the sight of every passing police car – and suddenly there were trillions of them, obviously having been called in from all over the state. And to ease our nerves a little, we would invent stories of a nationwide search for three hardened crims on the run.

0593 Fortunately, the day ended better than it began, largely due to the roaring success, during our meeting at Bowen Baptist Church, of replacing the teacup example with that of a toothbrush. This not only created some delightfully uncomfortable moments – when our *volunteer* needed reassurance that this *was* a clean toothbrush – but produced a sterling performance. It made the point; we all use *only* our right hand for cleaning our teeth (well, those of us who *are* right-handed that is). We *never* use our left hand. We *can* use our left hand but it's not effective, feels clumsy and we choose not to do it. Everyone at the meeting understood clearly why we *can't* just teach them English. The Bible *has* to come to a person in his or her language of preference, the mother tongue.

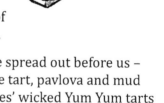

The array of desserts that were spread out before us – lamingtons, strawberries, apple tart, pavlova and mud cake, not to mention Mrs Hughes' wicked Yum Yum tarts – also went a long way to cheering my spirits at this, the beginning of my *middle mile.*

Day 23
The foundation

Wednesday 15 September

Most days we walked a little over thirty kilometres which came to eight hours pounding the pavement. Some people spend eight hours a day working; we spent eight hours a day walking. Bernard finds that walking up to thirty kilometres per day can be as pleasurable as *une douce drogue*, 'a soft drug'.

It was one of our average eight-hour days, starting at 7 am and finishing at 3 pm. However, what transpired between start and finish was anything but average, and anything but a *douce drogue*. Thankfully, this was the only time it would happen during our whole Walk.

Anyone driving along the Bruce Highway south of Bowen looking for Wiggles shirts at around 11.30 am would not have found them. Instead they would literally have driven right over them. After four hours tramping in the hot sun, with not a hint of a cloud or a wisp of a breeze to bring some respite, we were desperate for shade. We finally found it right under the highway in the form of a culvert large enough to walk into. As we stepped out of the sun, the relief was instant, much like walking into one of Myer's air-conditioned stores, which always seem to cater more for penguins and polar bears than human beings. Once our eyes had adjusted to the dark and after a careful glance to be sure there were no other creatures also taking refuge from the heat, we sat, flushed and sweaty, leaning against the wall. Without talking, we breathed in the cool air. I pulled out my water bottle and raised it to my lips for a quick swig. Nearly empty, it flipped up easily.

Only a couple of centimetres of water remained.

We had miscalculated. We hadn't counted on what turned out to be the hottest day of the month, and weren't used to carrying large quantities of water. Added to that, there had been no service station or store for the previous sixteen kilometres, so no possibility of a quick top-up. We could have benefitted from one of Bushy's roadside deliveries, but he and his chocolate milk were 150 kilometres back.

I slowly and carefully peeled off my socks, revealing flushed, burning soles with layers of skin slowly being rubbed away from constant friction. I held onto the sole of one foot and the contact with the relatively cool skin of my hand was soothing.

It would be three hours before our appointed pick-up and we had two choices: either sit it out in the shade or chip away at a few more kilometres. The former was tempting but we knew that the more kilometres we walked that afternoon, the fewer we'd have for the next day. I pulled on my socks and boots, sucked out the last drops of water, hauled the backpack over my shoulder and stepped out into the blinding sunlight.

The first kilometre or so, after even a short rest, was always challenging. While at rest, all the nerves in the soles of my feet, desensitised by the relentless beating against the road, would wake up. Then when I'd stand and walk off again they'd scream profanities at me and violently object to yet another dose of torture, leaving me to hobble and limp in pain.

'Pain is just weakness ...,' began Dave, but with less conviction than normal.

'I know, I know,' I cut him off, and added quietly in my middle mile misery, 'I've had a lot of weakness leave my body today.'

We ate some remaining morsels of dried mango, trying to

imagine them dripping with juice. I also tried to imagine a cool breeze picking up. I was unsuccessful on both counts, my usually vivid imagination failing me dismally. We stopped momentarily to watch a cane harvester spitting cane-leaf confetti into the air, envious of the driver enclosed in his air-conditioned cabin. We walked on. Even Dave's bounce had left him. Because of the heat, his liquid-crystal watch display was also malfunctioning. We tried not to think of our empty water bottles, but there's nothing quite like running out of water to bring on a raging thirst. As I walked I counted down the minutes. I also counted down the days till my family would arrive – three.

Three long hours later my head was feeling foggy when, right on cue, Zorrie, our hostess for the night, turned up in her little silver Honda CR-V.

'No,' she apologised, 'I haven't brought any water.'

I groaned, but soon discovered an old plastic bottle with water for the radiator under my seat. It was hot and looked like it had been there for months, and was exactly as expected – pretty ordinary! But it *was* wet.

Back at the house, Zorrie produced a few bottles of cold Coke and I lost count of how much I consumed. It didn't even touch the sides as it went down, and I wondered if I was going to discover what it was like to overdose on Coke.

Zorrie produced something more important than Coke though – a striking analogy from her work as a counsellor. Glass in hand, I listened fascinated.

She explained that in counselling, the foundational work done in people is like building a skyscraper. First you have to dig down deep to clean out all the rubbish and then very carefully lay the foundation. Only then can you put up the building. She said that the foundational work can take as long, if not longer, than actually putting up the building - and that it's all unseen.

She related that to the task of Bible translation.

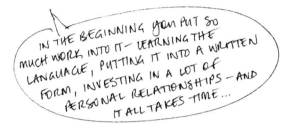

IN THE BEGINNING you put so much work into it— learning the language, putting it into a written form, investing in a lot of personal relationships – and it all takes time...

She had attended our meeting the previous night, listening wide-eyed as we shared how some Bible translations take several decades to complete.

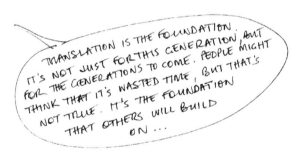

TRANSLATION IS THE FOUNDATION. It's not just for this generation, but for the generations to come. People might think that it's wasted time, but that's not true. It's the foundation that others will build on ...

I pondered that statement, *It's the foundation that others will build on*, which reminded me of the words of the late Kenneth Pike, eminent linguist and Bible translator, 'Dig the well deep and irrigate widely.'

It occurred to me that our mobile and fluctuating society doesn't encourage us to dig deep wells – we're content, instead, with feel-good splashing on the surface. It doesn't encourage us to put down deep foundations – it favours the superficial and the instantaneous. It doesn't encourage us to develop deep relationships – we nibble, instead, around the edges of thousands of Facebook friendships.

Lying in bed, I determined to invest my life in a *deep* way: laying *deep* foundations, digging *deep* wells and developing *deep* relationships.

I put my resolution into practice by falling into a deep sleep.

Day 24
Longest day

Thursday 16 September

I eagerly peered through the window for signs of clouds and breeze. My heart leapt – there was a little of both. Fears of a third consecutive scorcher proved unfounded. We had become unreasonably spoilt by the unseasonably cool weather. It would have been quite within the realms of possibility to be walking for three consecutive *weeks* in sweltering heat, and here I was anxious about the possibility of three consecutive *days*.

The clouds and breeze, however welcome, did nothing to remedy the ache in my feet that was kicking in earlier and earlier with each passing day, leaving me wondering if I really did have twenty-six bones in each foot after all. They felt more like blocks of bone than complex formations of flexible phalanges. Sitting down and standing up were uncomfortable but starting off after a period of rest continued to be downright painful. It was at that point a lot of weakness would leave my body.

0633   Even so, start-up pain was no deterrent to taking advantage of an opportunity to sit for a few minutes in an air-conditioned Red Rooster restaurant with a rapidly emptying Snack Box before me. That decision was made as soon as we sighted the familiar red and white insignia upon our arrival in Proserpine right on lunch time.

Licking my lips and preparing to leave, I produced one of our 2000 Walk presentation cards, hoping to strike up conversation with the check-out chick – nothing too serious, just a little exchange of intelligible speech. As it turned out, I would have had to strike a good deal harder to achieve some level of conversation. Maybe she was just having a bad day, or perhaps word had reached her about three crims on the loose and she was playing it safe. Or could it be that she was simply a product of the younger generation who don't do conversation nearly as well as they do texting, twittering, tweeting, twarting and twooting? Hence, I regretted my failed attempt, though not nearly as much as I regretted having oh-so-carefully informed her we were walking all the way to Stanthorpe – in the hope, perhaps, that she would help me achieve that momentary *awesome* status once more – and adding oh-so-clearly that we had another 1367 kilometres ahead of us. You see, as I terminated my monologue and took a few steps towards the door, more weakness than usual started leaving my body. Flinching and limping, I finally hobbled to the door. I must have looked like history's least-likely candidate to make it to the next crossroads, let alone another 1367 kilometres. I did *not* look back. I did *not* want to see the expression on Miss Rooster's face. Any status of awesomeness I may have briefly achieved in her eyes would surely have given way to derision and disparagement – though she may not have been familiar with either of those words. The irony of the moment, however, was not lost on me.

Note to self: keep trap shut until feet are functioning.

My feet, however, did eventually function again. And just south of Proserpine we came across, for the first time, another walker – backpack and all. We were excited – elated even! When the shipwrecked sailor on his desert island sees smoke and signs of life, he goes wild. The prospect of meeting and perhaps even walking with another idiot just like us was exhilarating.

143

We parted company and pressed on somewhat deflated, coming to the realisation that we really *were* the only idiots on the Bruce Highway. Over the entire 2000 kilometres, we wouldn't meet even one other walker.

A surprise was awaiting us, though, that would blow wind into our flagging sails. Ahead of me Carnsey was pointing at a billboard. It took little to amuse us. The slightest variation to the ubiquitous black road and white line quickly became a most welcome distraction. Billboards provided mega entertainment – something like a day-time, non-motion version of a drive-in cinema.

One billboard advertisement for a veterinary clinic asked: *Feeling pawly?*

Another one cleverly advertised a law firm with the question: *So you don't think you need legal advice?* Underneath, and by way of an answer, was a close-up rear-view of a pig's butt.

A work-wear ad for miners reminded me of the Chileans who had already been six weeks underground. That one caught my attention with the caption: *The air's thicker than a dead dingo's guts.* I could relate to that. We'd had to hold our breath and hurry around many guts but, to date, no dead dingo.

On yet another billboard, a fitness centre guaranteed results with *just thirty minutes three times a week.* With a puff of the chest, I calculated that *our* weekly quota came to *thirty* times their suggested time commitment.

My favourite though was a huge close-up of an exaggeratedly bloodshot eye, aimed at encouraging tired drivers to rest. An average driver, travelling at a hundred kilometres an hour – assuming that he mostly kept his eyes on the road – had only a few seconds to take in the message. By contrast, travelling at only five kilometres an hour, I had the luxury of being able to gaze at that monstrous, somewhat obscene eyeball for a few minutes. The effect was nothing short of spectacular – it was the yawn effect. I felt tired and rubbed my eyes, convinced that they too were bloodshot and swollen. We'd passed several giant eyes and it concerned me to notice that the yawn effect never failed. If it had that effect on me, I wondered whether the same was true of drivers, which could be dangerously counterproductive.

Carnsey was still gesticulating at the new billboard, trying to catch my attention. This one, compared to *the eye*, was much less in-your-face – a large stylised bunch of grapes with the caption: *We are the pick of the bunch*. Confused, I wondered why Carnsey was so excited about a bunch of grapes. Was he perhaps intimating that we, the intrepid 2000 Walkers, were the pick of the bunch? Then I noticed the secondary text at the bottom of the billboard. *Stanthorpe – Tidy Towns Winner*. My jaw dropped. My little home town was famous all over the state. Not only had we won the Tidy Towns award, but we were on a Bruce Highway billboard, putting us in the same league as pigs' bottoms, dingo intestines and monstrous eyes. I had reckoned we wouldn't see the first Stanthorpe road sign for another month, and even then, I imagined it would only be a small distance indicator.

Buoyed up by this experience, and with renewed eagerness for the remaining kilometres of the day, we decided spontaneously to walk two more hours than planned in order to take advantage of The 2000 Walk clouds and cool breeze. A recently harvested cane field provided a cushioned walkway, with its thick carpet of cane mulch. We usually didn't walk too close to cane fields, keeping out of the way of any Joe Blakes that might be hiding there. But we were safe in this open field. No snakes there.

Wrong!

We saw him before he saw us – a shiny, dark brown individual with light belly markings and thin pointed tail just two metres from us, head stuffed down a hole, intent on sinking his fangs into some poor unsuspecting rodent. Actually, my guess is that the rodent in question, at that point in time, was anything *but* unsuspecting. He was no doubt *very* suspecting and in the process of peeing his proverbial pants. I might have too had I known – as video footage later confirmed – that we were in the presence of a Coastal Taipan. I was blissfully ignorant though, and the *50,000-mice* statistic didn't come to mind. We just watched, entranced. Finally his head emerged and whipped around in our direction, round black eyes staring, tongue flicking. We dropped some clods of dirt near him to encourage a little action.

'What if he shoots this way?' I asked. Instead he melted away, as if by magic, and disappeared.

Apart from Mr Taipan, we discovered something else of particular interest. Over the weeks we'd had a series of road finds, including several pairs of sunglasses, a hammer, different types of hats, several magnetic 'P' plates and a full packet of cigarettes. But today Carnsey scooped up a new item – a long, elastic rope with hooks at either end. While it was familiar to me, I had no idea what it was called. The ensuing new topic of conversation served to remind me I have holes in my vocabulary bank – a consequence of years spent outside my country speaking languages other than my own. Carnsey

said it was called an *occy strap* but, being too much of
a stimulating conversation topic to keep to ourselves,
we decided to use a lifeline and phone a friend. We had
instant confirmation of *occy strap*, and also the addition
of a more common name: *bungee strap* which can also be
spelt *bungy* or *bungie*. And not only that, but it is often
known as an *octopus* or *shock strap* (not to be confused
with jock strap). I would discover later that these straps
were first used even prior to the First World War as
lightweight suspension for aircraft undercarriages.
During the last hours of the day, we would discover an
equally worthy, wholly new function for this whatever-
you-like-to-call-it.

Remembering the words of our indefatigable coach,
Extreme Janine, we suddenly saw in this humble bungee
strap a potential tow rope. I was definitely dragging
the chain and ready for a pull. With one hook clipped
on Carnsey's backpack and the other on mine, we were
off! While this arrangement didn't propel
me into turbo mode, it did allow me to
maintain a consistent cruise speed.

In tow-rope mode, we crossed the O'Connell
River with me peering down onto the sand
banks in the hope of catching sight of a croc, reputed
to be up to five metres long in this part of the world.
I played a little private mind game called: *Is it better to
get bitten by a crocodile or a taipan*? It's a marvellous
game to play when you have time to kill because there is
no real solution. It simply goes on forever.

We unhitched the tow rope, with at least one of us
singing its praises, and returned to Proserpine just
in time to set up for our umpteenth meeting. We had
clocked up forty-three kilometres – the
highest count of any day during The Walk.   0665

Our meeting attracted only two people – the lowest count
so far.

Day 25
Death

Friday 17 September

I readily admitted – due partly to the recent demise of Mrs Ibis – that I was now scared to death of walking along the Bruce Highway. And with very good reason.

The Bruce had recently been named the most dangerous stretch of road in all Australia, accounting for one in six deaths on the entire national road network. As a response to these alarming statistics, the RACQ launched its biggest campaign in more than a century to fix the highway, including eleven billboards mounted on the 1600 kilometre route between Cairns and Brisbane. They featured the shock message: *Driving the Bruce Highway may result in death.* And walking it may too. Of the 1368 people who lost their lives in 2010 on Australian roads, 173 were pedestrians – one in eight.

The road improvements to The Bruce came too late, however, to be of benefit to us. They were also too late for Hilda, Mary-Anne, Sandy, Duncan and Perry.

It was right on midday when we rounded a curve and noticed several white objects on the side of the road ahead. I stopped alongside these crosses, in silence, and noted the names. At that location, right where I was standing, in April 2005, those five people lost their lives. Hilda and her two teenage daughters were travelling with a friend, Duncan, when their car collided head-on with another vehicle, driven by sixty-eight year old Perry. Life snuffed out in an instant!

I waited for a gap in the vehicles hurtling past, crossed the highway and checked out Perry's cross. Underneath his name, there was the phrase: *The road goes on forever*

– an allusion no doubt to Robert Earl Keen's country and western song of the same name, perhaps a favourite of Perry's. The title struck a chord with me. Yes, the Bruce Highway certainly did seem to be never ending.

But, in fact, it does *not* go on forever – neither the Bruce Highway nor the road of life. People are *destined to die once,* the Bible tells us, *and after that to face judgement* (Hebrews 9:27). These are God's words, carefully passed down from generation to generation and transcending culture and language, telling of judgement, but also of hope – hope *beyond* death, and life *after* death – regardless of whether death comes to us on the side of the Bruce Highway or in an old people's home. *God loved the world so much that He gave His one and only Son, that whoever believes in Him will not perish but will have eternal life* (adapted from John 3:16).

These words have changed millions of lives. It is estimated today that there are more than two billion people in this world bowing the knee to Jesus. In some countries it can feel like we are a minority, but we are part of a huge worldwide movement of believers guided by God's Word. Yet there are still hundreds of millions of people who can't hear this message because it hasn't been translated into their languages.

Those white crosses impressed on me the brevity of life, where we have no rehearsals and no repeat performances – we have just *one* chance to perform, *one* chance to give, *one* chance to invest. I decided, again, that I wanted my life to count. I can think of fewer more worthwhile tasks to be involved in than sharing God's Word with those around me, and helping translate it for those who still don't have it in their language.

We pressed on down the highway, under our continuing cloud cover, with the images of those crosses firmly imprinted on my retina.

Two hours later, a passing motorist recognised us and

brought his car to a stop abruptly beside us. It was a hasty decision that confused the truck driver following too closely behind. We turned with a start as the truck braked and swerved. Another close call! I was shaken.

I was counting the days and the kilometres till I'd get off the Bruce Highway and shake its dust from 0692 my weary feet. While that countdown would continue for another month, the countdown for my wife and sons to arrive was almost over.

Day 26
Drag

Saturday 18 September

The word for the day was *drag.*

I was *dragging* the chain.

The minutes *dragged* by.

The whole Walk had become a *drag.*

I was *dragging* a cow rather than riding a horse.

What's more, I had to admit, I'd become a bit of a *drag* myself.

The word *drag* was on my mind when I came across an empty two-litre Coke bottle on the roadside, conveniently attached to a five-metre cord. So, I did. Drag it, that is. It trailed out behind me flipping and somersaulting, skidding and sliding, jumping and jerking. It took less than a kilometre for me to become emotionally attached to my Coke bottle. It had become obvious we would have no other human company on this Walk so I had to be content with lower life forms.

Dave flipped open the video camera to interview me. 'Why are you pulling along a Coke bottle, Sav?'

'Walking along the Bruce Highway is not the most stimulating of activities in life,' I replied, 'and one can go several kilometres with very little of interest to amuse oneself. Today I found this gorgeous Coke bottle lying in the grass looking very, very lonely. It seemed like the two of us were made for each other, and now this little Coke bottle looks very happy. I don't think he's been this happy for a long time. I haven't chosen a name for him yet, but personally I think everybody should have a friend like him.'

On and on I dragged it, waiting (I am slightly embarrassed to admit) to see how long it would take for its little guts to rip open from the constant hitting and flicking against the bitumen. Surprisingly, it took a long time for even the label to rip and detach itself and it was with relish that at last I finally witnessed the remains of the flapping paper come unglued and flick off onto the road. The bottle itself, however, was made of some sort of transparent titanium and refused to die. I eventually abandoned it, along with its rope, on the side of the road. Maybe in a few years another walker might pass that way and take up where I left off.

By then I was only hours from being reunited with my wife and sons. I had walked 200 kilometres in the six days since my last day off and I was exhausted. I arrived home, closed the door behind me and collapsed in a heap.

Home is a relative term. Over the eighty days of The Walk we obviously didn't have the same home to return to each night but neither were we *homeless*. In fact, we had multiple homes. Sometimes we slept under the stars or in tents, caravans, sheds, cabins or huts, but mostly we stayed in *homes*. Even months later, a kaleidoscope of faces, voices and smiles would fill my mind as I'd recall with gratitude the wonderful people who opened their homes to three sweaty, weary walkers: young people, couples, families, pastors, priests and retirees.

However, in that kaleidoscope of faces there is one missing. It's not that I am ungrateful to this lady, but simply that I never actually *saw* her face.

Madge is an elderly widow who heard an announcement in her church that I was looking for a place in Mackay to stay with my wife and boys for a week. She responded, not by opening the door and welcoming us in, but by walking out and closing the door behind her, leaving *us* the key so we could let *ourselves* in. We slept in her bed, sat at her table, showered in her bathroom, shaved at her mirror (at least I did), cooked on her stove, fed her goldfish and even drove her car – but we never saw her face.

The following day would be my day off and I'd spend it with my family. The days after that I'd still be walking, further and further away from the family, and getting a lift back to Madge's house each evening.

So this would be our first evening together. It was just a few hours before they were due to arrive by taxi from the airport. I leapt into action. After a shower, a shave and a clean change of clothes (*not* a royal-blue Wiggles shirt) I was off to the shops. I forged my way up and down the aisles whistling to myself and clicking my heels together as I filled my trolley. Heads turned in amusement and I think I even heard a little dog laugh to see such a sight.

I continued my strategy, carefully planning the menu, and choosing the finest ingredients, which included a *magret de canard* (duck breast) imported from France, *fromage blanc* and herbs to accompany the cream and a familiar brand of North African couscous – a family favourite. Next came an assortment of fruit to make a fresh fruit salad and ice-cream for the boys – six different exotic flavours. I knew they'd go wild.

Deciding to forego a taxi, deeming it more fitting to the *hero* status my reception would earn me, I lugged the two overflowing bags home on foot. A bouquet of red roses from a florist en route completed my foray. This was Hollywood at its best.

The kitchen became a hive of activity, a working bee of one, as I literally buzzed with excitement – *Julie and Julia*, eat your heart out. The dessert was ready in the fridge, the vegies were bubbling away nicely and the amazing aroma of roast duck sent my salivary glands into a frenzy.

Right on cue, I heard the happy voices of my boys and the doorbell rang.

In a perfect world, and if I was a perfect husband and father, all of the above would have been true. My wife would have arrived and, at the sight of the spread table and under the charm of the aromas wafting in from the kitchen, would have embraced me. We'd have eaten a sumptuous meal and lounged around basking in that happy puppy feeling, the adoring children bestowing thanks and hugs on their darling Daddy.

Alas, it was *not* true. I *had*, however, summoned the energy to wash off the day's sweat and at the same time check for non-resident beauty spots. I *had* managed to drag myself to the corner store and home again carrying a small bag of instant noodles, sausages and eggs, but *nothing* else. In spite of good intentions, my battered body and brain just weren't up to the challenge.

My wife and boys arrived late, tired and starving. While Hélène was possibly not expecting a *magret de canard*, couscous, vegetables and fruit salad, neither was she expecting to find an almost-empty fridge and a bare table. Her month as sole parent hadn't been easy. We were two needy people looking to the other to meet our own needs, and off to a bad start.

But tomorrow would be another day.

Day 27
The day I ran

Sunday 19 September

It felt good to wake up with my family. It also felt good *not* to wake up with Big Red and Sky Blue who were no doubt thinking the same about Royal Blue. It also felt good, *very* good, not to be on the road.

It was Sunday. In France our Sunday morning routine includes walking to church – past our block of neighbourhood houses hidden behind hedges and down the hill past the 16th century *château* that is home to the Council Chambers. Hélène and I enjoy the Sunday morning walk, the boys usually do too once they get past their customary initial grumblings. On wet days we take the car, but those days are rare. In our corner of the country we enjoy 300 blue-sky days a year – the French sunshine record.

It started out as a blue-sky Sunday in Mackay, but we weren't going to church. Instead we wandered to the beach within walking distance from Madge's house. The boys pointed out that The 2000 Walk had already redefined for me the term *walking distance.*

Through the town, past Queen's Park, over the ridge, and one kilometre later a massive expanse of wet, low-tide sand lay before us. We had been warned that tides can be upwards of eight metres in this part of the country, which means at low tide the beach can be 200 metres wide. On the other end of the scale, the tides in the Mediterranean are the smallest in the world, peaking at a weenie two to three centimetres.

No, this is not the beach in Mackay. I cheated - haha.
It's a drawing I did of Coolum Beach in 16 BG *

Hélène
and I sat
and chatted.
The harsh rays
of the sun were
soon blocked by
heavy cloud cover and it
was wonderfully cool. Flynn
and Joseph wandered happily
away exploring pools and rivulets.

The unspeakable beauty of the
seascape captivated me – the watercolour
hues, the curls of the waves, the low-tide
swirl patterns in the sand, the salty whisper of
the water and the wind coming soothing and soft.
This was where heaven and earth met, where the
blue above touched the blue below. It was impossible
not to think of the divine – *The God who made the world
and everything in it is the Lord of heaven and earth* (Acts
17:24a). Simple words that undergird my faith and life
and everything I do. All this beauty did not happen
by chance. Sitting on the beach there was a spiritual
connection, no less real and no less important than if I'd
been sitting in church or even in a grand cathedral. The
vault above *was* His Grand Basilica.

* "Before Google" – which was founded
on Sept 4th, 1998.

My thoughts took me back to Africa, to the mighty Basilica in Yamoussoukro, Côte d'Ivoire, the largest church in the world, bigger by far than St Peter's in Rome. At a cost of US$300 million – with seating for 7,000 people and standing room for a further 11,000 – it was built, it is said, *to house God*. I shudder at the audacity, recalling when I first laid eyes on it, rising obscenely, 158 metres high, in the midst of impoverished Africa.

There on the beach, watching the boys playing away happily, I pulled out my Bible and read the words of the Apostle Paul. *[God] does not live in temples built by hands. And He is not served by human hands, as if He needed anything, because He Himself gives all men life and breath and everything else* (Acts 17:24b, 25).

Hélène and I sat happily in our Beach Basilica and chatted for a stress-free hour, grateful that our boys, no longer little, were able to entertain themselves. We were particularly grateful they had each other, both for their sake and for our peace of mind. We never would have allowed either one of them to wander so far or for so long on his own, but we were relaxed about letting the two of them head off into the distance together. After some time, we casually turned and scanned the beach for two boy-shaped dots. There were a few dots at different points, none of which had any easily distinguishable form. We checked the time and decided we should be heading back. A few minutes later, walking along the beach, the first ember of panic flickered. I was certain now, scanning as far as the eye could see, that the boys *weren't* there. They weren't on the beach. The swings? The park? We quickly made a plan and separated. In less than a minute, our staccato conversation had fanned the ember into flame. A few minutes later, I phoned Hélène. Not there?

No! Not here either! I broke into a run. No sign of them. I phoned again.

'You go via the park, I'll run back home in case they've somehow headed back.'

'But they won't know the way.'

I ran fast. For almost the first time since I'd left Cairns, my legs moved faster than a walk. Every few minutes I stopped and phoned. Nothing! No sign!

'But they wouldn't have gone home.'

'Do you want me to go back to the beach?'

'Yes, check again.'

I kept running, desperately hoping I'd find them at home, but knowing I wouldn't. They'd never done anything like this before.

I arrived at our locked house. No boys waiting outside. I panicked. Tears stung. I tried to talk calmly on the phone to Hélène who almost shrieked into my ear that they weren't anywhere on the beach.

'I'll phone the police,' I told her.

Horror stories of news reports surfaced like unwelcome bubbles and popped somewhere in the back of my mind. I tried pushing them away but they kept appearing in high resolution before me. I started punching buttons on my phone. Frightened, I turned once more, confused, to peer into the house. Grabbing hold of the bars, I rattled the security gate loudly and screamed:

A slight movement caught my eye. Against all hope, I pushed my face against the bars of the gate and peered through the lounge room. On the back verandah two surprised little faces appeared.

They told me their story. When they began to feel hungry, they looked for us and thought we must have headed back already. Without missing a beat they started off, winding their way through unfamiliar streets until they came out at an intersection they recognised and then to our house, only to discover we weren't home at all.

'We tried a thousand ways to break in,' Flynn said.

They ended up climbing over the high fence and sat quietly on the back verandah waiting for us to arrive with the key.

Apart from racing past putrid road kill, that was the only time during The Walk I broke into a run. And I will *never* forget it.

Day 28
Torrential rain

Monday 20 September

Before my alarm rang or my eyelids had a chance to slide open, I heard it – rain! Not a light summer shower, but serious storm rain drumming hard on the roof. I smiled.

As a child I loved the sound of rain beating on galvanised iron. My heart would leap and I would feel enveloped and loved, surrounded and protected, warmed and cared for – by my family, by our house and by the rainmaker Himself. There was definitely also an accompanying element of fear and reverence related to the power unleashed by storms, the cracking bolts of lightning and the deafening claps of thunder. In a strange, paradoxical way, all of that only served to intensify my passion and exhilaration.

The first poem I ever wrote, as an eleven-year-old, was about a storm:

> Thunder booms + rain pelts down
> lightning flashes and I hear the sound
> of hailstones crashing on our roof at night
> that give me such an awful fright.

My heart gave that old familiar leap of excitement. The sound of the storm signalled that we wouldn't be walking and I could stay curled up in bed and linger longer, which is always nice when you have someone to linger with.

Suddenly the reality sank in. This rain was not likely to stop in a hurry. We would miss walking our miles and have to make them up. The relentless itinerary before us was like an email *inbox*. You can ignore it but it won't go away. Nobody else was answering my emails, and nobody else was walking my miles. This dismal thought threatened to spoil the day off with my family when, with a remarkable act of will, I managed to dispel it post-haste and get on with the business of lingering.

The local evening news would tell the full story. Mackay had been hit by an *unseasonal downpour* and *flash flood* which lasted five hours and unleashed an unprecedented 182 millimetres of rain. The region was inundated, which was bad news for cane farmers in the middle of harvest. It was also bad news for motorists as the Bruce Highway was closed.

The newscaster's word *unseasonal* was not chosen lightly. September is normally the driest month of the year in Mackay, with an average rainfall of only nineteen millimetres. Ten times the monthly average in just a few hours was truly *unseasonal*. In many ways, we were not surprised, as the weather had actually been unseasonal for all four weeks of The Walk so far.

After lunch, the storm subsided. The violence and clamour gave way to silence. The darkness gave way to brightness and we looked out on a clean new world, like the child of my poem:

> When the rain is finished I crawl out of my shell
> I look out the window . then I can tell
> that the storm is over and the ground is like clay
> and I stay inside for the rest of the day .

Unlike that child, however, we didn't stay inside. We were men on a mission and sprang into automatic routine action – boots, backpack, blister kit – and we were on the road, redeeming the time and pounding out a few more miles. I chose a back road that circumnavigated the city, a last-minute executive decision which did not impress Dave. All was awash with cleanliness and crisp afternoon light. The storm had even scrubbed the sky clean and the air that I sucked into my lungs was pure.

We *splashed* through puddles, *walked* alongside fields transformed into lakes, *stepped* over rivulets and *marched* alongside tumbling water in drains and rivers. The otherworldliness caught me in its spell.

There was not a breath of wind as dusk lowered itself gently over the cane fields – newly planted and totally drenched – transforming them into watercolour tones of milky-mauve and pink. Only the very occasional swish and spray of passing cars, headlights reflecting on the wet road, disrupted the concert of hundreds of happy birds and millions of extremely happy frogs. And as if on cue, the chirping of the birds subsided as they settled down to roost before sunset.

We too went home to roost, Dave and Carnsey to yet another cousin's place and me to my waiting family.

Day 29
Royal boys

Tuesday 21 September

At 8.30 am, there were six walkers at the drop-off point – not only Big Red, Sky Blue and Royal Blue, but also Mrs Royal and our two Royal boys.

Hélène and I discussed the possibility of Flynn and Joseph joining me for the very last of the 2000 kilometres. And as we marched along together as a family, it occurred to me that I could share those last-kilometre moments with my sons in a special way.

'Could I find,' I wondered, 'child-size, royal-blue shirts, identical to mine?'

I tucked that thought away, imagining the additional thrill for all three of us *Sav men* being identified by the same shirts at the end of this marathon. I was stoked at the *togetherness* of this idea.

Filled with these noble father-son thoughts, I slipped out my compact video camera and filmed an interview with Flynn. I was less than stoked by his response:

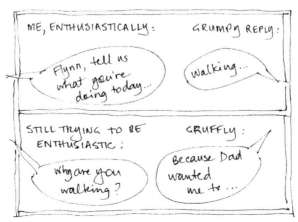

He popped my bubble. Miffed, I snapped the camera shut, stuffed it in my bag and walked off ahead in a mini, only-half-disguised huff. Ungrateful brat! It took me a little while to get over his smart comment. Few things can hurt a parent like the careless words or actions of a much-loved child. The Taruuba people have a proverb about that, likening children to fingers: *My own finger poked me in the eye.*

Flynn had poked me in the eye big time. Mind you, I didn't hold it against him – he was just trying to be funny, and at eleven years of age the line between *being funny* and *being smart* is pretty blurred.

Apart from that incident, I did enjoy having my boys with me as walking companions. I also enjoyed having them participate in the meeting at Mackay Baptist Church. The pair of them volunteered to hold up two stats signs. What a pair of dags they looked – Flynn barefoot with his cheeky grin, Joseph wearing the tightest of tight black jeans. I swelled with pride just looking at them!

Flynn held up the sign **Complete 451**, representing the number of languages with the entire Bible translated. Joseph held the one with the more impressive figure of **NT 1185**, representing the number of languages with at least the New Testament. One of the signs that kept people guessing was the smallest one, **NV 188**. I lost track of the creative guesses for this one – *new version*, *non-verbal*, and even *night vision*. It actually referred to the 188 languages considered *non-viable* for Bible translation purposes. There are two main reasons for this.

Firstly, if a language is dying out with only a few older speakers still living, no Bible translation project will be undertaken. Sad as it is, many languages *are* dying out.

The second reason not to undertake a Bible translation project would be if nearly all the speakers are bilingual, and the Bible already exists in their other language. Dave always did a good job in our meetings explaining this situation:

> *'Bilingual doesn't mean that they learned the other language at school or that they can speak a few words they picked up somewhere. Rather, it means they can fully communicate and fully understand basically everything in the two languages.'*

However, having said that, there are not many truly bilingual communities in the world.

Following on from the *bilingual community* explanation, there was the inevitable question: *Why don't we just teach them English?* By way of response, Dave pulled out his trusty toothbrush for the demonstration, and we discovered yet again, that North Queensland has talent! However, I needed to take this question one step further, wanting our audience not only to *know* that it's not enough to teach them English, but to actually understand *why* it's not enough. I'd devised another activity for that purpose and was looking forward to trying it out on the Mackay mob.

With Flynn's help I'd formulated a short paragraph written in a strange font style, designed in such a way as to be readable but at the same time difficult *enough* for the volunteer to find it hard work. The point of the exercise was to reproduce a feeling akin to the effort of speaking and functioning in a second language.

This is the text. Try reading it aloud:

> *This is a short paragraph that is written in a way that is not very easy to read. You can more or less manage to read it, but it's not easy. This is a little bit what it feels like operating in a language that is not your mother tongue. You can do it OK. You can learn to talk another language but*

UNLESS YOU BECOME A VERY FLUENT SPEAKER IT IS PROBABLY GOING TO BE QUITE HARD WORK A LOT OF THE TIME. THAT'S ALSO WHAT IT'S LIKE TRYING TO UNDERSTAND THE BIBLE IN ANOTHER LANGUAGE. PERHAPS YOU COULD LEARN THAT LANGUAGE WELL ENOUGH TO BE ABLE TO READ, BUT IT WILL MOST LIKELY BE HARD WORK — AT LEAST IT WILL BE HARDER WORK THAN READING IN YOUR OWN LANGUAGE.

I followed this exercise with a series of questions:

The majority of people will probably never want to either *read* or *listen* to the Bible in any language other than their own mother tongue. It is simply not enough to teach them English.

Day 30
In the dark

Wednesday 22 September

For over a month I had been happily whipping out my beaut little Sony video recorder, my compact companion, proudly immortalising all those kilometres for posterity's sake. I was totally satisfied with the results in spite of Mr WIN TV cameraman turning up early to film us, flaunting *his* equipment.

His was a two-hand job slung over his shoulder, causing him to swagger a little under the weight. He looked ridiculous, all pomp and arrogance. Who did he think he was impressing? Seriously, what size lens does one really need to film a stupid interview with three guys on a footpath? And as for those totally-pretentious, mega-zoom, extension lenses! He didn't fool me for a minute – there wasn't one thing he could do with his apparatus that I couldn't do with my no-frills mini-model.

The interview was filmed in a light misty drizzle. Big Red answered several questions about the physical aspects of The Walk – blisters, shoes and the like. Sky Blue got to talk about the motivation behind it all, while the questions addressed to me focussed on the 2000 languages we were harping on about.

'Where are these languages found?'

'The majority are located in Africa and Asia. In Africa, some countries have more than a hundred languages. For example, in Cameroon there are 230.'

'Why is it important to be concerned about these languages?'

Cameroon

'The people who speak these languages are often marginalised minority groups, neglected, hidden, unseen and sometimes exploited and underprivileged.'

'Can you elaborate on that?'

'Well, let me give an example. I lived in the Sahara Desert for a number of years with the Taruuba people. On several occasions, Taruuba friends, knowing I'm a linguist, asked me if their *talk* is really a proper language or just some sort of primitive gibberish. By way of response I was able to describe to them some of the intricate aspects of their language. For example, in English we only have one word for camel but they have more than fifty. Their verbs are conjugated in more than a hundred different ways, and their language is possibly the only one in the world that doesn't have adjectives. What we know as adjectives in English are verbs in Taruuba. For example, instead of saying *the blue tent* they say *the tent that blues*. Their language is unique, complex, complete and very beautiful.'

'So why would people tell them otherwise?'

'Denigrating comments about a minority language are common, and are often attempts to discourage the people from speaking their language, which is a violation of human rights. Every person has a right to speak and be proud of the language he was raised with.'

'What about the Bible?'

'Every person has the right to hear God's Word in his or her language too.'

The fine drizzle was still falling when Mr Cameraman packed his equipment away. We sheltered a few minutes under the awning of a florist shop where a sandwich board on the footpath caught my eye.

As Carnsey and I put our boots to the bitumen and knocked down the first kilometres of the day, I was still thinking about the importance of attitudes and in particular, the attitudes people have to language. In the past, Australians have had very strong and not particularly benevolent attitudes to other languages. I was walking with a friend through a park in Sydney one day when we passed a group of Chinese people deep in what was obviously warm conversation – Chinese conversation, of course. My friend was indignant and declared, 'If people want to come to Australia then they should only speak English here.'

I was dumbfounded and asked, 'When you came to visit us in France, did you speak French with us?'

Thankfully some negative attitudes *are* changing, and that change *is* contagious. As more and more of us talk about the hidden languages, the invisible languages, the ones whose names we have never heard, the tide of apathy *will* turn. As we model an appropriate attitude of care and concern, others *will* catch it. We *can* be agents of change in our communities as we advocate on behalf of the hidden minorities of the world who are often trapped behind language barriers. Trapped, like the miners in Chile.

It had been one month since contact was made with the thirty-three miners, confirming they were still alive. For seven long weeks they'd been trapped, cut-off, and in the dark – a horrible experience but a very fitting analogy for many minority language groups.

Little did I know that by the end of the day I'd have my own *in the dark* experience that would remind me of the thirty-three miners *and* of the 350 million Bibleless people.

The day was, once again, cloudy – almost defying belief. It was the third consecutive day of near-perfect walking conditions! We moved along quiet back roads, including a short cut that sliced off ten kilometres. The smallest things became welcome distractions – an old microwave serving as a letterbox, a dog that wanted to have us for dinner, a flock of squawking parrots.

As the sun sank lower and my feet moved slower, Carnsey and I watched and waited for Dave to turn up in the support vehicle. The minutes ticked by. We kept walking. Every car that came was Dave. Except that it wasn't. He was half an hour late for the appointed pick-up and we were worried about being late for our meeting in Sarina. With no phone coverage, we couldn't find out what was wrong. We just kept walking until it was too dark to walk anymore. Then we stood by the roadside until we were too tired to stand anymore. After conferring together, Carnsey and his socks disappeared into the darkness heading towards the pin-prick light of a farmhouse up the hill. I stayed by the road, accompanied by a night full of insects buzzing and chirping, humming and droning. The lights of a car would slice the night and I'd step forward so Dave could see me, but Dave still didn't come. I kept thinking of the people who were waiting for us at the Anglican Church in Sarina.

Each of these meetings took us about an hour to set up – data projector, book display and the rest. The local organisers often spent *weeks* planning prior to our arrival – publicity, posters, contacting churches, radio announcements and newspaper articles, not to mention meals and showers for the Wiggle walkers.

A light appeared in the window of another house a way behind me. I could just pick out a sinister silhouette on crutches limping back and forth on the verandah. Dogs barked. A few minutes later a weak torch beam came bobbing down the driveway completing the setting for an Alfred Hitchcock movie. The obviously frightened woman behind the torch bravely asked what I was doing. After managing to convince her that I wasn't a crim on the run, she confessed, 'I was pretty worried to see two guys all the way out here without a vehicle.'

To be honest, I was pretty worried to *be* one of those guys all the way out there without a vehicle. She confirmed there was no mobile coverage and explained that in wet weather the landlines go down too. With that encouraging piece of news she turned, taking her beam of torch light with her and leaving me in the dark with my insect orchestra.

I was hungry, tired, footsore and smelly. We didn't know where Dave was. It'd been half an hour since Carnsey had melted into the night and I didn't know where *he* was. What's more, I didn't even know where *I* was. And the people waiting for us twenty kilometres away at the meeting had no idea where *any* of us were.

Occasionally the glow of an approaching vehicle would expand into a beam, which was my cue to step close to the road so as to be seen. This rewarded me every time with a shower of dirty spray. Just when I thought I couldn't take another whoosh Carnsey's socks materialised out of the blackness. He'd managed to phone Dave who'd been barking up the wrong road. Fifteen minutes later Dave appeared in the Land Cruiser and we were on our way, already preparing our apology.

G'day bloke

Kari, a born organiser, was not expecting her finely-tuned plans for this 2000 Walk meeting to be almost foiled by the inconsiderate, disorganised walkers appearing nearly two hours late. We wolfed down her sumptuous meal in record time, dispensed with the shower (sorry Sarina-ites) and set up for the meeting in a record six minutes flat.

Thank you Kari for being patient with us – at least outwardly.

(one of Mum's little poems!)

PATIENCE IS A VIRTUE
POSSESS IT IF YOU CAN
SELDOM FOUND IN
WOMEN
NEVER IN A ___

Day 31
Last day before break

Thursday 23 September

An uneventful day. We walked the prescribed thirty kilometres.

0830 · I was exhausted and really looking forward to our only *block* of three days off!!
Woo hoo!

It was a full moon, but I couldn't see it for the clouds.

Somewhere I lost my wallet.

Day 32
First day of break

Friday 24 September

Day off.

It had been fifty days since the Chilean miners were trapped, which is longer than anyone in history. Work had been continuing on the evacuation shaft for almost a month. They estimated it would still be a few more weeks till they could be lifted out. They weren't *out of the woods* yet or *out of the inn* as we say in French.

The saga of the missing wallet continued.

'Flynn and Joseph, have you boys seen my wallet?'

Day 33
Second day of break

Saturday 25 September

Second day off.

Still didn't find my wallet.

Hélène had to pay for everything. Hahaha!

Day 34

Third day of break

Sunday 26 September

Third day off.

Went to church.

I stopped looking for my wallet.

I hoped it would turn up when we packed to leave.

Day 35
The National Trail

Monday 27 September

The Bruce Highway is an ugly, in-your-face, 1700 kilometre scar ripping down the eastern flank of Australia. In sharp contrast, *The Bicentennial National Trail* winds like an invisible artery, stretching three times that distance, from Cooktown to Healesville, passing – as the website boasts – through some of the most magnificent terrain and unsurpassed scenery in Australia. It is open to horse riders, mountain bikers and walkers, and in most sections, is *not* open to any form of motorised vehicles.

Two years earlier, while still in France, I had pored over maps of the National Trail and drooled at the idea of spending weeks in the Australian bush. It was not to be. Dave and Carnsey had persuaded me to focus on meetings in the cities along the coastal route, so my trail became a highway, and my horse turned out to be a cow. However, I had doggedly refused to totally wipe the National Trail from our itinerary. Five of our eighty days of walking *would* be on the Trail. And those five days were about to start!

I was nearly beside myself with excitement, though it was somewhat *less* exciting to have to farewell Hélène, Flynn and Joseph. Cleaning the house and packing our bags in readiness for our separate departures was a cheerless affair. What's more, my wallet still stubbornly refused to be found. I guessed it had somehow slipped in with my family's luggage and was on its way back to Stanthorpe. It would turn up when they unpacked.

It was sad to see my family go. They had been my life-saving desert island. I had washed up on the shore into their arms, a wreck after my weeks adrift on the Bruce Highway. I hoped these next days on the National Trail would also prove to be another refreshing island experience.

Before leaving Mackay, however, I had a little unfinished business. Convincing the cousins, we returned early to the city centre and found ourselves standing before a two-metre-high structure – four bold red letters spelling the word YUWI. A small plaque at the base of this eyesore caught my eye:

> 2009
> The artwork is a considered look at the presence of the Yuibera people who once densely populated Mackay.

The word *once* deeply affected me as if it was something from a fairytale or an ancient history book. Actually, as recently as when my grandparents were born, this proud

people roamed free, custodians of a unique culture and language.

A rap at the red, metallic Y with my knuckles rang hollow, as did the pathetic *considered look* at the demise of the culture of one of God's unique peoples. Apologising to the indigenous people of Australia is high on our political agenda but it's too late to apologise to all those who've gone. However it's *not* too late for the thousands of similar ethnic groups around the world who *are* still alive, though perhaps not well. Will we invest the effort to take the Word of God to them? Time will tell. Of course, unless we are aware of the situation of these groups, nobody will speak up or stand up in their defence.

I wondered if locals were aware of the recent history of the Yuibera people right in their own backyard. Did they even realise that their own Cathy Freeman, gold-medal Olympian and Australian icon, is herself from the Yuibera tribe? I decided to interview a few passers-by and find out what they knew about this *considered look* artwork. My interviewees confirmed my suspicions:

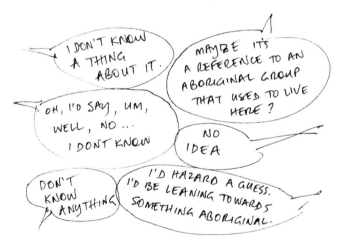

With a shrug of her shoulders and a hand gesture that said, *Don't know, don't care!* the last of them was gone.

After the disillusionment of my YUWI experience, I too turned tail and was gone – with great expectation – to find my Trail. I wasn't disappointed. The *island feel* was almost immediate.

The inhospitable cars were replaced by curious cattle – wide-eyed, tails a-swishing and disproportionately large ears a-flapping – reversing to let us pass. Instead of bitumen underfoot, we were crunching on sand, which sounded something akin to munching on cornflakes. The birds were no longer silent flecks in the sky, but colourful, raucous flocks in the branches all around. The friendly gum trees closed in from all sides, welcoming us, casting shade over our path and embracing us. Inspired by the stark beauty of one particular individual, I embraced him back, though I led Carnsey to believe that I was merely taking his girth measurement. He was one of the lemon-scented gums which are only found in this region. Because of his smooth, pale skin, without a blemish, I nicknamed him Mr Temple after Roald Dahl's character in *The Landlady*.

There are hundreds of unique species of gum trees in Australia, each *kashaa* continuing to reproduce according to its kind as commanded by God and recorded in Genesis. I love gum trees. They are so *steadfast,* which inspired this verse of a poem I wrote some years ago:

> Something there is that loves a gumtree;
> A kindly never-changing host in seasons all,
> A faithful friend throughout the year
> whose leaf won't fall,
> with loyal and unassuming inner beauty.

The National Trail? I was hooked.

Day 36
Timely deluge

Tuesday 28 September

Before embarking on the National Trail we'd made a plan.
For the first time without homes or hosts or meetings
for three days, we'd be camping. We'd need food, water,
cooking gear, a tent and sleeping bags but there was
no way we were going to carry all this on our backs –
especially not on *my* unreliable back – for an average
of thirty-five kilometres a day. Instead, the plan was for
Dave to go ahead by car and leave the provisions hidden
in strategic locations where the Trail was accessible by
vehicle. Since Dave wasn't walking with us for those few
days, he had to clearly communicate with Carnsey and
me exactly where, along that one hundred kilometre
stretch, he was concealing our precious provisions. On
top of that, there would be no phone coverage at any
point, so it was essential for the details to be coordinated
well in advance. We needed to be able to find each pack
by sundown. The identifying mark, we decided, would be
a length of blue tape tied around a white guide post or, in
the absence of such, a tree.

'She'll be right,' Dave chirped, 'Easy as!'

It had been a hot, sultry morning on this, the second day
on the Trail. At 2 pm, if you'd been peeping from behind
one of the Mr Temple gum trees, you'd have seen two
strange animals, tails up and heads down in the cool
water of a creek.

'The nicest creek we've come across so far,' Carnsey
moaned, from the sheer hedonistic pleasure of cold
water on a hot face. This was also perfect timing to fill
our water bottles – flowing creeks were few and far

Flat out like a lizard drinking – literally!

between. As were people! During our six hours on the Trail so far we hadn't met a soul. However, an hour later the drone of an engine in the distance and the glint of a 4WD announced the arrival of humankind and soon brought us face to face with a woman understandably suspicious of two guys walking so far from civilisation.

'I thought there must have been a breakdown or a car to pull out of a ditch.' There was a question mark both in the tone of her voice and in her eyes which was only accentuated when we told her about The 2000 Walk. She was, however, much more polite than Mr Cool Cop. We seized the opportunity to glean information about our chosen camping destination for the night, Six Mile Creek.

'You're about four or five kilometres away,' she said. 'The creek is flowing so you should be right for water,' and then looking skywards with a chuckle added, 'but you're going to get some water on top of you before then!'

We followed her eyes and noticed, for the first time, the darkening horizon.

After another half hour of pleasant cornflake crunching, the wind began to seriously pick up and we realised, to our horror, that the black clouds overhead were looming ever darker and nearer. If we didn't make it to our packs and pitch the tent before the rain hit we were in for a long, wet night. The race was on. The only problem was that my feet didn't *do* race. It's true, they did in Mackay when I thought my boys' lives were at stake, but now not even the prospect of spending a cold, wet, hungry night in the open would drag them out of first gear. Phys Ed teacher Carnsey, however, would save the day. He sped ahead, Granny socks a-bobbing. And I was alone.

To some, *alone* is a dirty word, but to me, it conjures up warm, fuzzy feelings. Hélène has sometimes jokingly commented that if I enjoy being alone so much maybe I shouldn't have got married! Personality-wise, my batteries only get charged to the full by time out. Now

 the menacing sky only served to intensify the pleasure of my own personal Bear Grylls experience. The wind whipped up stronger. High above, someone turned the dimmer switch and the world darkened. I loved every moment of it. My heart was racing even if my feet weren't. From within me a connection was made between the Creator One and the created one. I sang at the top of my voice, joining the wind in giving glory to Him who sits above the circle of the earth and displays His power in the brewing storm. I was safe, in Him, enjoying the roar of thunder in amazing surround sound. My spirit soared.

Round a bend, the road sloped down to a causeway, immediately recognisable as Six Mile Creek where Dave was to have left a pack. Carnsey would have found it and, somewhere nearby, he would be waiting for me with our tent set up. Perfect timing! In a minute or two I'd be sitting high and dry and none too soon, because the water-laden canopy above me was about to rupture. I scouted around for Carnsey and the camp site – nothing. There was no mistaking this *was* Six Mile Creek. There were white guide posts where Dave should have left the blue tape marker. No sign of the tape, but perhaps Carnsey had removed it when he picked up the pack. I called out – no answer. I walked ahead – nothing! I walked back – nothing! I called again – nothing! At that point the word *alone* took on a slightly more sinister tone. I decided to continue walking.

In the dimness, way off to the left and appearing wraithlike out of nowhere I made out a homestead. Could Big Red have gone in there? And left me out in the dark? Wouldn't be the first time! Confused, upset and disappointed, I kept walking. Suddenly ahead, he came into sight, still running, obviously having been a long way and now retracing his steps – no pack, chest heaving, he hadn't found the blue tape. No sign of the pack anywhere.

The first heavy drops of rain fell and at the same time, out of the blue, a woman appeared on a quad bike. We pinched ourselves in disbelief. I think she was doing the same.

If we thought the driver of the 4WD had looked a little concerned, Lady Quad appeared positively disconcerted. However, with the loud, hard rain now falling in sheets, she wasn't insensitive to our predicament. That, combined with the hospitable nature of country folk imprinted in her DNA, dispelled any fears she may have had.

'Yes,' she yelled into the deafening roar, 'we have a shed where you can stay the night.'

There was still the question of the missing pack. Lady Quad confirmed seeing a vehicle, earlier in the day, back at Six Mile Creek. So in the blinding, stinging rain, and already drenched to the skin, boots full of water, we sloshed off back to the causeway at Six Mile Creek. Where *was* that tape? We sniffed around the base of every tree like tracker dogs. Sherlock Holmes couldn't have done any better. Our evening meal and night's sleep depended on finding the tape. We looked once, twice and then did the rounds a third time. Carnsey looked. I looked. Then we looked at each other, shrugged, gave up and trudged back to the homestead, boots heavy with mud.

Lady Quad's mother-in-law showed us to their workers' quarters. The workers were long gone but the quarters were still there, and to our surprise, complete with hot showers, mattresses and simple cooking facilities. If our eyes had popped out any further they would have rolled onto the bare wooden floorboards. By then the rain had stopped and we bundled into mother-in-law's flat-back truck to return to the Six Mile Creek causeway, very aptly named, as it was the sixth time I had crossed it in just a couple of hours. Mother-in-law indicated the exact spot where she had seen Dave parked. Now there were three pairs of eyes scouring the terrain for the elusive blue tape. The concealed packs were *finally* discovered fifteen metres from the road totally hidden from view in long grass. And the tape? Back at the causeway and in a moment of inspiration, we looked *up* – and there it was, four metres up in a tree. We left it there.

By then we didn't care – the sky had brightened, we had our pack and a hot shower was waiting.

Mother-in-law told us we were lucky.

'If it hadn't rained,' she explained, 'I would have put a match to that long dry grass this afternoon. It is getting to be a fire hazard and needs burning off.' She was talking about the grass where our packs were hidden – they would most certainly have been burnt to cinders.

We were grateful for that rain.

And there was more to come.

Day 37
Tent pegs

Wednesday 29 September

The day dawned bright and clear over Marylands Station. The wet, white curtain of rain that had veiled the glory of the place the previous day had vanished, revealing a sparkling world of pristine beauty. The crisp morning air was filled with carols of bush birds, rising and falling, including the cheeky grey and pink galahs – my favourite Aussie birds – screeching their greetings to the world. Hélène and I had chosen grey and pink as our wedding decor, in honour of the galah. Now, twenty years later, the antics of these feathered acrobats fascinated me once more.

Mother-in-law appeared at our door to see us off, along with her son. His impressive Akubra, so broad that it shaded his whole face, attested to the fact that he was manager of Marylands. Who said that size doesn't matter? In the Taruuba world it certainly does. For countless centuries, the Taruuba men of the Sahara Desert have worn turbans covering their entire faces, leaving only a letter-box slot for the eyes. Without any religious significance, these turbans are traditionally worn twenty-four hours a day from the teenage years. Some women never see their husband's face, only his seductive eyes. And yes, the bigger the turban, the better, but not everyone has the *right* to a big one.

When I first settled in a Taruuba township in the sub-Sahara, a local friend bought me my first turban, which measured two metres. It only wrapped around my head twice, with not enough left to hang down over my chest, as I'd seen others do. As it happened, this was the *beginner's* version. Teenagers, for example, wore two-metre turbans like mine. As a then thirty-two year old, I was humbled, but complied with what was a cultural norm. After all, I was not a Taruuba and, in the early days, my place in their community was often more that of an infant than a teenager. A year or so later, however, another friend suggested I change my turban, and presented me with a five-metre model, giving me the distinct impression I'd just been promoted. Some of the older and more respected men, however, wear turbans measuring as long as ten metres, wrapped many times around the head in an impressive and imposing construction of folds, the loose end draping almost to the ground. No, there is no mistaking the ten-metre men. If Mr Akubra had been a Taruuba, he would have worn a ten-metre turban.

In the inimitable, affable way of the man on the land, Mr Akubra casually warned us about lightning strikes.

'We had six cows electrocuted not long back,' he drawled pleasantly. 'They were leaning against a wire fence with metal posts. Found 'em fried the next day.'

Note to self: keep away from metal posts.

Mr Akubra informed us of the day's walk ahead, which involved climbing a steep ridge known as Beattie's Pinch. 'The only bit of bitumen for miles around,' he explained, adding, 'Without it no truck would ever get over.'

'Have you ever walked up there yourself?' I asked.

'No,' he replied, 'You two'll make it though. You look fit.' The shade of his Akubra, however, failed to hide the wry smile which did little to encourage me.

We asked how many people used the section of the National Trail that traversed his property. He said that he'd only ever seen a couple of groups on horseback.

Had they ever seen people *walking* through there before?

Mr Akubra: 'I can't remember any.'

Mother: 'Never.'

A few kilometres down the road, we startled a family of emus that took to the bush, long legs propelling the parent bird out of sight, chicks trailing behind, scurrying through the long grass and nearly tripping over their striped pyjamas in an effort to keep up.

Unlike those of the fleeing emu, my legs were not exactly propelling me along, but at least I was still able to put one foot in front of the other. Three hours later, we were glad to pause for lunch on the 0900 rocks beside a creek. The heavy, still, sultry air was weighing us down, suggesting the likelihood of another late afternoon storm. Thankfully we now had the tent, so unlike yesterday, we weren't going to be caught out. While Carnsey proceeded with great relish to remove his shoes and Granny socks, proclaiming them to be a fashion statement, I worked on lighting the fire. A million wet twigs and a hundred matches later, a trickle of flame appeared in the midst of a small column of smoke and eventually turned into a decent fire. There wasn't a breath of wind and not a leaf stirred as we sat and watched and waited till the billy boiled. Once again I found myself framed in a Frederick McCubbin oil painting. And I loved it. I also loved our instant noodle lunch eaten with a ridiculously small plastic fork. Suddenly, we both had the uneasy feeling that someone was looking over our shoulders. A glance behind revealed, to our dismay, that another storm had crept up and was about to unleash itself on us. How could neither of us have seen it coming? Bear Grylls would *not* have been proud of us. We immediately started shouting instructions to each other and scrambled to extract the tent. In no time, the wind was whipping the words away from our mouths and the first heavy drops of water were pelting down. As Carnsey flung the tent open it began to flap wildly in every direction. He held on to the bucking tent with one hand, eyes half closed against the driving rain, while we both groped in the bag for the pegs. Then ensued a shouting match, due to the noise of the wind and the rain as well as our mutual annoyance with each other:

The only way to keep the tent from blowing away was to get into it, which sounded like a great idea, except for the fact that a lot of water had already beaten us to it. It didn't matter though because we were already soaked. We managed to crawl into this flapping excuse for a tent, and sit in the water with our packs squashed up beside us. That's when we discovered that this two-man job had been designed by one of the pygmy tribes in Africa.

 The absurdity of the whole situation hit us just before we began hitting each other. I laughed till my sides cramped and my face hurt.

'Someone forgot the tent pegs!' was repeated amidst laughter for the next ten minutes, while the rain bucketed down on our useless tent. Then, as quickly as the storm had hit, it passed. We crawled out, laboriously repacked the tent and set off again. Oh, and I believe it is irrelevant to the narration of the incident to identify which of us had forgotten the tent pegs, so let's just keep this story moving along.

On the subject of moving along, it was becoming more and more difficult for me to walk. For the last hours of the day I was limping and it actually occurred to me that I might be doing permanent damage to my feet. When the infamous Beattie's Pinch loomed ahead, I doubted whether I'd make it. Thanks, however, to Extreme Janine's advice and the bungee cord we still carried with us, I hooked up behind Carnsey who dragged me all the way to the top of the twenty-degree gradient – the steepest climb of our walk so far.

By nightfall we *still* hadn't found Dave's blue tape – *again* – even though this time we'd wised up and were craning our necks to scan the trees to a height of ten metres! Thankfully though, we *did* still have a little water left so we set up camp, cooked what little food we had with us and sat chatting in the dark for a couple of hours. To the crackle and glow of the fire, our conversation was interspersed at regular intervals with, 'Someone forgot the tent pegs.'

Before slipping off into the land of nod, with the last embers of the fire dying and the crickets still chirping, Carnsey's last words were, 'We should do more of this, you know, instead of staying in plush houses.'

I readily and wholeheartedly agreed with him.

But who was I kidding?

Bring on the plush houses!

Day 38
St Lawrence

Thursday 30 September

A few minutes after setting off bright and early, toting our seemingly heavier-than-ever backpacks, we spotted the elusive blue tape – literally just around the corner from where we'd camped. It wasn't in the branches of a tree either, but tied around a guide post. It led us to the water supply, which then weighed down our backpacks even more.

There was a certain lightness in my step, though, because I knew that we had a plush-house night ahead of us. We had already walked two days on the Trail with three more to go, but we'd planned to step off the Trail for an evening meeting at St Lawrence, not to mention a real meal and a real bed.

I was keen to see this well-known little coastal town, located on St Lawrence Creek, which flows into a vast bay known as Broad Sound, noted for tides of up to a massive nine metres in the summer.

I saw St Lawrence sooner than expected. After several kilometres of great walking on undulating hills along the ridge of Connor's Range, the view opened up below us. The town lay bejewelled in the sun against the backdrop of the Pacific Ocean, perhaps twenty kilometres away – impressive!

Impressive was also the word that described the following segment of the Trail – the descent down the range. We'd been told by Mr Akubra that over a distance of one and a half kilometres, we would drop 600 metres. Images of the terrible descent in *The Man from Snowy River* came to mind. If Mr Akubra's statistics were accurate and if my calculations were correct, the average gradient was forty degrees, slightly more than *The Steepest Residential Street in the World* – Baldwin Street, Dunedin, New Zealand – at thirty-five degrees. No, I certainly didn't need a tow rope to help me with the descent – gravity was more than sufficient.

Dave picked us up later in the afternoon and gave vent to a good belly laugh over our tent peg incident. He is organisation personified, and such negligence – like losing a wallet – is unknown to him. He then shared some news of his own that would forever change the way we three walkers would relate – Dave had a girlfriend. This had apparently been on the backburner for some time, but now he wanted to tell the world. Although physically Veronica was thousands of kilometres away in old Sydney town, from now on she would be *with us* on The Walk.

Crossing the Bruce Highway, we drove the six kilometres into St Lawrence and back into Optus coverage. My first call was to home and, no, there was *still* no sign of my wallet. We met up with Kari again, as she had organised *this* meeting too. I was thankful we were on time today, but it wouldn't have mattered because, in spite of a lot of effort on her part splashing this little town with advertising posters, we didn't attract a crowd. This was our poorest attended meeting – apart from Kari and her husband, *zero* attendees.

Kari and Graeme took us home to their *plush house* and filled us in on the local scene – the lie of the land, the road we would be walking the next day, and, *the death adders*.

For some reason, perhaps fatigue, the latter must not have registered!

Day 39
Death adders

Friday 1 October

The death adder is a nasty piece of machinery. They don't come much meaner than this – broad, flattened, triangular heads, thick bodies and vertically slit eyes. Unlike other snakes, the death adder doesn't shy away when approached, but lies in wait – often for many days – until a meal passes. It hides in leaf litter, making itself inconspicuous, lying coiled in ambush. When an animal approaches, the death adder strikes, injects its venom and waits for the victim to die before eating it. This ambush hunting makes the death adder a particular threat to humans. From its typical coiled resting position, it can make lightning fast strikes on prey or potential aggressors. Of all Australian snakes, it has the longest fangs – up to 6 mm – and the most developed biting apparatus. And this is the part I like best – when it bites a target, it tends to *hang on*. As I said – *nasty!*

I knew *none* of the above when Dave and I set out that morning for another two-day walk. Nor did I know that by the afternoon we would be walking – and camping – in death adder country. Blissful ignorance!

Apart from finding out an awful lot about Miss Veronica, the first hours of the day on that segment of the Bruce Highway were relatively uneventful. However, three incidents occurred that broke the morning monotony – and all involved Dave.

 We called in to a Driver Reviver stop, one of the 220 around Australia – particularly at holiday time – manned totally by volunteers. I'd *driven*

192

in to several of these stops over the years, but this was the first time I'd *walked* into one.

'Do you revive walkers too?' Dave chirped cheerily at the ladies behind the counter, bouncing a little between syllables.

'Of course we do, love,' they smiled at him, barmaid style.

Tea, coffee and biscuits are available at these stops, free of charge – a very good thing for me seeing as all my money was somewhere in the elusive wallet. Drivers take the opportunity to revive by walking around and stretching their legs. We got our tea and bikkies and revived by sitting down and giving *our* legs a break, which also gave me time to wonder why our barmaid had smiled at Dave and not at me.

2 A little further along, Dave pounced on an Army Reserve camouflage hat he'd spotted in the grass beside the highway.

'Did you know,' he most kindly informed me, 'that you can get charged in the Army if you get sunburnt? It's called dereliction of duty!'

No, I didn't know, and I had to confess that I didn't even know the word *dereliction*. That wasn't the first time Dave had been instrumental in increasing my vocabulary.

Note to self: don't play Scrabble with Dave.

3 Just before turning off the Bruce Highway for another long-awaited quiet stint on the National Trail again, we came across a recent road kill. It was a big buck grey kangaroo, still intact. Seizing the opportunity to break the boredom, Dave grabbed the stately gentleman by the ears and hoisted him up most unceremoniously, flapping the flopping head up and down accompanied by his own rendition of evil laughter. I'm embarrassed to admit that I found it amusing.

The last hours of the day, off on dirt roads, were awesome. As the light drained from the sky, an amazing array of pastel colours washed in. Sleepy-eyed horses raised their heads to watch us crunch past. A flock of bleach-white egrets lifted as one and swung lazily above a group of grazing Brahman cattle, before circling back and out of sight. Hiking through this little piece of Eden was mesmerisingly beautiful.

We identified and skirted the Crocodile Lagoon, distanced ourselves from the only house in sight, crossed the railway line and found a grassy spot for Dave to pitch his tent. He industriously set about extracting the tent from the bag, pointing out that *he* hadn't forgotten the pegs, and was about to show me how a real tent was erected. However, much to his silent chagrin, Dave discovered that the poles were somewhat less than solid.

'Dodgy', he called them. In fact they were so limp they were incapable of supporting the weight of a tent. He tried oh-so-valiantly to make them stay up, using string, sticks and even *Elastoplast* from our medical kit – all to no avail. While verbally castigating himself he set about to execute Plan B – a lean-to *gunyah* – thanks to some strategically positioned saplings. It would at least provide a covering to keep off the morning dew and was more than adequate – a credit to Dave's ingenuity.

After boiling the billy and enjoying a hearty meal, we retired to our improvised *gunyah.* Lying on the ground, half in and half out of our sleeping bags, we enjoyed easy conversation – mainly about Veronica – inspired by a cloudless, starry sky.

As I drifted off to sleep, bare arms stretched out on the ground, it actually *did* occur to me that we might *not* be alone.

Day 40
Leaf litter

Saturday 2 October

At 5 am the countryside was already awash with the first soft light of day and the trees were alive with the tinkling of the first small birds on their piccolos and glockenspiels. The plovers joined in on the strident strings and the crows on the cello. The orchestra was finally complete when the kookaburra pulled out all the stops and signalled it was time to rise. And so the sun did.

'You texting someone already, Sav?' Dave opened an eye. 'You'll wake 'em up.'

'If *I'm* awake, why shouldn't everyone be awake,' I retorted, smiling.

I stood and stretched, drinking in the golden glory of the new day, while sucking on an orange juice. Rehydration and elimination were both important to start the day. The latter usually required no more etiquette than turning away for a minute. At times, however, it did take a little more. Armed with the now-battered roll of loo paper and leaving Dave still pulling himself out of sleep, I wandered off a good way and chose my spot in a gully, under overhanging trees which had dropped a good layer of leaf litter. If at that very vulnerable moment you had asked me, 'What hides itself inconspicuously in leaf litter, lying coiled in ambush?' I wouldn't have known. And if you had asked, 'Which Australian reptile bites its target and hangs on?' I wouldn't have known that either.

Life is like a roll of toilet paper. The closer it gets to the end, the faster it goes.

All went according to plan however, as did the day's walk under a very welcome cover of cloud, including another segment along a train track. Shhh! What the Gumlu Nutters don't know won't hurt 'em!

Dave alternated between talking to me *about* Veronica and sending text messages *to* Veronica. He was besotted and our repertoire of conversation topics narrowed down to one.

At the very end of the day, I revelled in coming face-to-face with an odd species of very large bird that I'd never seen before. I immediately recognised it, however, because of its similarity to a smaller cousin found in the Sahara Desert with the same peculiar stance, head tipped back and beak pointing upwards – the Australian bustard. The Saharan bustard is known for its distinct lack of personal hygiene. One humorous Taruuba proverb compares its dirty bottom to unsavoury speech: *Man's mouth is a bustard's butt.*

Kari and Graeme welcomed us back again, necessitating a pick-up from seventy kilometres away. It was worth it to be back in their plush house where we 0998 enjoyed recounting our two-day hike and I calculated we were just two kilometres short of our halfway mark. An incredible feeling! We also enjoyed recounting our evening camp, but were puzzled when their voices dropped slightly, their eyes grew wide and they began questioning us a little more closely.

'Was there a white house just as you turned that corner?'

'Yes.'

'And you crossed the railway line and camped just on the other side?'

'That's right.'

That's when they informed us we had entered death adder country, big time, and they filled us in on the sinister nature of the beast. Apparently the inhabitants of the white house never venture out at night without a strong torch to check the ground for unwanted visitors, of which they have many.

I hadn't known any of this, of course. However, now that I did, I relived my very private moment of the close encounter with the leaf litter as a nightmarish flashback. I had visions of myself rocketing out of the bush, screaming like a stuck pig, with a slit-eyed hitchhiker firmly fastened to my nether regions.

It would be a long time before I could bring myself to sit on a toilet without first checking under the seat.

Day 41
Neck and neck with Bernard

Sunday 3 October

Graeme and Kari's plush house is a marvellous, rambling
weatherboard homestead at the end of a long dirt
driveway, off a series of unpaved country roads, miles
from anywhere. It's an amazing creation, having been re-
modelled and re-shaped a dozen times during its lifetime
– and it draws you in. I love these old Aussie homesteads
and could think of no place where I'd rather wake up
with a whole day off ahead of me.

What a luxury not to have to jump out of bed and pull on
my boots! Once I managed to suppress the unsolicited
and unpleasant thoughts of slit-eyed hitchhikers,
I reflected on our Walk tally: 998 kilometres. Yes, I had
just walked almost a thousand kilometres. Me! Little old
Sav! The reality struck. I felt a warm, self-congratulatory
flush sweep over me at the amazing achievement – as an
old man – of making it this far. Even if I fell by the wayside
in the following days, and Dave and Carnsey took over as
the only walkers, with me driving the support vehicle, I'd
feel I had achieved a great personal goal and would go
away a happy consolation prize winner. There was great
freedom in thinking I had already succeeded.

Suddenly I realised how quiet the house was. Our hosts
were out all day, Dave was off visiting a rellie somewhere
and Carnsey was plonked in front of the TV, where he
ended up spending much of the day watching footy. This
meant I could enjoy some wonderful *alone* time again.

I helped myself liberally to the contents of Kari's fridge,
wondering if she always kept that much food in there.
Then, while Carnsey was enjoying his sport fix, I decided

to have a little fix of my own – a reading fix. I joined Bernard again via the pages of his *Longue marche*. I had barely read a couple of paragraphs when I was jolted bolt upright. I couldn't believe my eyes. Bernard! My mentor, my walking companion ...

I dropped the book in utter disbelief and burst in on Carnsey's footy match to announce the amazing news that Bernard was *also* up to the thousand mark. We were neck and neck. Actually, first I had to introduce Carnsey to Bernard, which didn't elicit a massive response. No, Carnsey was singularly unmoved by this extraordinary meeting of the ways. To his credit though, he did turn his head away from the match and in my direction for a few brief seconds. Unperturbed by his superlative lack of interest, I returned to my reading, wondering where else I would meet up with Bernard during the days and kilometres that still lay ahead for both of us.

The day slipped by at a leisurely pace with a series of snacks, naps and emails. I *finally* got around to checking on my net-bank site that no-one was using my credit card, which I had lost along with my wallet. And I announced on our blog that early the next day we would cross the 1000 kilometre mark.

However, heeding Extreme Janine's advice to *not* stop walking even on days off – in order to prevent muscles from clamping up – I also went for a stroll around the property and out along the deserted roads. It was a pleasure beyond compare to be flopping along in thongs, toes free in the fresh air and wriggling happily, just because they could.

Thongs, it bears mentioning, is one of those unfortunate words that creates confusion across the continents. In other parts of the world they are called *flip-flops* or *jandals* – a New Zealand contraction of *Japanese sandals*. In Singapore they're called *sandals* and in

199

South Africa, *slops*. To an Austrian, they are *schlapfen* and to a Frenchman, *claquettes*. All these remarkable names are onomatopoeic, replicating the sound made when walking with them. Of all of them, however, the one that was most descriptive of my little stroll that afternoon was the South African name: *slop*.

Slop, slop, slop, slop.

I slopped down the road, casting a long shadow, when my eye was caught by a large flock of the now familiar magpie geese, a gaggle of clerics congregating on the banks of the dam, enjoying the last of the sun's warmth. This was obviously their regular day residence. The contrasting black and white brought to mind the amusing geometrical ink drawings of Escher, and even more so when they took to the wing and flew hooting and honking out of sight. As dusk fell, transforming the lazy windmill into a silhouette, and painting the vault above in a thousand shades of mauve and purple, more groups of geese rose in V formations from distant unseen dams. They climbed their way laboriously across the sky, blowing their discordant trumpets to egg themselves on, as they headed to the safety of their night residence.

I followed their example and headed to mine.

Day 42
The halfway mark

Monday 4 October

I was up early but the magpie geese had beaten me to the first worms. By the time I was on the road, they were already back at their day residence and honked at me as I walked past.

Kari drove us all the way back to where we'd finished our walk two days before, so we could continue from where we'd left off. Dave's Dad, who'd come up all the way from Stanthorpe, joined us at this halfway mark.

G'day Bloke

'G'day, bloke,' Dave chirped at Russell, who responded without batting an eyelid. Hmm, not the way I would have greeted my father, but I guess the times, they are a-changing.

We were all happy to have new blood on The Walk, even though only for a day. It was also great that Russell could be with us for the momentous 1000 kilometre milestone, especially as we'd come up with an idea to mark the occasion and needed an extra arm – literally. Kari photographed us, the three Wiggles, standing side by side, with our arms held up, curved to form three zeroes and Russell stood beside us with his arm forming the number one. 1000. That was the last of Kari's many acts of service before we sadly waved her off. She drove north up the highway and we set off walking south.

It was then my phone beeped – a text message. Then Carnsey's phone. Then Dave's – and for a change, it wasn't a message from Veronica! For the remainder of the day our phones were out of our pockets as much as they were in, as hundreds of texts rained in from all around the globe. Lots of people were *with us* on this Walk. The effect of this collective encouragement defied description. I was so buoyed up that I kept a record of some of the silent cheers that came my way.

WOW.
whoopeee
well done, Dad.
Woohoooo! Congrats. wow
DAD
yAH. PTL! yeah.
Yippie Ai Ay.
Onya fellas. I pray you're encouraged. Awesome

That last one, from my doubting cousin, Pessimistic Pete, was particularly heartening. In spite of his open doubts – he's completed some amazing walks himself and knows only too well the reality of it all – he was on the sideline cheering me on, along with all the others.

We alternated between squinting at our text messages as they continued to beep in, and stopping every now and then to pore over our map. I had insisted we get off the highway and try what appeared to be a few quiet, dirt roads. By my calculations, taking that route would *add* a kilometre or two to our day but the alternative of staying on that nerve-racking highway was likely to take a year or two *off* my life. I had made the decision and Carnsey and Dave had tried, unsuccessfully, to hide their displeasure. So there we were – lost! Our map showed a through road. However, since the publication of that map, a lot of private properties and fences had sprung up – there was not a sign of a through road anywhere. We had to backtrack. The additional one or two kilometres turned into six and, on top of that, we got to enjoy – *not* – every single metre of highway madness after all. Needless to say, the camaraderie at this part of the day was not the best it had ever been, and neither was the weather. It was stinking hot.

I was relieved to finally make it to the end of the day, arriving at the Marlborough Caltex service station, and ecstatic to make acquaintance with their one, basic shower. If the other smelly, sweaty walkers hadn't been eagerly awaiting their turn, I could easily have spent half an hour enjoying the cool hydro-massage on my hot skin.

After swallowing huge portions of takeaway junk food – Dave's father paid for mine as I was still wallet-less – we went through the motions of yet another meeting at the local hall. This was now our sixteenth meeting but it felt like our hundredth. Our interesting stories and statistics, while new and fresh for our audience, were becoming old and stale to us. If Dave had dropped dead in the middle of his presentation, telling of his time trekking in Nepal, I could have picked up, word for word, and continued his story. At least he couldn't be accused of embellishment – same gestures, same intonation, same words and same sentences. It was like watching a re-run of Bugs Bunny over and over again. And the cousins got a kick out of taking the micky out of me too, as I gave my awesome (haha) account of an important Taruuba word, *talast*, and illustrated it by talking about a well caving in.

'What do you do if you're in a well that is collapsing?' I would ask. 'Just get out of there!'

I heard Carnsey and Dave repeat that line back to me, complete with my thumbs-up *getting-out-of-there* gesture more than I ever said it myself. But I couldn't change it. Like a stuck record, I subjected each audience to my own well-performed Looney Tunes routine. This didn't matter of course, except for those few particularly enthusiastic folk who followed us to the next town to hear us again. If they expected to hear different stories, they were sorely disappointed. We never did have anyone turn up for a third dose.

The highlight of the day? Taking half an hour to do a close inspection of some little finger paintings. You know the sort? The ones you find, for instance, on a preschool wall. The idea is for the kid to get as many bright colours as possible, lipstick red being compulsory, onto that one piece of paper.

The finger paintings I was looking at were all perfectly identical. It was dusk and they were lined up on a bird feeder, dipping their little heads up and down into the wet bread. The artist was not a youngster in a preschool class, but none other than the Ancient of Days, the Master Artist himself. I wondered though if His palette had run dry when he got to painting the dull, drab European birds, where the most you can hope for is a touch of watercolour blue on a wren or a tiny tinge of rusty red on a robin.

These little Rainbow Lorikeets were living up to their reputation as the clowns of the parrot world, both from their antics and their attire. They were plastered in glossy acrylics – brilliant green, blue, orange and yellow.

And their stout little beaks were, of course, bright lipstick red.

The Rainbow Lorikeet's wardrobe:

(Gaudi would have approved!)

Trousers: royal blue with green legs
Shirt: orange/red
Jacket: green with a yellow collar
Balaclava: bright blue
Lipstick: bright red

Go on – bring them to life with some colouring pencils.

Day 43
Brazilian cyclist

Tuesday 5 October

Even before we took to the road, we knew the day was going to be a shocker. The forecast was for a hot one and for once – with all due respect – the people at the weather bureau were spot on.

1040

By the time the sun was burning down from its zenith, I was walking on wood. The arches of my feet were hard and sore. Instead of the regular smooth rhythm of weight exchange from one leg to the other, I was beginning to *clump* from one foot to the other. Gone was the ease of walking made possible by the coordinated effort of happily functioning muscles, bones, ligaments and tendons – the machine was malfunctioning. The combination of heat and sore feet made it hard going. If pain *is* weakness leaving the body, then how come I was getting weaker and my pain level was increasing? Explain that one to me, Dave!

I tried not to think of 960, the number of remaining kilometres. I also tried not to recall that my only real break was now behind me – I'd used that card up. There was far too much time for thinking however, and think I did. There were five more weeks to walk and in all that time I would only have four days off. I repeated to myself, 'I won't make it. I can't make it.'

I was badly in need of something or someone, other than my fellow Wiggles who were already sick of my complaining, to take my mind off my feet. That's when a cyclist breezed onto the scene.

Like the bicycle he was peddling, Danilo was a lean machine. Decked out in a legionnaire's sun-safe hat, and wearing a bright orange sun-protection jersey, he looked everything I didn't feel like. Greeting us with a cheery magpie-goose honk on his horn, he rode across the highway and stepped off smoothly beside us.

Olive-skinned Danilo, from Belo Horizonte in Brazil, was sporting a day's dark stubble and when he flashed his smile, I thought I recognised him from a Colgate advertisement. The predictable questions ensued from both sides:

WHAT FOR? WHERE FROM? HOW LONG? WHEN? WHERE TO? WHY?

We told our story and listened with rapt attention to his – my aching feet momentarily forgotten. Danilo was cycling around the world, raising awareness and sponsorship to combat child trafficking and poverty in his country. He had already completed two of the three years it would take him, Australia being country number forty-five. These statistics, by comparison, made our Walk look like a stroll through the botanic gardens.

'Where's your tent?' he asked curiously, eyeing our relatively small backpacks. His tent was neatly packed under his saddle and was obviously well worn. He told us he almost always camped, sleeping on a mat in his tent. We had to confess that we almost always stayed in plush houses, slept in comfy beds and ate sumptuously.

He began his epic ride on 08/08/08 and would finish it on 11/11/11, exactly one year, to the day, after we were due to finish our Walk. By the end of his ride, he would have cycled a total of 43,000 kilometres which made our 2000 kilometres look rather paltry. My feet began to feel better by the minute.

We talked about the Chilean miners, the progress on the drilling of the evacuation shaft, and the ordeal of both lots of men – the ones sitting down in the dark and those working against the clock up in the light. Comparing their challenges to our own he asked a probing question:

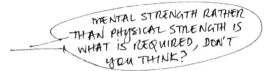

MENTAL STRENGTH RATHER THAN PHYSICAL STRENGTH IS WHAT IS REQUIRED, DON'T YOU THINK?

I wondered which of the two I most needed right at that moment – probably a great deal of both. The roar of two double semitrailers meeting exactly where we were standing drowned out any possibility of a reply, and nearly blew us off the shoulder of the road.

With a wave and another cheerful honk, Danilo rode off. In our six weeks of walking to date, that was our first conversation with either a cyclist or fellow walker. It only lasted fifteen minutes, but it kept me going for the rest of the day.

So did the scruffy General Store that appeared like a mirage ahead of us. After wending our way through the obstacle course of crates and fridges, boxes and shelves, all stacked around outside – more reminiscent of a house-moving than a store – I located the cold drinks. Chocolate milk! It was Carnsey's shout – 'cause I still hadn't found my wallet.

A tame Blue Indian Parakeet on top of a pallet, no cage in sight, eyed me suspiciously, head cocked to one side, and pursed his cherry-red beak.

Lipstick was obviously fashionable in the parrot world.

Day 44
Styrofoam pet

Wednesday 6 October

I hadn't slept well. My feet, hard and sore during the day, were now hard and sore during the night as well. The alarm clock rang far too early and it was getting tougher by the day to get out of bed. I was slowly spiralling downwards.

During the long boring walking hours, I was desperate for anything to keep my mind off my feet. I even would have been happy to talk about Veronica, but Dave was having a day off. As it happened, a lump of Styrofoam tied to a rope did the trick. Reminiscent of the resilient Coke bottle two weeks back, I found this little baby lying by the roadside, waiting patiently for someone to take him for a walk. I instantly adopted him and dragged him along behind me.

I don't know whether it was the fact that the rope was quite thin, or that the Styrofoam reminded me of a fishing float, but it felt as if I was trawling for a catch. And after just one hour I got my first bite.

Dorian explained that when he drove past and saw me dragging something his curiosity was piqued. So he turned around, drove past us again from the opposite direction, turned again, and parked beside the highway to intercept us – he'd taken the bait.

When I saw him stepping out of his car, I wondered if it was Mr Bowen Policeman, wearing civvies, who'd finally caught up with me! My relief upon realising that wasn't the case, turned to embarrassment when I discovered that Dorian was hoping to get a juicy scoop on my stupid

Styrofoam. I don't like disappointing people but I needn't have worried, because it turned out we shared a common interest – languages.

He told us he was on holidays from Melbourne, which his accent readily confirmed: in the rest of the country we drink *milk* but Dorian and his fellow southerners drink *miwk*. What his accent didn't give away however – being Australian born – was that he was of Greek origin, which perhaps explained his interest in languages. And not just languages, but translation! And not just translation, but translation of the Bible! We had barely begun to explain why we were walking when Dorian jumped right in.

'Some people say the return of Jesus is imminent,' he said, 'but to know when the end will come you've got to look at the facts.' The facts, for Dorian, meant the Bible. He quoted from Matthew chapter 24: *This gospel of the kingdom will be preached in the whole world as a testimony to all nations, and then the end will come.*

He insisted, 'So the end won't come until the gospel has been preached to all nations.' He explained that the Greek word in this verse, *ethnos*, which is translated as *nations*, would be more accurately translated as *ethnic groups* or *races*. The word *nations* gives the wrong idea of political divisions or countries, whereas it is referring rather to *people groups* having their own language and culture. Then, in a twist of events, without realising that he was preaching to the converted, he gave an impassioned appeal. 'There are so many tribes and ethnic groups in the world that don't have the Bible – thousands.' He didn't give us a chance to get a word in edgeways. We just smiled while he talked.

'They don't know anything of God's Word,' he said, 'because it hasn't been translated into a language they understand.'

I immediately wanted to enlist Dorian to join our travelling band to speak at our meetings. He was a natural. If I hadn't already been converted to the cause, I would have been by then. Finally there was a chance to join the conversation, and I picked up on a related theme.

'People tend to think that the gospel has gone out into the whole world,' I added, 'because they've heard that Christian radio is broadcast into every square kilometre of the surface of the earth.'

'Yes,' he said, finishing the story for me, 'but the people in thousands of language groups all over the world can't understand a *word* of these radio programs that aren't in their language. It's like if I was speaking to you in another language, you wouldn't understand me.'

With passion and conviction he concluded, 'The work of Bible translation doesn't happen overnight. It needs a lot of skilled and dedicated people.'

I was still thinking of a way to sign him up for our presentations when he wished us well, said goodbye and drove off leaving us scratching our heads. That was the only time during our eighty days of walking that someone would preach to *us* about the need for Bible translation.

Dorian successfully took my mind off my feet for a time, as did the middle-aged British guy, the second cyclist in as many days who stopped to greet us. His response to Bible translation was less enthusiastic than Dorian's.

'Oh well, it's OK I s'pose. At least you ain't 'armin' nobody are y'? Just doin' y' own thing, like.' And he was off, looking oh-so-small and vulnerable sharing that narrow, single lane of the beastly Bruce with traffic hammering past. At least *we* could walk off on the side.

The rest of the day stretched interminably ahead of us, presaged by an unremarkable hand-painted sign:

TAKEAWAY
FOOD
FUEL,
16 KMS
ON LEFT

For passing motorists sixteen kilometres was only ten minutes down the highway. For us, however, that welcome pit stop was still three hours away, giving me ample time to think about my feet again. The only relief from boredom was Carnsey's occasional conversation, my Styrofoam pet and a swooping magpie. Even the bird seemed to pick up on my lethargy and, after a couple of half-hearted attempts, gave up.

I couldn't believe that at 6 pm I was still walking. I dragged my poor, battle-weary feet through the doorway of my new home, to face a challenge of a totally different nature – a six-year-old coffee thief.

1085

Day 45
Coffee thief

Thursday 7 October

One of the joys of our crazy Walk, apart from getting to limp on stiff and painful feet day after wearying day, was meeting up with friends from the past. Few of the friends were as *past* as Ewan. We grew up in Stanthorpe, attended the same high school together and have remained in contact ever since. He is the one responsible (along with his lovely wife, Jo) for bringing into the world Dougie – the young coffee thief.

Ewan did warn me in advance that I would be a potential victim. Nothing prepared me, however, for the lightning-speed strikes that would ensue. Invisible to the naked eye, something akin to *Road Runner*, Dougie would descend on any unattended coffee cup and drain it dry in less than a nanosecond. For a six-year-old his timing was impeccable, his attack plans, flawless. James Bond doesn't hold a candle to my little mate, Dougie. Over the few days I would stay at Ewan and Jo's, I lost count of how many times I raised my coffee cup only to find it disarmingly light.

But before my readers cry parental abuse, appalled at caffeine consumption at such a tender age, I hasten to the defence of my friends.

'We pick our battles,' Ewan explained. Not only has Dougie been diagnosed with severe autism and is unable to communicate verbally, but both his brothers have Asperger's syndrome, a higher functioning form of autism. This means that each, in his own way, is extremely *quick* – coffee pilfering for instance – but they face some major challenges with social interaction and they present unusual behaviour. Little five-year-old Rory, for example, in his own obliging way, woke me up two hours before my alarm was due to ring by knocking on my bedroom wall – with his head! Never mind. I had already learned to get by on six hours sleep instead of eight, so maybe I could also learn to survive on only four. Yes, life is a challenge for my friends – Sergeant Ewan and Lieutenant Jo are always on duty.

At 7 am I stepped out of their battlefield onto my own – the asphalt. About that time, back in Stanthorpe, Hélène was yawning and waking up. We were celebrating our twenty-first wedding anniversary – over 900 kilometres apart. We'd come of age. There I was with my feet on the road, and there she was with her feet up in bed. Guess where my feet would rather have been?

Actually, sometime during the morning, my feet abandoned me and in their place I was walking on plaster casts. Not only was I struggling to keep my mind off the pain, but an unwelcome, insidious thought had implanted itself there, and was repeating over and over:

What if it was true? What if my feet actually never did recover after this? I had to decide whether I should be listening to this voice or not, as the thoughts swirled in the dark morass of my sleep-deprived mind.

All three of us were walking today, which, ironically, provided me with the opportunity to walk alone as the cousins were striding it out ahead again, (probably talking about Veronica). This was a regular routine on the days all three of us walked. Occasionally one of them would look back and realise that the distance between us had increased. They would then politely wait until I caught them up, at which point we would resume our routine with me once more bringing up the rear.

It was nice, for a change, to be in built-up areas most of the day as we approached Rockhampton. It was even nicer to walk on some grassed areas – my feet were extremely grateful for that. An added bonus was crossing the Fitzroy River on the Neville Hewitt Bridge, affectionately known locally as *The Old Bridge.* I love bridges. I don't think I've ever met a bridge I haven't liked, and this was no exception. At her opening sixty years ago no fewer than 30,000 people – more than half the population of Rockhampton at the time – crowded in and danced on the new river crossing. They celebrated the connection – the passage – the way over – the link. People and goods could travel in a way and at a speed previously not possible. A bridge is like a language really – it opens the way previously closed. In the same way, the Bible translated into the heart language of an *ethnos*, a people group, opens the way to God that has been previously closed. The Fitzroy River Bridge cost £600,000 – a great deal of money in those days – and countless man hours. A Bible translation is also a costly endeavour, in both time and money, but the end result is a *bridge* for generations to come.

1113   We celebrated our crossing in a rather ignoble manner, by pausing midway for a spitting competition, aiming at passing branches in the water below. This was not as idle an occupation as you might imagine and took a deal of careful calculation of height, speed of the current and wind direction.

Note to self: never admit to doing this.

Just hours later, however, we *were* forced to admit it. In casual conversation with some young ladies, Dave said, 'Tell them, Carnsey, what we did off the bridge today!'

It took less than a second and a quick glance at the inquiring faces to realise that an answer to that question was necessary to appease their suspicious minds. We quickly and gladly owned up to merely spitting.

And the topic of *bridges* surfaced again. Back at Ewan's, airing my red and calloused soles and leafing through the newspaper, my eyes fell on a photo of the now very familiar *Burdekin Bridge*. With a quick mental calculation, I shook my head with the realisation that it had been already a month since the three of us walked across it. I read with keen interest that it had just received the *Engineering Heritage National Landmark Award* in celebration of one of the great feats of engineering in our country. The article read: *It must have lifted the soul of the peoples of Ayr and Home Hill as they walked across the bridge after the cutting of the ribbon.* It lifted my soul the day I walked across it, as it lifted my soul to walk across the Neville Hewitt this afternoon.

I folded up my newspaper as the aroma of grilled lamb chops drew me from my reverie. How could Jo possibly have known they were my favourite? Immediately, the look in her eye gave it away – they were Hélène's wedding anniversary gift to me. And my gift to her? Well, I'd make it up to her somehow.

Soon after, I discovered my coffee cup was unexpectedly empty – again. That was a good thing actually because I badly needed to sleep – very, *very* badly.

On the other side of town, Dave was skyping his little Sydney honey into the wee small hours of the morning. How did I know? Well, he didn't go out and buy a web-cam, a powered USB hub and card reader for nothing now, did he?

While he was skyping, I was sleeping.

Day 46
Podiatrist or cleaner?

Friday 8 October

On the other side of my bedroom wall, my personal alarm clock *banged* right on cue. The night was short. About four hours too short. My downward spiral continued.

After breakfast, also right on cue, a red-eyed Dave called to pick me up.

G'day bloke

He took advantage – while I was preparing my backpack – to circle the breakfast table and swoop like a hungry seagull on the leftovers.

'Didn't you have breakfast this morning, Dave?'

'Sure did, Sav. But I hate to see anything go to waste. Veronica says hi.'

Sometimes we were clocking up meetings at the rate of one a day, which was often one too many for my liking. On this particular day we topped the record with three, the first two being at schools and the third, a combined churches' meeting.

The first was part of the weekly assembly at Heights College – a pretty big affair. The auditorium was full of uniformed teens belting out some slick Christian songs and running quickly through a full and well-coordinated program – impressive! My head was spinning as we leapt in for our few allotted minutes and slicked our way through a very much abridged version of our program – stats, video and a story. The whole assembly went off like clockwork, so much so that I wondered if any of those kids would even remember anything we said. We were just a little tick in the middle of a lot of slick ticking and tocking. I reminded myself that we were in the business of sowing seeds, and it doesn't take more than a tick or a tock to sow a seed.

The second meeting, on the other hand, was all for us. Ewan's oldest son, Andrew, attended St Peter's Primary School and so with that insider connection, the school principal mustered the troops for a special meeting. I was looking forward to this one.

I must admit to having a soft spot for Andrew. He's a likeable lad. He and the rest of the kids were on the edge of their seats and didn't have the don't-throw-any-more-information-at-me look on their faces that some of the Heights kids did. The St Peter's bunch was all tuned in. I later discovered they'd already been following us on our website and were really anticipating our arrival – nice!

We went through the routine of our stat signs, comparing Bible translation – already in thousands of languages – to Harry Potter – only translated into sixty-eight languages. Then came the fun part – the questions fielded from the kids!

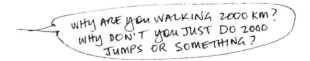

DO you WALK ALL DAY AND ALL NIGHT OR DO you STOP & SLEEP?

No, we'd walked around the clock without sleep for forty-six days – or at least that's what it felt like! I thought that little guy was going to ask if we forewent toilet stops too.

WHY ARE you WALKING 2000 KM? WHY DON'T you JUST DO 2000 JUMPS OR SOMETHING?

Indeed, I was beginning to wonder myself. It would have been all over in three hours, instead of torturing myself for nearly three months!

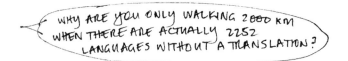
WHY ARE YOU ONLY WALKING 2000 KM WHEN THERE ARE ACTUALLY 2252 LANGUAGES WITHOUT A TRANSLATION?

Now if only someone could get that kid to walk 2000 kilometres, then we'd see if he'd be up for another 252.

Nevertheless, that last question was a good one. The number 2252 is, at best, a close estimate. Since the goal of The Walk was to have people simply remember *the big number*, i.e. there is a *lot* more work to do, we chose to round it off to the neat 2000. Also, we hoped that in not too many years, the number would be down to 2000 anyway.

In Rockhampton, the most memorable meeting of all was with the *foot specialist*. Ewan, seeing the state of my feet, had insisted on making an appointment for me with their family podiatrist who, incidentally, was away on holiday – which kind of invalidated the recommendation. I saw his replacement instead. It was extremely hard to stifle a laugh when I was welcomed into the consulting room by a guy decked out in a T-shirt and a cheap pair of rubber thongs (as in *slops*). After talking with him for a few minutes I was still looking around for the hidden camera. Was this some kind of practical joke Ewan had orchestrated? Was this actually the cleaner who just happened to step in at the wrong moment? But as the minutes ticked by, I had to face reality – this was indeed the man who was going to cure my foot woes. I found it hard to take him seriously.

True, I did get to sit in his comfortable chair. I also got to tell him my story – how many kilometres I walked each day, the planned schedule and details of the pain I was experiencing in the arches of my feet. Dr Thong-man then, to my bewilderment, proceeded to repeat back my entire story, getting the distances wrong and mixing up other details of the schedule. I corrected him, wondering why I was bothering, because I already *knew* the story and he didn't *need* to know it. No word has yet been invented in any of the languages I speak for the emotion that was welling up within me – something between anger and amusement. It got worse. I would have the privilege of coughing up forty dollars for his words of wisdom, 'Your feet are telling you that they need a rest.' This sentence was repeated three more times, in as many minutes, until I was beginning to wonder if he was a master in the art of verbal torture.

I humoured Dr Thong-man when he asked me to stand and walk a little, while he observed my gait.

'I'm saying you're normal,' he announced importantly.

Before he hit me with it again, I got in first and declared, 'I think my feet are just telling me they need a rest.'

He beamed, visibly delighted that I had understood. He relieved me of my forty (borrowed) dollars and released me back to the Bruce Highway. I shook the dust off my feet on the way out.

My visit to Dr Thong-man had done nothing to reverse my downward spiral.

And I still think he actually *was* the cleaner.

I named my son after this man. See Day 16.

Day 47
Thumbs down, thumbs up

Saturday 9 October

It was cloudy and cool all day. My diary entry reads:
A near perfect day. The word *perfect,* however, only
referred to the weather and certainly not my feet – which
now felt like they'd been injected with plaster and had
solidified. Neither did the word *perfect* refer to the
information we gleaned from Google Maps.

At 7.30 am we were at our starting point on
the highway, ready for action. Well, Dave was
ready. I was resigned. He was brandishing
a wad of small pieces of white paper on
which he'd carefully outlined the day's plan
of attack, thanks to a careful study of Google

1143   Maps. If we followed his plan carefully we
would gain a few hours on quiet back roads,
which, to me, was the equivalent of winning the lotto.
Good on y' Dave! I think he must have overheard my feet
telling me they needed a rest, but since that wasn't going
to happen, the next best thing was to get them off the
highway. The first twenty kilometres would be bitumen
but, beyond that, Dave's fistful of little papers promised
us an afternoon of bliss on peaceful back roads.

My faith in Google Maps had taken a nosedive in recent
days but, like a drowning man clutching at anything that
happened to float by, I was clinging on to those maps for
dear life. Nevertheless I needed a tad reassuring.

'Dave, do you think we're actually going to find those
roads without getting lost again?' I quickly added, 'Look
me square in the eyes when you give your answer. What
are the chances?'

Dave met me eyeball to eyeball and confidently affirmed, 'One hundred per cent, Sav. We're going to find these roads without getting lost.'

I didn't believe a word of it but, at that stage, I didn't care too much about facts, being quite content to be lulled into a false sense of security.

As for Dave, he announced first up in the morning that he and Veronica had just gone *Facebook official* which is a little bit like getting engaged except *heaps* less serious and you tell *heaps* more people – basically everyone you've *ever* met, not to mention countless others you've *never* met and who couldn't give a fig. With his new status, Dave didn't really care what roads he'd be walking on because he wasn't really walking on roads anyway. He was walking on cloud nine.

But I cared. So I perused Dave's papers, carefully studying the roads he'd mapped out for the end of the day. The very names evoked images of bliss in much the same way ice-cream flavours entice the young – and they lured us on. Sisalana Road, Tounda Road, Twelve Mile Road and Rocky Road[1]. With these quiet roads to look forward to in the afternoon, I mustered the courage to surrender myself yet again to the Bruce Highway for the entire morning. How could I begin to describe the effect on my brain of further incessant hammering by passing vehicles, of the pounding of the air rush in the wake of trucks? I was counting down the days till we'd step off The Bruce and onto quieter roads, once and for all – still eleven more days to go.

The only thing that broke the monotony of the morning was Dave finding a half-decent soccer ball – which he then proceeded to dribble along the narrow strip of bitumen between the white line and the shoulder of the road to a spectator crowd

this is worth watching – just to see our glorious clouds ha ha ↙

---

[1] 'Rocky Road' - my poor attempt at a joke

of probably one hundred passing motorists. When the ball scudded across the white line Dave deftly retrieved it with a quick flick of his foot. An oncoming motorist communicated his displeasure by sitting on the horn for a full, deafening, ten-second blast. That unnerved me totally and Dave kicked the ball back into the grass.

After four hours of highway torture we still had not seen any of the ice-cream flavours promised by Google Maps. I was close to pain-induced, sleep-deprived tears. Dave had gone quiet too, but for a different reason – he didn't like to think his plan of attack wasn't working. Twice we slid off onto side roads in the hope they may have been the magical detour but we soon did an about-turn back onto The Bruce.

'It all looks so easy on the maps,' Dave mumbled.

'Thumbs down for Google Maps,' I added. Discouraging, with a capital D.

At midday, looking up, Dave bellowed, 'There's our road!' As we drew near we knew we'd hit the jackpot. We did an Irish jig. Well, if you'd been watching you may not actually have picked up that I was *jigging* – but inside, at least, I was.

Once off The Bruce, I said cheerily to Dave, 'What do you see on this road?'

'Nothing,' Dave countered, bursting with renewed confidence in himself, 'No traffic, no trucks, no cars, no B-doubles, no trains, no motorbikes, no bitumen – only sand and gravel!'

We barely had time to initiate a game guessing how many snakes were in the grass beside us – Dave guessed ten, I guessed OVER 9000[1] – when we realised this little road was turning suspiciously in a semicircle and seemed to

---

[1] What? There's no way that can be right!

be looping back. Ten minutes later, the familiar stream of highway traffic was just ahead of us and Dave muttered, 'That's not what my map says.'

We were back on the highway.

'Hey, Dave!'

'What?'

'Let's see how many synonyms we can come up with for the word *walk*,' but I quickly added, 'and if you say sprint, I'm going to thump you.'

Dave is good with words and this got him going – tramp, dawdle, stagger, saunter, amble, trail, stride, march, toddle and stroll.

'You forgot one, Dave.'

'What's that?'

'Plod!'

Plod has always been one of my favourite words. To some it might have negative connotations of joyless or dry resignation, but to me it speaks of the high and lofty qualities of perseverance, resolution and doggedness. The title of one of my favourite *plodding* books is *A Long Obedience in the Same Direction*, by Eugene Peterson of *The Message* fame. Both the word *plod* and the title of Peterson's book seemed to be appropriate to what I was going through.

And then we saw it – one of our ice-cream flavours on a road sign – Sisalana Road. Thumbs up for Google Maps! Sisalana turned into Tounda and Tounda turned into Twelve Mile and it all turned into a near perfect afternoon, which gave me an opportunity to hear a whole lot more I didn't already know about Veronica.

Day 48
I can plod

Sunday 10 October

I spent most of the day just sitting. No walking, trudging, meandering, strolling or even plodding.

It began in the morning church service with Ewan and Jo and their three dynamos, and was followed by a sit-down lunch – which was quite a novelty after our usual on-the-hoof lunches. I forfeited yet another cup of coffee to Road Runner and then enjoyed an afternoon rest. Nice. The advantage of a day off is not only resting but also having time to think. The hours spent walking are not really productive *thinking* hours. And so I enjoyed simply *thinking*, and the topic of my thoughts was the word *plod*.

The classic story of a *plodder,* forever indelibly etched on my mind, is that of William Carey. He began his work in India in 1793. It took perseverance over many years for him to build cultural bridges that nobody had built before. He learned indigenous languages, wrote and printed grammars and dictionaries, and translated the Bible. There were no back-up copies and, in 1812, in a single day, his years of work vanished in smoke. A fire in Carey's print shop consumed his entire library, his complete Sanskrit dictionary, part of his Bengal dictionary, two grammar books and ten translations of the Bible. Over seventeen years of work were gone. After the fire Carey knew what needed to be done. Despite the heartache and discouragement, he knew that he and his fellow workers would begin all over again with page one. And he did.

'I can *plod*,' he said. 'I can persevere in any definite pursuit. To that I owe everything.'

The evening broadcast of WinNews buzzed with the latest update from the Atacama Desert in Chile, another *plodding* and *persevering* story. After forty-one days of drilling and three separate rescue plans, the 700-metre-long escape shaft had finally broken through to where the miners had been entombed for two months. I watched the euphoric scenes of celebration right across Chile. In just a few days these men hoped to see sunlight again.

Speaking of light, when I finally switched mine out – and in the very short time before my eyelids crashed in sleep – I realised that one of the best examples of plodding was my host family. Parenting is a plodding experience at the best of times, but more so for Ewan and Jo who deserve a *plodding* medal. Indeed they were recently awarded the *Queensland Creative Futures Parent Award* for their relentless effort and amazing commitment in raising their three young men. Bravo!

William Carey plodded. The Chilean drillers were plodding. Ewan and Jo were plodding. And, still on my middle mile, I too was plodding.

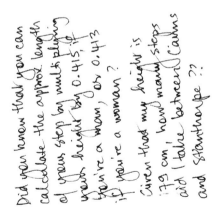

Day 49
Gentle Annie

Monday 11 October

It was sad saying goodbye to my old mate Ewan and his family, depressing to find myself once again on The Bruce and worrying that my feet now felt like they had rocks in them. Three strikes! But still not out.

1179 The countdown continued – only nine more long days until I would at last turn my back on big, bad Bruce. And the rocks? I was convinced by then that they were not only in my feet but also in my head!

Google Maps struck again. The promise of a lovely series of back roads led us on a wild goose chase over several kilometres, largely because Carnsey's print-out had a tiny corner missing which turned out to be the key piece of the puzzle. We phoned two friends whose internet searches on our behalf put us back on track, only to find that further ahead the road petered out at a sign: *Private Property. Do Not Enter.* So we didn't. Once more the sweetness of the quiet roads turned to bitterness as we had to backtrack out of there.

'Those maps are nothing but rubbish,' Dave remonstrated, his annoyance at my insistence on getting off The Bruce only slightly concealed. But insist I would! I was in survival mode.

1190 A few hours later Google Maps came through for us. *Gentle Annie Road* led away from The Bruce, up over a steep little ridge and then back onto The Bruce again. The deviation added four kilometres in return for the privilege of a few hours of peaceful country walking. Dave and Carnsey were silently unimpressed but to me, *Gentle Annie* was worth every one of those extra four thousand steps.

Henceforth *Gentle Annie* became synonymous with *quiet back road*. Each one was a life-saving reprieve on this long middle mile.

Gentle Annie roads are advantageous for a few reasons, one of them being that when a man has to do what a man has to do, he has a million quiet places to do it. As we climbed towards the summit of the ridge, we came unexpectedly into phone coverage and the cousins decided to set up in a shady spot to take care of a few pending calls. I decided to take care of a call of my own – one of a more personal nature. I walked ahead a little.

There was no need to glance around as I would hear any vehicle long before it came into view or before I came into the driver's view. I was alone. Right?

Wrong.

I stepped away from the road and, standing and looking out over the view and casting caution to the wind, proceeded to enjoy one of life's little pleasures with great gusto. At that moment the ground in front of my feet exploded. A thrash of a slithering tail and a flash of scaly skin burst out of the pile of dead leaves and whipped away into the bush. This had the effect of a bullet being fired. I let out a yell, yanked my shorts up and leapt back onto the road. Heart pounding wildly, I stood shaking and stunned. At that point I became aware of an embarrassing wet patch, the result of having been interrupted mid-stream. Thankfully the cousins' calls took longer than mine, which gave my heart time to settle down and my shorts time to dry off. The only consolation to this traumatic incident, which some days later would cause me to break out into spontaneous laughter, was picturing Mr Snake, minding his own business, enjoying a quiet moment beside Gentle Annie, being so rudely and unexpectedly interrupted by a warm shower.

1211   Thanks to Gentle Annie I made it to Mount Larcom. The *Café and Collectables* store at the entry to the town was a sight for sore eyes, as were the handwritten signs all over the walls: Big Mama's Pies, Pizza, Fish & Chips. I can't remember what we ate – I think it might have been all of the above. Carnsey paid, because I still had no money. The hard, wrought-iron seats out the front, where we sat to eat our health food, couldn't have been more comfortable if they'd been leather lounge chairs. The shower at our caravan park, in all its concrete glory, was five-star luxury. But – horror of horrors – there was no internet! By 9 pm the internet withdrawal symptoms were kicking in – trembling hands, slurred speech, blurred vision, involuntary mouth spasms and frothing. We jumped in the support vehicle, laptops open, dongles hooked up by the windows and we drove. Randomly. It was fifteen kilometres before we found an Optus connection, parked the car and switched off the headlights. The black of the moonless night that instantly engulfed us was only challenged by the glow of our computer screens. The silence of the night that settled on us was broken only by the tinkling of a million tiny insects and, of course, the tap of fingers on keyboards. No prizes for guessing who Dave's fingers were tapping for!

Email fix successful, all was well with the world. We drove back and sank into our bunks.

Day 50
Lovely young boys

Tuesday 12 October

We had been called a lot of names during The Walk (as per Mr Cool Cop) – possibly more behind our back than to our face – many of which we probably deserved. There was, however, one name that never ceased to amaze me and, in my case at least, was totally *un*deserved – *boys*. I was two years short of fifty and I don't think anyone – apart from my mother – had called me a boy for two or three decades. But we were *boys*. Literally hundreds of people referred to us as boys – in person, in meetings, in television and radio interviews and in the written press. Boys! The boys of The 2000 Walk! By virtue of participating in this crazy venture, I had regained the status of boyhood. Reflecting on this intriguing situation, I came up with three possible reasons.

First, because I was walking with two single, younger guys, by association, I too qualified as a boy. Second, because The Walk was a physical adventure there was a *young* ring to it. I mean, *old* people don't do this sort of thing; it's for the boys! Third, people warmed to us and, by way of cheering us on and encouraging us, referred to us affectionately as *the boys*. At first I found it unsettling or strange, but it rapidly grew on me. It was a little like suddenly and unexpectedly discovering the elixir of youth.

However, dear Grannie of Mount Larcom, originally from the South Pacific Islands, pushed the *boy* appellation to the limit. Grannie Island and her friends were looking after us very well and, before we set off, had the self-appointed goal of feeding us such a feast that we wouldn't be able to get off the starting blocks – bacon, eggs, sausages, juice, Weet-bix, toast, tomato, coffee, tea and melon. A veritable feast. Dave commented between mouthfuls, 'If we ate a breakfast like this every day, we'd be as big as a house.'

 Then Grannie Island came out with it. Wiping her hands on her apron and smiling broadly, looking charming with flecks of silver in her tightly knit hair, she called us – wait for it – not just *boys*, but *lovely young boys*. I liked it instantly. I wanted a badge with this new title for the entire world to know I was a *lovely young boy*. I couldn't wait to tell my wife she was married to a *lovely young boy*. She would no doubt find it hard to equate any of the three words of my new title with the man she knew, but maybe it would grow on her as it had instantly grown on me.

With those few words, spoken in her unhurried island lilt that reminded me of gentle waves lapping onto the beach, Grannie Island blew wind into my sails and launched me into the day with her very astute and accurate description of me and my fellow walkers. In fact, it occurred to me that we could replace *Jolly Good Fellow* with *Lovely Young Boys* to create our very own theme song.

1234   Five hours later however, footsore and already weary, I found myself standing on the roadside arguing with Carnsey about our route for the afternoon and feeling more like an *ornery old goat* than a *lovely young boy*. It happened like this:

Because we had a meeting that night in Gladstone, Dave and Carnsey had insisted we walk all the way into the city, even though we hadn't planned on it. Gladstone was off the highway and this idea would add several more kilometres. I didn't like it. We'd already added extra kilometres on Gentle Annie roads, but I was *not* in favour of adding any kilometres on not-so-gentle *main* roads.

'It just seems more authentic,' they argued, 'walking right

into the town where we're holding a meeting.'

They won and we set off walking into Gladstone. But my feet and I changed our minds halfway when I saw a side road that looked like it might cut back to the highway even though we had no map, and no idea where it went, or how long it was. We tried phoning a friend for information from Google Maps. No answer. Another friend! Same thing. We weren't even really sure how we would describe our location. Carnsey wanted to continue walking, saying that things were becoming too complicated – if we didn't walk into Gladstone we'd have to get someone to pick us up somewhere on the road. I dug my heels in. Neither of us was enjoying this moment. I pulled my *seniority* card (which always went down like a lead balloon) and waved down a car. We were duly dropped off at the side road I'd seen five kilometres back, and we found ourselves on another very quiet Gentle Annie, perfect for walking. Calliope River Road took us through the tiny township of Yarwun which, for some reason, I really liked. There didn't seem to be anything or anyone there, which is probably why I liked it so much.

Three hours later, having thoroughly enjoyed Calliope River Road and not regretting my decision for one second, we emerged much further south on The Bruce, to find our pick-up waiting to take us into Gladstone. I was happier driving in than walking in, and we had saved ourselves a few kilometres to boot. 1247

Three cheers for the three *lovely young boys* at the end of the fiftieth day of our Walk.

Answer from map : 2 693 734 stars ii

231

Day 51
Trivia games

Wednesday 13 October

We woke to the news that after sixty-nine days underground the thirty-three Chilean miners were about to see daylight. The massive rescue operation, watched by millions around the world, was a historic moment.

I felt a particularly close bond to those miners and not without reason – Chile is one of my all-time favourite countries on earth. I've been there several times and I have wonderful Chilean friends who are very dear to me. As well as that, my second daughter was born there. So there is a part of me that will always be Chilean. And now there was another part of me that related to these miners – we were partners in *endurance*. These men had endured so much – uncertainty, fear, confusion, regret, fatigue.

They were on my mind when we walked through the *Fatigue Zone*. As part of a campaign to counteract driver fatigue on one long and boring stretch of highway, the Queensland Department of Transport and Main Roads implemented the novel idea of Trivia Games. *Trivia games help you stay alert*, they claimed. Strategically placed along the highway were signs displaying different trivia questions and each was followed a few kilometres later by the answer.

1. *What is the highest mountain in Queensland?*
2. *Who was Queensland's first Premier?*
3. *What is the floral emblem of Queensland?*
4. *Where in the world is Sav's wallet?*

Of course, in a car travelling at one hundred kilometres an hour, you'd only have a couple of minutes to ponder the question before the answer sign came into view. On foot, however, we had the best part of an hour to ponder each question. By the time we came up to the answer sign, we'd forgotten what the question was. This had the added benefit of providing us with a second trivia activity – guessing the question that went with the answer.

I wondered what trivia questions the Chilean miners had been asking 700 metres underground, in the dark, for two whole months. As for the road sign trivia questions, I knew three of the answers. How about you?

The day continued dull and cool with clouds hanging low and damp. Ironically, when we least needed them, our scavenger hunt produced three pairs of sunglasses. Modelling them, we voted Carnsey the winner with his large, plastic, white-rimmed babes with a missing lens.

At our host's place, along with an estimated one billion others around the world, we glued our eyes on the scenes of jubilation, hugs, cheers and tears as, one by one, the thirty-three miners, squished up in their missile-like escape capsule, ascended to the surface and emerged into the daylight.

I was temporarily teleported to Chile with my own cheers and tears.

1. Mount Bartle Frere
2. Robert Herbert
3. The Cooktown orchid
4. Nobody knows

Day 52
Frogs

Thursday 14 October

Early in the morning I met a young French couple. Even though part of my personal motivation behind The Walk was to refill my *Australia* tank, I was very happy to meet these folk and top up my *France* tank as well.

The van stopped opposite us on the highway and, dodging the speeding cars, a young couple crossed over to offer us bananas. Louis XVI and Marie Antoinette had seen us walking and, even without the lure of a Styrofoam pet on a rope, curiosity had got the better of them. We told them our story and they trumped it with their own – fifteen thousand kilometres around Australia on a tandem bicycle. Said bicycle was, at that moment, travelling in the back of their van. I never actually saw it but I took their word for it.

I was aghast! Safety conditions on the Bruce Highway, bad for walkers, were even worse for cyclists as there was often nowhere for a bicycle, let alone a tandem, to get off.

Curious, I asked, 'What has been the hardest thing for you?'

Without a word or a second's hesitation, Louis XVI looked me in the eye, knowing full well we were about to share a deep and meaningful moment together and, with a communicative gesture that spoke volumes, simply pointed pitiably down at the highway. I nodded.

'Wherre arre you frrom?' the monarch asked, regally gargling his rrrrs.

'Frrance,' I replied. Louis cocked his head to one side and

looked at me doubtfully with one beady little peeper.

'But you speek Eengleesh wizout zee Frrench accent?' his rising tone was inquiring.

The look on his face was priceless when I continued the conversation in the language of Napoleon, though possibly with a less-than-Napoleonic accent.

When King Louis drove off, and for some hours later, I could still see him pointing miserably at the highway. I only had six more days to endure it. In my book, that was six too many.

The next person I greeted, a few hours later, was a distant cousin I'd never met before. Kathryn is my second cousin twice removed. If you're into family trees and genealogies you'll know what that means. If you're not, you won't care. Cousin Kat is a poet and author of children's books with titles like *This is the Mud*. One of her cute little poems goes like this:

> *Ping-pong, ping-pong.*
> *Even frogs sing in the shower.*

Love it.

Kat says her goal, as a writer, is to find the perfect word for every situation. I think she does too, because as she and her husband opened the door to welcome me in, she said, 'You know we're related, don't you?' And that was just perfect. And so was the meal, the great conversations, the fun with their two lads and the warm bed in their caravan parked in its own little shed. Kat reminded me of a big family reunion just two weeks away, but I had to confess that I wouldn't be at it. Even though it wasn't far from where I'd be at the time and it fell on one of my days off, I wasn't sacrificin' that rest day for nobody or nothin'.

In the evening the Chilean miners surfaced again. Well, not literally, but Carnsey mentioned them at our meeting in Miriamvale.

'How amazing it has been to watch the miners in Chile emerge after their underground ordeal,' he began and all thirty eyes locked in.

He continued, 'I don't think many of us would like the feeling of being trapped for that long underground. Have you ever been trapped? Stuck in an elevator? Stopped for hours in a traffic jam? Stranded in a flood?' Then he got to his point, 'Those thirty-three miners are no longer trapped – they've been released – they're free! But there are 350 million other people still trapped – trapped behind seemingly impenetrable walls of minority languages, cut off from the rest of the world and in the dark, cut off from the life-giving words of the Bible.' He concluded, 'Over 2000 language groups don't have these life-giving words. They are trapped.'

Carnsey's trumpet call was loud and clear. No-one missed it.

I went to sleep thinking not about miners though, but about frogs – frogs singing in the shower and Frogs riding a tandem bicycle down the Bruce Highway.

Day 53
Bypassing Bundaberg

Friday 15 October

Once more, we walked past 600,000 gum trees,
4000 white dashes on the road and met 2000 cars –
approximately. And somewhere we crossed
the 700-kilometres-to-go mark. At the end   1300
of it all, it suddenly dawned on me that my feet hadn't
been hurting quite as much as in the previous few days.

While they were still very sore, the painful hardness had
gone and some suppleness had returned to replace the
blocks of plaster. I could have cried for joy. Not only was
it a huge relief to be relatively pain-free, but this marked
improvement went a long way to convincing me that
perhaps I *hadn't* done myself a permanent injury after all.
But I was still struggling, both with the highway and the
schedule.

Bruce had become a four-letter word.
I couldn't bear to talk or think about it   # % @ $
except to count down the days till I was
off it – only five to go! It had been too
long, too noisy, too much. I thanked God for the Gentle
Annies – without them I doubt I'd have made it this far.

Our schedule provoked yet another confrontation among
us three Wiggles. The first thousand kilometres saw few
such show-downs, probably because the route back there
was more straightforward, with few alternatives. Now
I seemed to be questioning our planned route almost
daily, as many attractive options leapt out at me.

I pored over maps and came to the startling realisation
that if we didn't walk all the way into Bundaberg, but
took some of the smaller roads that kept us more or less

walking in a straight line due south, we would cut off a lot of kilometres – a full fifty-five! At our average walking speed of five kilometres an hour, that translated to a whopping eleven hours. Faced with a choice of walking eleven hours or not walking eleven hours, I didn't need to deliberate. To me it was a no-brainer. Not so for Dave and Carnsey!

'But it doesn't seem right *not* to walk into Bundaberg when we're having a meeting there.'

'We never said we *would* walk into Bundaberg!' I countered.

'But our kilometre tally will be down. If we cut corners we won't clock up the 2000 kilometres.'

'In the first place our tally was going to be about fifty kilometres over the 2000 and no-one was complaining then,' I interjected, 'so what does it matter if we end up a little under? It's just a round number. The important thing is that we walk all the way from Cairns to Stanthorpe.'

'But we don't mind walking the longer route.'

'I mind!'

With all the sensitivity of a scrub bull, I pulled my seniority card *again*, which did a superb job *again* at dampening team spirits. However, since all three of us were lovely young boys, there was never any nasty confrontation, just an uncomfortable mild simmering somewhere, which had somehow, at some point, eroded something of our comradeship. A sadness settled over me like a shroud and seeped into my bones at the same time motivation leached out. I felt dry and empty. I downloaded a flurry of warm electronic accolades from all over the world – though in my current condition, I felt anything *but* deserving of them.

Back once more in our little caravan, as bedtime approached, even the sky grew forebodingly dark

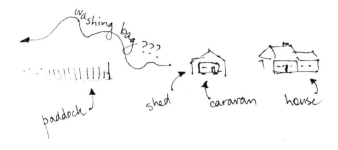

and gloomy. The wind picked up to almost gale-force proportions and the caravan, in spite of being tucked inside its little protective shed, was buffeted back and forth. The roof of the shed amplified the pounding rain to a deafening roar. I loved it. I felt a sense of exhilaration at the power of the storm, only heightened by my vulnerability as a human being in the midst of it. Dave suddenly remembered our washing bag was outside. He stumbled out of bed to rescue it, defying the elements, only to return with the report that it was nowhere to be seen. He declared it was probably blowing away out in the paddocks.

I declared it was time to sleep and thanked the Lord for my sore feet because they were only *sore* and no longer actually *painful*.

Day 54
Boring

Saturday 16 October

We woke to a clear, blue sky and a world washed sparkling clean. I knew at once it was going to be a hot one.

We retrieved the washing bag, not soaking wet in the middle of some paddock as predicted by Dave, but safely inside beside the washing machine. Kat had plucked it up as the storm first hit – bless her. Cousin Kat and I said our goodbyes, mentioning again the oh-so-important family reunion that I wouldn't be attending, and we took to the road.

By 8 am, my predictions about the weather were proved wrong as the sky was already under total cloud cover. Woo hoo! It remained that way for the entire day, making for perfect walking conditions.

Just the same, the day proved to be very long. It was also very *boring*, which is one word that, surprisingly, rarely left my lips.

1326 We'd put most of the day's quota of kilometres behind us when my phone vibrated – it was always on vibrate mode because I would never hear it ring over the noise of the traffic. It was my mate, Steve, from the Sunshine Coast. I often found it discouraging how few of my mates phoned me during The Walk. For some interminably long days I wouldn't hear from any of them. But there was Steve. He'd picked up the blower to talk to a foot-sore friend. I found that uplifting.

In his refreshingly unconventional way, Steve took a

different tangent by asking me to describe what I saw around me. His question jolted me out of my walking trance, forcing me to look up and around. My reply, with pauses as cars and trucks tore past, was less than scintillating:

> 66 We're been walking now for six hours. We haven't seen a single house or property entrance. We haven't seen a car or a horse. There hasn't been a service station or a rest area or even a bridge to cross - just the black road, the white lines and a lot of cars. We hadn't even seen a billboard until a few minutes ago. 99

Is it actually possible that I walked for six hours and saw none of the above? Perhaps I was in automatic pilot mode with the blinds down and the lights off. One day I'll re-walk that stretch of highway to resolve the question of my journaling accuracy once and for all. For the time being, I can only believe what I wrote.

Oh, and at the end of our call, Steve confessed that he hadn't actually *meant* to phone but had accidentally butt-dialled me. I found that a little *down*-lifting.

The word for the day: *boring.*

Day 55
Turtles and lizards

Sunday 17 October

Waking up in different beds had become something of a routine and, paradoxically, a novelty and generally quite fun. What hadn't been fun, however, was waking up far too early to the now detestable phone alarm.

However, while I woke up in yet another bed, there was no alarm and, when I crawled out to face the day, the sun was already well up – bliss! In the quiet of Brian and Caroline's little downstairs apartment, I could feel the accumulated stress and fatigue begin to dissipate. These extra sleep hours on my days off were a survival *must*.

It was quiet because it was Sunday and everyone was out at church – Carnsey and Dave by choice, Brian and Caroline because he is the pastor which kind of means that he doesn't have much choice. So, that morning the whole house was empty except, that is, for several other *residents* safely locked away.

My first stop was the cage with the scaly ones, the eastern bearded dragons. I'm a bit embarrassed to

admit my ignorance, but I actually thought they were frill-necked lizards. Brian soon set me straight on that one, explaining that dragons are smaller and don't have the large, loose frill around their necks but rather a sort of tiny beard that puffs out a little – their name says it all.

For a long time I sat staring through the wire mesh at these unblinking, bearded residents, thinking how well they played dead. It occurred to me that, from their side of the wire mesh, they were possibly thinking the same about me.

The dragons won the staring competition and I moved my attention to the turtle tank, where I sat for therapeutic hours, admiring these aquatic butterflies crawling through their hypnotic bubble bath in slow motion.

I enjoyed the inactivity of my morning watching the dinosaur-like dragons and the aerobic turtles. I also enjoyed inspecting Brian's imposing book collection. Brian is a bookworm, or as we say in French, *un rat de bibliothéque* (a library rat), and each of his four thousand volumes is neatly covered with plastic, categorised and catalogued. Standing before that wall of books, I was deeply disturbed as I thought of the thousands of ethnic groups in our world that don't even have an alphabet or a writing system, let alone a *single* book in their language.

My day ended reading some of Brian's books and walking some more kilometres with my friend Bernard in Turkey.

Dave's day ended with a long midnight Skype chat to Sydney, which kept me awake.

Day 56
Ma and Pa

Monday 18 October

One day off was not nearly enough to satisfy my body's need for rest or allow my feet to even begin to recover. It only served as a cruel reminder of the depth of my exhaustion. Long before I was ready, my detestable alarm rang and we were back on the road, the scant benefits of the day off being soon forgotten.

I consoled myself, however, with the fact that my feet were still holding out. Also, in spite of the clear sky with not a breath of wind, walking conditions were good. They got even better when we stepped off the highway, at my insistence, onto one of the disputed short cuts. Carnsey, good sport that he is, didn't protest too much. I suspect he too was happy walking on *Duck Pond Road* where cars came by at the rate of one every ten minutes instead of every ten seconds.

We never did come across the pond or the ducks, though we did come across a fresh road kill. Sprawled out in the middle of the road, pretty, even in death, was an orange whiptail wallaby. The whiptails, also called pretty-faced wallabies, are distinguishable by the white stripe on both sides of their faces which this fellow had very  obligingly revealed by throwing his head back. Our pretty-face obviously came off second-best in the impact, but we had proof that his opponent didn't get off totally scot-free – somewhere there is a vehicle driving around without a number plate. Carnsey picked up the incriminating evidence and laid it with great aplomb atop the corpse.

A few hours later, a more familiar number plate – firmly attached to its silver Camry – came into sight. The driver gave a long blast on the horn and came to an abrupt stop in front of us. Carnsey was taken by surprise, but I wasn't – his folks had been cooking up this roadside drop-in for some weeks and had made me privy to their plan. It was just as well, because at the rate I kept changing walking routes – sniffing out Gentle Annies and Duck Ponds – they would have been hard-pressed to guess where we might be.

Carnsey's Ma and Pa had travelled all the way from their fruit orchard, just south of Stanthorpe, to pop in on their lovely young boy and bring him some encouragement and nourishment – he seemed pleased enough at least for the latter. So was I. Within minutes we were settled in a beautiful spot on the sandy bank of a flowing creek taking the weight off our feet. We were also able to boost our calorie intake, which continued to be one of the more gratifying obligations related to The Walk. Homemade fruit cake, mangoes and ice-cold Fanta sent my blood sugar level spiking and my pancreas working overtime. All in the call of duty!

Ma and Pa calculated the distance they'd travelled from home as 540 kilometres – from their homestead and from the next-door cottage where my family was living. It was actually right there, on their property, in just under three weeks, where our journey would end. So I was walking home – literally, right to my front door. And seeing as Dave's family lived just around the corner, we were, all three of us, Dave, Carnsey and I, walking home.

But because we would be taking inland roads, our itinerary would be around a hundred kilometres longer than the highway Ma and Pa had taken. And while it took them just six hours to drive, it would take us twenty-four days to walk.

Our day's walk was aborted not long after that at a mere eighteen kilometres for us to be rushed into Bundaberg for an interview with the City Mayor. I felt as sorry for the Mayor as I did for myself, having to interrupt more important activities. I suspect she may not have been any more excited than I was about the encounter, but she found some appropriately positive things to say about us – while not really knowing what to say about Bible translation. The local newspaper appeared to struggle too, reporting we were walking *to raise Bible awareness*.

1349   I was cheesed off at having to cut short our kilometre quota, being acutely aware that it would only take *one* little thing to go wrong, *one* spanner in our carefully calculated works, to put me off my feet and out of the ~~race~~. From the beginning I'd hardly dared to believe I might make the 2000 kilometres but now I was beginning to believe that I actually would. As a result I was starting to sense some pressure building up.

One of the magic words that was always music to my ears after a sweaty day's walk was *shower*. Now I added another one to my inventory – *painkillers*. I can't imagine why I hadn't thought of them before. A friend supplied me with a little box of these magic beans that go by the name *Nurofen* – one bean every two to three hours. I had a feeling they would be an essential component of my daily survival kit.

Under the effect of the magic bean, I was lulled to sleep by the muffled voice of Dave from the next room. He was going his hardest, getting his money's worth out of his new webcam and sound card. Ain't love grand!

Day 57
Faith in any language

Tuesday 19 October

By 11.30 am, Carnsey and I had already been on the road for hours while Dave was still in bed just waking up after his late Skype night. That worked out well for Dave since it was his turn to stay home and look after some housekeeping and logistic details, largely the never-ending phone calls organising upcoming meetings. Without Dave's tireless efforts, we wouldn't have presented at half these meetings.

Speaking of which, we'd just chalked up another one, an encouraging gathering of forty-five responsive people – including Ma and Pa – from several different churches. The folk really engaged with the message, particularly the paragraph written in a weird font showing why *teaching them English* is not an alternative to translating the Bible into their language. After reading the paragraph, our volunteer 'reader' explained that she didn't enjoy the experience at all:

IT WAS QUITE AWKWARD. I LOST THE CONTEXT BECAUSE I WAS CONCENTRATING ON EACH INDIVIDUAL WORD AND NOT THINKING ABOUT THE MEANING.

She proved the point admirably that reading in another language can be hard work, so much so that you miss the meaning.

On the topic of *meaning*, I introduced a new illustration based on personal experience. It happened like this:

Back in France our translator and I were working side by side on our computers. This young man, because Taruuba is his mother tongue, does all the first drafts of the Bible translation before we work on checking them together. But apart from Taruuba, he is also fluent in French, Arabic and Spanish, knows some Hebrew and can understand me if I talk to him in English.

Given that he consults Bibles in all these different languages, he generally has a good grasp of the meaning of the text and his first drafts are usually of a high standard.

However, as I checked through Alher's first draft of Luke, what caught my attention was an Arabic word inserted in the text. It's true that some *loan words* are quite valid, for example the word for *boat,* for which there is no equivalent in the desert language of Taruuba. Consequently, when Jonah embarks on his fateful sea voyage, there is no option but to use the Arabic word *elbabor,* as it's the only word the people know for boat.

On this particular day, the Arabic word our translator had inserted in his text was *faith* as in إيمان the phrase *to have faith in God.* I was curious as to why he would have used an Arabic word for *faith.*

His reply: 'Because there isn't a word for faith in Taruuba. Faith is a religious term and so we have to use the Arabic word.'

I challenged him. 'You mean there is no word in your language for faith?'

'That's right!' he replied, leaving no room for negotiation. I was somewhat surprised, but when I came across the same Arabic word further in the text, I brought up the subject again, to be given the same adamant response. Not prepared to give up, I checked my 1500 Taruuba proverbs wondering whether there might be a word that could at least start us on the track to explore the idea of *faith* as it might be expressed in the Taruuba language. The closest I came was a proverb that referred to *talast*. The proverb could be translated: *Don't have talast in a well that is caving in.* An old Taruuba lady explained this, describing the scenario of a man down a well, cleaning it out or retrieving something, and looking up to see the sides of the well beginning to crumble and cave in.

'He doesn't wait,' she said. 'He just gets out as fast as he can.' She went on to explain, 'This proverb is applied to a bad situation in life, an unhealthy friendship, or a risky business deal. If there is no *talast*, you don't sit around thinking – you just get out of it.'

I investigated the word with our translator at the first opportunity. I was greeted, once again, with even firmer opposition.

'That word *talast* is just a common word,' he explained with exasperation. 'It's not a religious word,' he pressed. 'It just means trust, like I would trust you if you promised me something or if I tell you a secret.' He assumed he had ended the discussion once and for all, and he had, but not in the way he expected.

'You know what?' I said to him quietly.

'What?' he asked, intrigued.

I felt goose bumps as I explained, 'I think that's our word for faith.' Alher looked surprised and said, 'You mean that's all that faith means? Trust?'

After a little more discussion together to verify it once and for all, we locked it in.

You see, Alher had read those verses in four or five different languages. He thought he had understood the word *faith* in each one of them but, in actual fact, he had little or no understanding of the word at all until he finally heard it in his own mother tongue. If Alher, of all people, didn't *get it* with his multi-language reference library, what chance does the average Taruuba speaker have of *getting it* via a word from a language not his own? In this case, the Arabic word would have actually communicated a wrong *religious* meaning, when the gospel writer simply meant *trust.*

People loved this story. Giving people the Word of God in their mother tongue is not only a question of *preference* (as per the toothbrush), or even of simply *making it easy* (as per the weird font). It is much more than that. Without God's Word in their mother tongue, there will be important parts that people simply *just won't get!*

All in all, it was a great meeting.

Back at home, Dave turned the conversation to *the* subject, again. By then, I was more than a little irritated that his radio was only ever tuned to *Veronica FM*, broadcasting it over his loud speakers all day and half the night: *Veronica AM* and *Veronica PM.* No, I hadn't forgotten that at his age I too fell in love and subjected all and sundry to my new-found heaven on earth. But as chance would have it, Dave's *all and sundry* sometimes amounted to just little old me!

Long after I had finished updating our blog I could still hear the muffled cooing of the young lovers' voices on their long nocturnal Skype chats. I knew that the next day I would be walking just with Dave. Suddenly I had an inspiration – I groped for my phone in the dark and sent him a text message through the wall.

> *Hey Dave. Suggestion for our walk tomorrow – how about we spend the morning, up till midday, talking about something or someone other than Veronica?*

I swallowed a magic bean and smiled myself to sleep.

Day 58
Goodbye Bruce

Wednesday 20 October

The big day had arrived when we would turn off the highway. My heart was light and there was a spring in my step. The countdown was over and by late afternoon we would part company, once and for all, with Bruce. I couldn't imagine being any happier on the day we would finally cross the finish line in Stanthorpe, three weeks down the track.

Two weeks previously we'd celebrated the *invisible* landmark of one thousand kilometres. This landmark, however, was palpably *visible*. For me, it was the most important of the entire Walk.

My bright mood and light heart were soon to be shattered by a text message from Hélène with the word *cancer*. A phone call followed. A medical check had revealed suspected breast cancer – a further test the next day would be more conclusive. She was calm and taking it well. It wasn't totally unexpected as her mother had very recently died with breast cancer that had spread to her bones. The memory of that ordeal was still too much alive and the 600 kilometres that separated me from my wife suddenly seemed more like six million. She told me she'd already had a little talk with the boys. Joseph's response was, 'Does this mean you are going to die?' I felt as if I'd been hit by the Gumlu train. I was glad to be walking while I talked with Hélène – somehow the motion helped. I said nothing to Dave about the phone call – I needed time to recover from the impact of that bombshell.

And Dave said nothing to me about my midnight text message. He had obviously understood though because, after a full half an hour, Miss Sydney still hadn't surfaced in conversation – not a word. It did occur to me though, that in my somewhat sleep-deprived state, I had perhaps been just a tad insensitive in what I wrote. Maybe I had offended him, though it didn't appear so as Dave was his usual bouncy self. Right through the morning our conversation flowed easily, but not in the V-direction. I was glad. If ever there was a time I didn't want to hear *young love* stories, this was it. As the minutes crawled towards midday, I braced myself ready for the V-topic to arise. But it didn't. Not at midday, and not all afternoon. Neither of us mentioned her, which opened up other conversation possibilities.

My thoughts were never far from home though and I was walking in somewhat of a daze, with my sunglasses fogged up from the inside. Then suddenly, Dave came out with an amazing statement about how people make such a fuss about dying.

'There are so many appeals for heart and cancer research. We should just accept that we all die and not invest so much into trying to stay alive.' He couldn't know how his words pierced my heart!

As the shadows grew longer, my calculations said we had less than an hour to go on that dreadful highway. And that was when I saw my first crocodile!

1397   We were a lot further south than what is normally considered croc-country, so it took me by surprise. Dave hadn't seen it until I pointed it out – a small one, concealed in the long grass only metres off the highway. At first I considered simply getting as

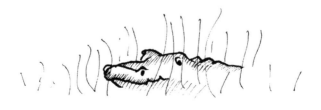

close as I could to photograph it, but, when I cautiously approached and realised it was less than a metre long, a crazy idea surfaced. I would catch it and keep it for my son Joseph, an animal lover like his Dad. Having never handled a crocodile before, I had no idea how difficult this endeavour might be, or the dangers it might entail. I did know that a crocodile has the strongest bite of any animal; the muscles that *close* its jaws are fifteen times more powerful than a Rottweiler's. But I also knew that the muscles that *open* its jaws are amazingly weak. So I figured that the most important thing in capturing this croc would be to immobilise its jaws. With heart beating fast I inched forward – Steve Irwin style – and pounced on the closed jaws, holding them tight. I swung the little animal, which proved to be amazingly light, out of the long grass and onto open ground. It put up no fight whatsoever but lay staring up at me with beady little eyes. Yes, with a few minutes in a washing machine and some disinfectant, this little fellow would be a perfect gift for Joseph. I did feel sorry, though, for the child who had perhaps inadvertently tossed it out of a car window.

Soon after, the soft croc safely tucked under my arm, the long-awaited intersection came 1400 into sight. I hardly dared to believe it. It was surreal. I unsuccessfully fought back the emotion – all the tension, pain, noise, danger and stress of fifty-eight days on the highway somehow started leaking from my tear glands.

Marking this momentous occasion, I threw the stuffed croc aside, whipped out my video camera and recorded the following heartfelt anti-epitaph to Bruce.

'Over behind us you can see we have a sign that says Bruce Highway. For the last 1400 kilometres we've been walking almost entirely on this highway and, without a doubt, for me that has been the hardest part of this Walk so far.' In the video, I have the same beaten expression on my face as that of my French cyclist friend, Louis.

I continued, 'We've counted, on average, one vehicle every ten seconds and that makes for very annoying and very stressful walking, and we've had a few close calls.' As I spoke, the vehicles, right on cue, roared past in quick succession behind me, drowning out my voice.

The fatigue was written on my face, 'And today, right at this minute, we come to the end of the Bruce Highway. Our longstanding relationship with Bruce comes to an end – right now. And we're not unhappy about it. We're very happy to say goodbye to Bruce and to be going down another road that is quieter and nicer. So, we are officially saying goodbye to Bruce and we don't ever want to set foot on him again.'

It was 6 pm, the end of the day. And the end of Bruce! And also, I sensed, perhaps the end of my *middle mile*. Up to this point I had been, as Vance said, 'too far from the goal to be inspired by it,' but now we had left The Bruce, the goal was in sight.

The pick-up vehicle whisked us off to our new hosts, Ned and Anne. Then I remembered Joseph's crocodile that I'd tossed to the side while filming.

I hoped it would still be there the next morning.

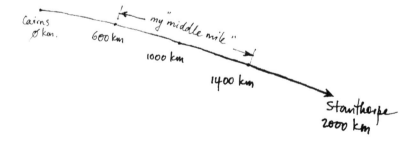

254

PART FOUR

Over the hump

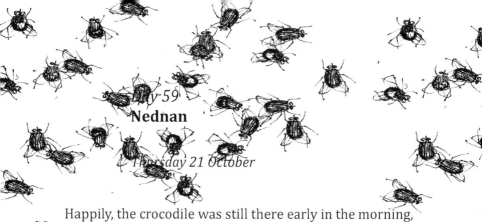

Day 59
Nednan

Thursday 21 October

Happily, the crocodile was still there early in the morning, lying in the long grass where I'd thrown him, which presented me with the opportunity of catching him all over again.

We found something else too, or rather, they found us – flies! Swarms descended on us, covering our packs and backpacks. It appears they didn't like the Bruce Highway any more than we did, the difference being that they were smarter – they kept away from it. Now, just spitting distance off the highway, they were all over us like a rash.

Carnsey's voice reached me from behind. 'It would help if Sav had a shower from time to time.' I ignored him.

My thoughts were grateful ones, however. I was glad that for those first 1400 kilometres, along with everything else, we didn't have to cope with flies. But my main thought, of course, was for Hélène and her test.

Then I got to thinking about our new hosts, Ned and Anne, which momentarily took my mind off both the test and the flies. When we turned up on their doorstep the previous night, they knew next to nothing about us, nor us about them. Unlike most of our other hosts who had been planning for our arrival for weeks, or even months, Ned and Anne filled in at the last minute. When we walked through their door, tired and hungry, Anne, like my cousin the poet, found the perfect words.

'There's food ready for you guys, the shower is waiting and I'll show you to your beds.' In less than ten seconds she had uttered those three vital words – *food, shower*

Italy
Sicily
Malta

and *bed* – which raised a laugh and made me instantly feel at home. There was a familiarity about these two that was hard to pinpoint at first – almost French, but not quite. I discovered it stemmed from a common Mediterranean connection; Ned is from a Sicilian background and Anne from that jewel of an island, Malta.

Showered and tummies full of delicious lasagne, we fell into easy conversation with *Nednan*, as we now affectionately called them, running their names into one easy, two-syllable word. I listened in silence as they shared the depth of their pain and anguish in raising an autistic child. Anne told us, through tears, of Troy's increasingly violent moods as he grew into adulthood and how it tore them apart to eventually have to entrust him to support workers in full-time care. The mixture of pain and love was visibly etched on their faces.

Anne said with genuine gratitude, 'Troy's been a real blessing, because without him we would have been really selfish people.' That simple statement was full of insight and faith, distilled through years of heartache. Pain, it seems, is often part of God's loving growth plan for us. I thought of Hélène and wondered what pain the future might hold for my little family.

Nednan, from the Catholic tradition, said that even through all the pain they never blamed God. Ned pulled out a Bible and read from Romans chapter 9: *But who are you, O man, to talk back to God?*

He turned to us, looking over his glasses, 'You know, we've never questioned God's will in giving us Troy.' He continued reading: *Shall what is formed say to Him who formed it, 'Why did you make me like this?' Does not the potter have the right to make out of the same lump of clay some pottery for noble purposes and some for common use?* As for lumps, I had one forming in my throat as he read.

Ned produced several more Bibles, proving to be a veritable Bible bowerbird. His eyes lit up as he pored over his precious collection.

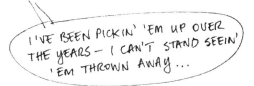

I'VE BEEN PICKIN' 'EM UP OVER THE YEARS — I CAN'T STAND SEEIN' 'EM THROWN AWAY ...

In all our encounters during The Walk, I never met anyone so obviously enamoured with God's Word and with God Himself.

The flies followed us all day – all forty kilometres of it – as did my heavy heart. I was thinking of Hélène at home and waiting for news of her test results – another twenty-four hours to wait.

1440

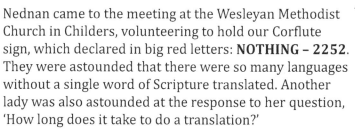

Nednan came to the meeting at the Wesleyan Methodist Church in Childers, volunteering to hold our Corflute sign, which declared in big red letters: **NOTHING – 2252**. They were astounded that there were so many languages without a single word of Scripture translated. Another lady was also astounded at the response to her question, 'How long does it take to do a translation?'

Carnsey gave the answer. 'It varies a lot – perhaps between five and fifty years.' Her jaw dropped open in shock, and stayed that way for the longest time.

After the meeting, my long-lost wallet and I had a rapturous reunion! I'm slightly embarrassed to admit though where it had been for three long weeks – on my back, tucked in an inside pocket of my backpack! A fitting proverb in the Taruuba language describes a camel carrying water bags from the well back to the camp: *The camel carries it, but can't drink it.*

I laughed to myself.

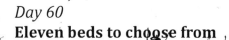

Day 60
Eleven beds to choose from

Friday 22 October

Our new-found friends, the flies, joined us again. Due to my heavy heart, my attitude towards these uninvited hitchhikers was considerably less charitable than at first. However, we only had to suffer them for twenty kilometres, as our new host picked us up early to take us to our isolated country abode. Actually, he was not really our *host* as such, because he just dumped us there, leaving us to our own devices. I, for one, was very happy to be dumped and left to my own devices. Up to this point, I had thoroughly enjoyed all our hosts but, now that we were alone in this rambling old farmhouse, I realised how much I was in need of silence and space.

1460

The awaited phone call came from Hélène. The planet stopped revolving while I held my breath waiting to hear her words. Her voice was calm. The results had come back negative. I let out a slow, silent sigh of relief and said something inane. At times like that words can be clumsy, impeding meaningful communication rather than facilitating it. Although the heaviness was instantly lifted and the world appeared visibly brighter, I knew it would take me several days to totally recover from 'what could have been'.

Now able to focus, I looked around and fell in love with this seen-better-days weatherboard house, which had an impressive choice of eleven beds – not counting the hammock. Showered and sprawled out in the hammock, I surveyed the sun-soaked beauty of the rolling hills around me, thanking the Lord for His grace in giving us life – and in giving me my wife. After recent rain the hills, as far as the eye could see, were washed in the first green of new grass. And I enjoyed observing our languid four-legged mower, just metres from my horizontal vantage point, swishing her tail and ripping at the grass.

My friend Bernard and I compared notes – we had both been through the proverbial wringer. I discovered, to my utter horror, that he had been walking *every single day*. Unthinkable! Impossible! He was at the end of his tether and could no longer keep up that pace: *Je me promets sans trop y croire de m'arrêter dorénavant un jour par semaine.* He'd at last made the decision to rest one day a week. I contemplated, with a shudder, what state I would have been in if I hadn't had my weekly rest days.

My eyes turned from the pages back to the hills – and to the lethargic cow – and to the willy-wagtail perched on her rump with his nervous, robotic twitch. It was indeed a perfect place to unwind or, as Carnsey said, 'to put our fingers to the keyboards.'

Yes, within the hour, all three of us were at different tables – emailing, skyping and blogging. The fact that we had coverage in such an isolated place for two nights was a real gift. Or was it? Here we were, for the first time, totally on our own in the perfect setting to really relax and we were drumming our little digits off.

Carnsey complained we were a boring bunch. 'Not only do we spend all day walking the road,' he muttered, 'but then when we get off, we spend our free hours with our fingers to the keyboards talking to the rest of the world.'

Then, to my great surprise, *he* came up with a plan for us to actually swing an *extra* full day off.

For once *I* wasn't the one suggesting changes to our schedule.

I think if it had been me, again, the cousins would have strung me up in the jacaranda tree or strapped me to the back of the bovine lawnmower where years later my bones would be found bleached by the sun. Carnsey's suggestion was to redistribute the kilometres. We would try to clock up as many as possible the next day – even as many as thirty-seven! In that way, in three days' time we would score a whole extra day off. My feet groaned at the idea of a thirty-seven kilometre walk day but my head and my heart instantly voted for the extra day off.

A check of my Excel spreadsheet itinerary showed that according to Carnsey's plan we'd be too far down the road to return to our quiet farmhouse for our day off. However, I realised it *would* mean I'd be at my cousin Bronwyn's place just outside Gayndah – my father's childhood home and one of my favourite, memory-filled places in the world.

'YES!' I exclaimed aloud. But this would only work if we powered along. The idea of an extra day off was already dispelling my lethargy and blowing wind into my sails – and would maybe also give wings to my soles.

A further incentive, according to my spreadsheet, was that we were only forty kilometres short of the 1500 mark. All being well, we'd cross that line in just two days. I was elated at the thought and particularly grateful to God that I'd had almost no back trouble. I realised that I hadn't *really* believed I'd make it to this point. Of course I'd *hoped* I would and I'd *planned* on it and I'd certainly *talked* about it. But in the deepest recesses of my heart I don't think I really *believed* I would. A lack of faith? A healthy dose of reality? Possibly both, but I like to think it was more of the latter.

Faith doesn't close its eyes to reality, and my eyes were wide open from the start, thanks to people like Rod with his blood-dripping chafe and Extreme Janine with her broken ankle. It was faith that took me to the starting blocks, faith that brought me almost 1500 kilometres, and faith that saw me through the dreaded, dreary middle mile. And I was counting on faith to take me home. Emotion welled up from deep inside.

fee-fi-
fo-fum

I began the day with flies on my back and I ended it with
a frog on my butt. Opening the lid of the toilet seat and
finding a huge, bright green tree frog stuck to the bowl
with his sucker-like toes, was somewhat disconcerting.
True, it wasn't a death adder and it was unlikely to latch
itself to my anatomy, but the fact of the matter is that
I prefer to be alone during my visits to the little boys'
room.

Without further ado, in an uncharitable moment,
I decided to dispense with him by flushing. Judging,
however, by his lightning-speed reaction to Niagara Falls
unleashed without warning, and his Thorpedo swimming
skills, I guessed he was well practised at this game. I felt
suitably chagrined in no small way by the reproachful
look in his eye when he crawled out of the whirlpool and
assertively re-positioned himself on the side of the bowl.

The frog stayed. We shared the toilet. It wasn't a
particularly pleasant experience for either of us.

Day 61
Ban Ban Springs

Saturday 23 October

 Early morning saw Dave hanging out the washing accompanied by our lawnmower friend and the cheery calls of peewees, plovers and crows.

As I watched him pegging up our Wiggles shirts I recalled his words about cancer research. I remember thinking exactly the same when I was young, but with age comes a different perspective. Life is a never-ending learning experience, the young from the not-so-young, and the not-so-young from the oh-so-young.

The neat rows of Wiggles shirts, three or four of each colour, were soon flapping happily in the warm breeze alongside jocks and socks. All would be dry in two shakes of a lawnmower's tail.

After another shared experience with Mr Frog, which gave me the opportunity to once again be impressed by his swimming prowess, we headed off, swept along by birdsong. Kilometre after kilometre I revelled in the piped-in, surround-sound music of nature, so rich and earthy compared to European birdsong. The perfect blue sky would have been cause for concern in the tropical north during our early days of walking but now at higher altitudes, the weather was noticeably cooler, and walking more do-able.

Several hours on, however, it began to feel a little *less* so. To momentarily escape the sun, we stopped to buy a chocolate milk at the one shop in the tiny village of Coalstoun Lakes, resisting the temptation to follow the intriguing sign: Coalstoun Lakes Volcanic Crater.

I was curious, as I was born and bred in south-east Queensland and to the best of my knowledge there had never been any volcanic activity in this region. However, as men on a mission with a day off at stake, we pressed on.

Right on cue, feet and faces hot and red, we saw the sign for Ban Ban Springs. At a crossroads in the middle of nowhere, it boasts little more than a Mobil service station and, of course, the springs. Long before white feet walked on Australian soil, water has bubbled out of the ground at Ban Ban. The name comes from the local indigenous Wakka Wakka language, and means *grass* of which there is always plenty around a spring.

I drowned my hat in the cool water – along with my feet – watching steam rise off them. As Carnsey filmed me, I was taken back to the time exactly two months before, when I cooled my feet in the crocodile river north of Babinda. I shuddered. My thoughts then took me four decades further back, to another incident that happened at this exact spot.

As a family, we were squished up in our Vauxhall Victor en route to visit my grandparents. Ban Ban Springs provided a convenient spot for my brothers and me to stretch our little legs and empty our bursting little boy bladders and, more importantly, for Mum to dress us up. She had sewn matching outfits for all five of us during the weeks leading up to our holiday and was understandably proud of her achievement – to her it was possibly something akin to walking 1500 kilometres. However, she was decidedly *less* proud when, decked out in my new outfit, I ran across what I thought was a grassy meadow, only to find myself chest deep in water. It was the springs covered with a thick blanket of water grass. Mum did not see the funny side of it at all. Nor did she appear even slightly grateful that I had only narrowly avoided death by drowning.

I was still smiling recalling that day as we sat down at the servo for lunch. Between the Chiko Roll and the Weiss mango ice-cream the phone rang. It was our young uni friend from Townsville, Mr Mediterranean, telling us he wanted to put on his walking boots and join us on the road again. The forty kilometres we'd covered together seven weeks back must have whet his appetite, because he announced he wanted to fly down to join us for the last day and cross the finish line together. Awesome! Carnsey and I started speculating about how many others might accept our blog challenge to walk the last stretch with us.

But of more immediate importance was our speculation about how many kilometres we'd cover by the end of the day. Reaching forty would take us exactly to our 1500 mark. After our foot spa and calorie overdose, I was up to the challenge and popped another magic bean for good measure.

1500   Four hours later, aching and limping down the last of those forty long kilometres, I reached the goal for the day, leaving exactly one quarter of our total distance to walk – approximately, of course, given that our *talast*[1] in Google Maps had seriously eroded over recent weeks. In spite of this uncertainty, we chose a somewhat random spot on a lonely road to commemorate our achievement. With my muscles complaining at the effort it took to bend over, we picked handfuls of blue heliotrope flowers to improvise a *500* sign to mark the countdown of the remaining kilometres. All hands on deck! Bad timing. A lone truck roared through before we could finish, blowing his horn in disapproval of us being close to the road, and blowing the blooms all over the place. We started again.

Our next meeting, in the big Memorial Hall at Biggenden, did not fill many chairs and most of the hair was grey, but

---

[1] For readers challenged with short term memory retention, see p 249

I was excited to be able to share the challenge again. We presented the weird script illustration and asked, 'How many of you would buy a newspaper if it was written in this script?' To the amusement of all, a local journalist in attendance called out, 'I'd be out of a job!' The point was taken – no-one would buy a newspaper if it was that difficult to read, neither would we read the Bible if it was written in another language equally difficult to understand.

Returning to our farmhouse for the second and last night there, I stood on the balcony, looking out over the hills washed white by a full, bright moon. I did a tally and realised I could now count the remaining days of The Walk on my fingers and toes – twenty!

And I wondered if there really was a volcano back at Coalstoun Lakes.

Day 62
Volcanic craters

Sunday 24 October

I convinced Carnsey and Dave to visit the volcano.

A quick Google search revealed there were two amazing craters, the only recognisable volcanic landforms in the entire region.

The support vehicle took us to the base of Mt Le Brun, a mere 200 metres above the surrounding countryside. In Australia it doesn't take a great deal to qualify for the title 'mountain'.

As we climbed the slope I was very happy it wasn't a Swiss mountain[1]. While Carnsey and I climbed, Dave ran – like a madman – making the summit in one minute and ten seconds. We challenged him to repeat the performance and improve on his time. He didn't take us up on it.

The view was surreal, reminiscent of a 'lost world' from a Jules Verne novel. We stood on the rim of the crater and stared down into a watery, lush-green arena surrounded by a mini rainforest. Even from our distant vantage point we could hear the frogs and birds below in their amazing unique ecosystem. Our short-lived tourist detour completed, we took to the road again.

The Veronica topic continued to be alive and well, though with greatly reduced airplay. And now it looked like that funny little naked fat fellow with wings had been shooting his arrows again – at Carnsey! In contrast to Dave, however, Carnsey was playing

---

[1] In fact, surprisingly, Mt Blanc, in France, at 4810m, is actually almost 200m higher than the highest Swiss mountain.

his cards close to his chest. I would need to wait and watch a few more days to really gauge what was going on there.

Our evening meeting in Gayndah was 1535 hosted by The Uniting Church, and drew an audience of forty representing seven different churches. I love it when God's people come together from different denominational traditions in a wider family gathering for a special occasion. And I love small country churches. *Simple* folk. *Sincere* folk. *Faithful* folk. I sensed the presence of God in a special way.

This meeting was also special because, for the first time, a lot of family members were present, including one of my favourite aunties – eighty-two year old Aunty Una. There were also several cousins and miscellaneous pseudo family members, the latter related by bonding rather than blood, as a result of being neighbours of Dad and his mob in Gleneden for four generations. That's how it works in the country.

Country folk love stories. When Dave told his story about another long walk he did the previous year in Nepal, you could have heard a you-know-what drop:

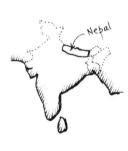

> *'I want to talk to you about a woman I met in a remote mountain village in Nepal and why I will never forget her. First, I spent twenty-six hours perched on the roof of a bus to get to the beginning of the trail.'*

Every eye was on him.

> *'From there we set off on our five-day trek along narrow mountain paths, often with a sheer vertical drop down into the valley. We passed village after village, hundreds of tiny houses made of mud and surrounded by rice terraces. They were sometimes built on slopes so steep that the terraces were higher than they were wide. An intricate system of canals*

flowed through them, irrigating the crops. It was in one of those villages that I met this woman. In my limited Nepali I offered her a copy of a gospel in the Nepali language. I showed it to her and told her it was a book about Jesus, but she just gave me a blank stare. I'd done this hundreds of times before – literally – so I knew that I could communicate at least these simple sentences. We'd given out 1500 gospels and the normal reaction was curiosity and wanting to see. Not this woman. She didn't seem to understand. My hiking buddy spoke something of a few other Nepalese languages, and he tried them all on her. Later we found out that this woman and her village were from a different people group, who spoke a different language – a language that doesn't have anything of the Bible translated. So it wouldn't have mattered if I'd had a copy of the gospel in every available language in the world, none of them would have been any use to her as she didn't understand any of them. Her village will never hear the message of salvation in Jesus, until someone goes and translates it for them.'

The audience was spellbound.

This little group took up an offering of $800 towards our expenses. I was *so* touched. They also provided a sumptuous country supper, which was great because I was *so* hungry. And over a cuppa, Aunty Una thrust a copy of the program for the upcoming family reunion into my hands.

'Next Saturday!' she said simply and I winced. That was my day off and I had serious plans – plans to sleep, eat, sleep, eat, and sleep some more. What's more, by then I'd be in Kingaroy, two hours' drive away.

'That's a lot closer than if you were still in France,' Aunty Una said simply without breaking eye contact. But Aunty Una had never walked 1500 kilometres and she didn't understand how badly I needed my days off.

Day 63
Bullocks

Monday 25 October

A wonderful thing it is to wake to the cawing of crows at 9 am. And even more wonderful, half an hour later, to find myself sitting on a verandah, the sole beneficiary of a truly sumptuous breakfast courtesy of cousin Bronwyn – potatoes, peas, avocado, lettuce, fried egg, mushrooms, pumpkin, sausages and capsicum. To think the French start their day with nothing more than a coffee and a croissant! *Tsk, tsk!*

This was my *extra* day off, purchased – literally – by sweat of brow and skin of feet. I intended to take full advantage of it. I did so initially – would you believe it? – by going for a walk. I poked around the old farmhouse, inside and out, where my Dad lived his childhood years. Memories from my own childhood visits fluttered out from a thousand places like a plague of butterflies:

- the shed where I witnessed the arrival of twelve pink piglets into the world.

- the outhouse where I never checked under the seat because I knew if I saw what lived there I'd never have been brave enough to sit on it.

- the tank stand where Aunty Una clamped the butter churn and we'd turn the handle till our arms ached.

- the pen where I encountered, for the first time, the noisy ritual of a mating boar.

- the hayshed where we'd romp and jump until the itching outdid the fun.

- the milking shed where Dad used to squirt the milk into my mouth straight from the cows' teats.

- the old piano, still standing, where I'd sit and tinkle away for hours.

- the paddocks where, according to my uncle, I wrecked his new little 100cc Honda by not changing out of first gear.

- the stairs leading up to the bedrooms.

My uncle was born in the room at the top of those stairs and, seventy years later, died of a heart attack sitting on the bottom step, taking off his boots. I wonder how many people can claim to have died within a few metres of their place of birth. ☺

The whole place exuded an intoxicating aroma of the past. No matter how many more years I might walk French soil, my feet will only ever scratch the surface, but there in Gleneden they are rooted generations deep.

My spiritual roots are there too – a nearby peanut farm belonging to another uncle was where I came under terrible conviction of sin and, at the same time, the amazing conviction of forgiveness of that sin. In Jesus! Because of His death. He died in my place. My life, as a seventeen-year-old, took a new turn at that point and, in many ways, it really just began.

the old farmhouse where my 'Dad' grew up

Rohan

As much as I loved strolling around my grandparents' old place and gently unearthing memory after treasured memory, surprisingly, this was not to be the highlight of my day. Young pseudo-cousin Rohan had invited us to wander up and see his bullocks. I like animals, so why not?

Rohan is a bullock driver, the second youngest of only a dozen or so 'bullockies' still left in Australia. Bullock teams are part of our Australian heritage and feature in our pioneer paintings, poetry and prose. But they have been relegated to our past – they no longer exist. Or so I thought until I met Rohan and saw him strut his stuff.

Whip in hand, looking like he'd just stepped out of a Tom Roberts' canvas, Rohan hitched up his six bulky bullocks – i.e. bulls without bollocks – and, to my utter amazement, manoeuvred them around like trained French poodles. With a 'Walk back' here and a 'Come up' there, those big boys lined themselves up, turned in unison and even stepped sideways. I was speechless. I knew that bullocks *didn't* have bollocks, but I had no idea that they *did* have brains, *and* the ability to comprehend and obey instructions[1].

I plied Rohan with questions about the keys to working a bullock team. He indulged me, in turn, with some gems applicable to parenting, business ventures, church life and, in fact, anywhere people have to work together.

'They have to know what you want,' he said simply, 'and *you* have to know what you want and be clear about it.'

And the most difficult thing?

'Getting them to pull together,' he stated without hesitation. 'Anticipation is important too,' he added. 'If they're about to hit a tree, it's too late then to try to get them to change course.'

---

[1] Check out the video gallery on Rohan's website: The Gleneden Bullock Team

Our shadows were stretching long and thin when we said goodbye to Rohan, his bullocks and his young family. Written on their birth certificates, his two small children have *Father's Occupation: Bullock Driver* – a claim to fame shared by few.

Before arriving home, and enjoying the three magic words *food, shower* and *bed*, we had another stop as cousin Bronwyn had spotted a frill-necked lizard basking in the last rays of sunshine. We stopped to investigate. Of course, now a specialist, I knew the difference between a frill-necked lizard and a bearded dragon. The scaly little number in front of us was actually the latter but I didn't bother to enlighten my cousin. After all, she's lived there for more than half a century and if she doesn't know the difference, chances are high it's not of earth-shattering significance.

☑ PLODDING

☑ PERSEVERANCE

☑ PAINS

☑ PANIC

☑ PRESSURE

☐ PADDLING.

Day 64
Pressure

Tuesday 26 October

I hate getting up early. I hate packing. I hate leaving.

As I swallowed my magic bean, I wondered when I'd be back again. Due to financial constraints and work commitments, I am only able to return to Australia every four or five years. Consequently, it was with a lump in my throat and leaden boots that I turned my back on Gleneden, my favourite 'out-in-the-sticks' place in the world.

As I took my first steps for the day, still thinking about Rohan and his six big boys, a line of Banjo Paterson's poem *The Uplift* came to mind:

> *Take a lesson from the bullock –*
> *he goes slowly, but he goes.*

Like Rohan's bullocks I was going *slowly* but I *was* going. I was plodding with perseverance, pain – and now *panic*!

These mild panic attacks had taken me totally by surprise, but seemed to be related to the realisation that, with only 465 kilometres to go, I actually *did* have every chance of making it to the finish line. During the early weeks of The Walk, I knew I had every chance of *not* making it and I'd prepared myself to concede defeat. However, with the middle mile behind me, and the finish line in sight, conceding defeat was no longer an option. Having survived the Bruce Highway, Crocodile Creek, man-eating tick, death adder country and Mr Frog, I was determined, for the first time, that I *would* make all 2000 kilometres of it. As a result, a regular rush of adrenaline would surge through my body, unfortunately not translating into power walking, my poor body being far too fatigued for that. Instead there was now pressure to perform. Pressure to achieve. Pressure to make it. I now *plodded* with *perseverance, pain, panic* – and *pressure.*

While I was *plodding*, however, Dave, on the other hand, was *paddling*. Several metres ahead, he was dragging his invisible oar through the imaginary water – first left, then right. He kept that up for the longest time. For some reason or other, I found it inordinately amusing.

Note to self: I think I need help.

The day was long and hot and we were glad to take a break with some folk who lived right en route. We enjoyed a few minutes of shade and numerous glasses of cold orange juice.

Finally, on the last stretch, some cloud cover along with shade from roadside trees, gave long-awaited relief from the sun – perfect. It was also perfect to arrive at our new hosts' place, after thirty-four kilometres on the road, to discover they had a swimming pool. I can't really be sure whether I actually greeted Russell and Mandy before stripping off and plunging in.

Mandy had read about The 2000 Walk in *Footprints* magazine. I'd never heard of that one but wasn't surprised. Our conscientious 2000 Walk writer had been faithfully feeding information all over the country, and we'd seen our mug shots – and boot shots – in lots of magazines and newspapers[1].

Russell and Mandy lived on a pig farm and, even though

---

[1] Global (Operation Mobilisation), New Directions (Presbyterian), QB (Queensland Baptists), Signs of the Times (Seventh Day Adventist), The Journey (Queensland Uniting Church), The Presbyterian Pulse, Warcry (Salvation Army), The Messenger (Presbyterian), Witness (Victorian Baptists), Enhance, Eternity, Focus (Brisbane Anglican), The Melbourne Anglican, Australian Prayer Network, Catholic Leader, Christianity Today, Mission Network and New Life.

the grunters were housed some distance away, when
the wind was right, the faintest hint of the deliciously
incomparable odour wafted delicately through my open
window. But I really didn't mind, as I was happily set up
with a desk, Wi-Fi connection, a lovely peaceful view and
a full tummy – how *do* you get steaks to taste so good?!

With both the occasional whiff of pig perfume and the
odd squeal drifting my way on the night breeze, I drifted
happily off to sleep.

did you know that
pig poo produces twice the
methane of cow manure?

Day 65
Pigs

Wednesday 27 October

I was woken by the porkers stirring in excited unison awaiting their Weet-Bix. It occurred to me, given their confined existence, that food was possibly the only exciting thing that happened in their lives. And although I didn't make quite as much noise about it, I could identify with them.

Mandy must have heard about my cousin Bronwyn's breakfast bonanza because she competed with her own prize-winning entry of bacon, eggs, sausages, banana, paw-paw, juice, toast – and *coffee*. But this was coffee with a difference. Bright blue and white, Coffee pattered around on the table, flew around the room, perched on our shoulders and sat on the edge of our plates nibbling scrambled egg. Little Coffee, who acquired his name after a nose dive into a mug of it, was as much fun as any budgie I'd ever encountered. Carnsey was relatively nonplussed and Dave said he was going to call the RSPCA if I kept feeding him egg.

Mandy said they'd had other budgies before but they had all been taken by carpet snakes. Once, when they'd had a major rat problem at the piggery, they brought in carpet snakes to keep down the rodent population. Then when the rodents ran out, the snakes took to snacking on chooks and budgies.

'There's still a big carpet out there somewhere in the piggery,' Mandy said. 'We spot it every now and then curled up on a rafter.'

I told her of the solution I hit upon when we had a rat invasion of apocalyptic proportions of our own, around our chook house in France. A friend had explained how she got rid of mice in her kitchen by bringing in a guinea pig in a cage, suggesting I try the same. I wasn't convinced until I read the same advice in *Les Misérables*, Victor Hugo's famous novel: *Il défendait une lapinière contre les rats, rien qu'avec l'odeur d'un petit cochon de Barbarie qu'il y mettait.* 'He protected a rabbit hutch against rats with nothing more than the smell of a guinea pig he put in there.' In desperation, I decided to try it. The effect of putting a pair of guinea pigs in the chook house was both immediate and nothing less than astonishing. The rat population vanished permanently. However, the guinea pig population increased exponentially, which gave us a different set of problems!

I suggested that Russell might like to have a guinea piggery beside his pig piggery. He wasn't convinced.

After following some fantastic back roads, some as straight as a gun barrel for over a kilometre at a time, we arrived at our destination, Wondai, having passed the four-hundred-kilometres-to-go mark. How to celebrate? It was Dave's idea – shoes! Soon, twenty, smelly, worn-out shoes and socks formed the number 400 on the footpath. Dave's feet looked like he'd had them in a tub of bleach – sock tan! I guess we'd had more sun than I realised, even with our sunscreen.

1600

And in the midst of the shoes, socks and smells it was confirmed – Carnsey was to have a visit from a certain young lady the following day. I wondered what she would think of the sock odour.

That evening we enjoyed another meal with Russell and Mandy – and Coffee.

I wandered around the piggery looking for Mr Carpet, but to no avail. However, I did enjoy the setting sun gilding the clouds like hot shimmering coals, the reassuring cawing of the ever-present crows and the jacarandas in full bloom. And the pig perfume.

Day 66
Reading on the hoof

Thursday 28 October

Caw, caw went the raucous crows overhead, paddling across the clear blue sky. *Crunch, crunch* went our feet, plodding along the red dirt track. And apart from that, there was silence. Except, that is, for the sound of Dave turning the pages of his book every now and then.

 None of the above had been part of our cruel Bruce experience, but now, on quieter roads, in spite of my constantly sore feet, life had taken on a more friendly face, even to the point of being able to read. Dave usually read silently but occasionally would read something aloud for my benefit.

'Listen to this,' he said laughing. 'John Wesley used to read going along too.' Dave was reading from *Spiritual Leadership* by J Oswald Sanders.

> *John Wesley had a passion for reading and he did so mostly on horseback. Often he rode fifty and sometimes ninety miles in a day. His habit was to ride with a volume of science or history or medicine, propped against the pommel of his saddle and thus he consumed thousands of books.*

Dave closed the book and laughed again. 'What do you think, bloke?'

What did I think? I thought I'd like to be on horseback myself to get the weight off my sore feet.

Dave was still carrying the book when we passed through the quaint little township of Wooroolin with the even quainter CWA hall, which looked like an overgrown doll's house.

'History's smallest CWA hall, with seating for three,' I laughed aloud. It would have been more than sufficient though for our Proserpine meeting where we'd only drawn a crowd of two.

Dave asked if I'd like him to read Scripture to me and proceeded to read through all of 1 Peter. It was no small feat for him to read aloud and walk at the same time but I thoroughly enjoyed it, laughing to myself at chapter 4 verse 12 – *Do not be surprised at the painful trial you are suffering, as though something strange were happening to you.* This seemed appropriate. Though Peter was obviously writing about more than painful feet it was a good reminder to me that hardship and pain are an integral part of the Christian experience and service.

On a *really* back road we came across a mystery plantation – an orchard of big, bushy trees. The leaves were narrow and elliptical in shape, and there seemed to be a type of fruit growing in small clusters. I'd never seen anything like them. Curiosity got the better of me and I jumped a fence to get a closer look, but having done so, was still none the wiser. We then found ourselves walking past huge paddocks full of tall, scraggly thistles – the most untidy section of The Walk to date. I reckoned someone should put a match to them.

From a small grove of trees on either side of the road emanated the music of multiple bird songs, including that of the whipbird – the long, high-pitched whistle followed by a sharp *snap* that resounds like the crack of a whip. Yes, the sound of whip cracking was heard in Australia long before the first bullock drivers took up residence. From the grove of trees the crack of the whip resonated a few more times and then our legs took us out of range. But the whipbird was stored as a sound file in my memory to be recalled at nostalgic moments when I would be far from my sunburnt country.

Carnsey, not terribly interested in my whipbird, was doing some bird watching of his own. The young lady in question was Natalie, who had driven from Brisbane to join us for the afternoon leg of our walk. More accurately, she'd come to join Carnsey. He seemed to be quite happy about it all, though I did wonder if we were crowding his space. However, we all politely stuck together like birds of a feather until we completed our kilometres for the day and were driven back to Kingaroy where we were allocated to different host families.

Natalie returned home to Brisbane, and like the three little pigs, each of us went off to his own house. I got a house of bricks that belonged to Steve and Jenny, my new hosts.

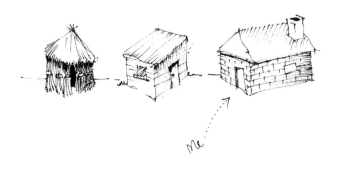

Day 67
A wonderful gift

Friday 29 October

Steve and Jenny presented me with a wonderful gift. It
didn't cost anything and wasn't gift-wrapped. I couldn't
eat it, touch it, share it or take it with me, but it was one
of the most wonderful gifts I had been given so far during
The Walk – *solitude*. Privacy! Space to myself. A whole day
of time alone. They walked out of the house before I was
awake, leaving me a fridge full of food, the Wi-Fi code and
a car. I thought all my Christmases had come at once.

Having hours on my own meant I could catch up on
important things such as hundreds of neglected emails
and an overdue blog entry. I was also able to indulge in
less important but infinitely more pleasurable activities
such as being horizontal and immobile – in bed and in
the bath. I spent hours in both. If the
activity of walking isn't conducive to
reflection, lying in a warm bath in a
quiet house certainly is.

During those reflective moments, the
first thing to surface like a slow bubble
was the conviction that I *had* to return
to Gleneden for the family reunion the following day. I am
part of this family and they are part of me. Under normal
circumstances, I would have been on the other side of the
world, a full twenty-two hour flight away, but there I was
just a two-hour drive down the road. Aunty Una's words
had probably been working away at me. I was glad. On
checking the family reunion program, I calculated that
to be there for the morning's activities I'd have to set my
alarm for 4.30 am. *Gulp*!

The second thing I realised, with a start, was that in less than a week I'd see Hélène and my boys again. My heart leapt. They'd be meeting me in Toowoomba. Realising I needed to look presentable for the occasion I took the car and went to get a haircut. The inexperienced young girl behind the scissors tried very hard to make interesting conversation and didn't pick up on any of the many cues I gave her that I really just preferred to sit in silence. It was, after all, my day of solitude.

And if Toowoomba was only one week away, that meant that Stanthorpe – and our finish line – was now only two weeks away. The adrenaline rush and panic hit again, and made my face flush and my heart beat fast. I couldn't fail now. So close, so close...

Steve and Jenny returned to find a much more rested and relaxed walker than the one they'd sent off to bed the night before. In conversation around the evening meal, I discovered that the mystery trees of the previous day were Duboisia, otherwise known as corkwood trees. Kingaroy is the corkwood capital of the entire world. These Australian natives produce a high concentration of alkaloids, which are used in several pharmaceutical products.

Thinking of how surprised Aunty Una would be to see me back in Gleneden, I crawled into bed – for the third time that day.

Day 68
Family reunion

Saturday 30 October

The alarm screamed pitilessly at the uncivilised hour of 4.30 am, at which point I seriously questioned my sanity in foregoing my day off for a family reunion. Then I remembered Aunty Una and tumbled *out* of bed and *into* Steve and Jenny's car.

Apart from a few kilometres around town in Mackay, that was the first time I'd been behind the wheel on the open road since the day I flew out of Brisbane with my knife-smuggling mother. I wasn't a stranger to vehicles travelling at high speeds, but for the previous sixty-seven days I'd been on the *outside* with my feet on the *ground*. It felt positively weird to be on the *inside* with my foot on the *accelerator*. It also felt weird to be backtracking over the same roads I'd just walked, passing all the familiar landmarks – the home where I overdosed on orange juice, history's smallest CWA hall, the long stretch without phone coverage, our piggery friends' home, the putrid road kill, the tree with the galahs and, of course, Ban Ban Springs. It was crazy to think that I had walked all this at five kilometres an hour and was now re-covering the ground at one hundred kilometres an hour. It was totally surreal, like watching a re-run in *rewind* mode. I kept thinking in disbelief, 'Have I really walked all this way?'

The day's activities of the reunion started with – a walk. Yes, there I was walking again! The irony was not lost on us and we all managed to see the funny side. A whole tribe descended on the appointed spot ready to walk where my great-granddaddy had walked exactly one hundred years earlier, retracing his steps over the ridge and into the glen beyond. It was quite moving to be a part of it all, to realise I was a part of all those people. I could sense the 'family belonging' in a tangible way as we walked and talked.

I was disappointed that Aunty Una wasn't surprised *at all* to see me. In her dry, slow voice she simply said, giving my hand a squeeze and squinting up at me, 'I knew you'd come.'

I loved her for saying that. Country folk don't use words unnecessarily. They've had to go sparingly to eke out a living off this land and they don't believe in wasting anything, words included.

Surprisingly though, Aunty Una's son, my cousin Trevor, must have missed out on that country DNA because he had enough words for everyone else put together. Even as a toddler he was an energetic and enterprising individual, and Aunty Una used to tie him to a post underneath the old homestead, to stop him from wandering. But Trevor was off his leash and was wandering everywhere to his heart's content, sporting a bright-red *look-at-me* T-shirt and a megaphone glued to his mouth, which is where the words were coming from. He was a cross between a roving minstrel, a court jester and a Master of Ceremonies. The megaphone crackled as he introduced the 200-strong gathering to his celebrity cousin, announcing that I was walking from Cairns to *Melbourne*! When he saw my face instantly contort in agony at the thought – as Melbourne was a further 2000 kilometres down the road – he realised his mistake and without missing a beat, added, 'But he doesn't know about the Melbourne bit yet!' Everybody laughed except me – I was still recovering from the shock.

As a result of Trevor's blunder, I realised just how much I was focussed on the finish line. With only a few hundred kilometres to go, I was counting down. If someone had moved the finish line even a short distance further away, I would have totally lost momentum and motivation and thrown in the proverbial towel. I also realised how difficult it would have been to plod on, day after day, without knowing *where* the finish line was, or even if there *was* one. I simply *could not* have done it. The pain and endurance were only possible knowing there *was* an end, and *where* it was. My whole life revolved around that famous finish line.

In honour of the little local school, which had long since closed, we sang *God Save the Queen*, which took me 'back to the past'. We also prayed the Lord's Prayer together, *Thy kingdom come, Thy will be done*, which took me 'back to the future'. After that we all feasted on hot damper and billy tea. Rohan brought out his bullocks again, to everyone's sheer delight – none more than mine – and the day came to an end.

I had to rush back to Kingaroy in time for our evening meeting. Zipping along at one hundred kilometres an hour, I amused myself by *again* recalling each of the landmarks, this time in *fast forward* mode.

Back at Steve and Jenny's, I finished the day with a delicious, steaming cup of coffee.

Bad move!

Day 69
Zombie

Sunday 31 October

Carnsey knocked at the door bright and early, took one look at me and said, 'Good morning, Zombie.'

He nailed it. Already suffering from long-term sleep deprivation, I had lain awake till 3 am while the recently ingested caffeine coursed recklessly through my veins, setting my system on artificial high alert. With my eyelids stubbornly jammed open, hours of precious sleep time had frustratingly ticked past. I was ready to give up even before putting on my walking boots. On the verge of tears, I set my feet on automatic pilot. For most of the day I wasn't exactly interesting company for my fellow walkers.

It was the last day of October – thirty-two years to the day since my father had died. Each year, this day marks the loss, not so much of what I did have, but of what I didn't. At sixteen there was so much more of a father still to be had. I continued to grieve that loss for the best part of two decades. Mum still grieves, but her pain has subsided to an occasional ache. 'Occasional ache' also pretty much described the state of my feet though they were gradually but steadily improving. The fear of having inflicted permanent damage appeared to have been unfounded since I was now walking with more confidence. Finish line, here I come!

Goodger General Store – tidy but long since closed down – was a sad reminder of what had obviously once been the hub of a great farming township. Peering in the window, with a bevy of parrots screeching in the gums overhead, Dave said, 'It'd be cool to live in a place like this.' I agreed.

Speaking of cool – it was. The heavens had provided total shade cover. Walking conditions could hardly have been better. My silent sighs were constant prayers of gratitude. In just another four days I'd be with my wife and boys. I was desperately hoping I'd be in better shape to meet them. I couldn't wait to present them with my roadside treasures. There was the Army Reserves camouflage hat for Flynn that Dave had kindly surrendered and the crocodile for Joseph. However my scavenging for Hélène had been fruitless, the only possibility being an old straw hat. Given my pathetic non-effort for our wedding anniversary, I didn't think the hat was likely to make amends. And then, like manna in the desert, the solution to my dilemma appeared before my very eyes. Flowers! Everlasting daisies! Bright golden buttons dotted the roadside at irregular intervals, and with the little energy I could muster, I was on the chase for the biggest and the best – a bouquet for my bride of more than two decades.

G'day bloke

Dave, bless him, was on the lookout for ways to brighten my obviously not-so-bright day. Aiming the video camera at me, he made a great show of being Mr Important Television Interviewer.

'What have you got there, Sav?'

'Everlasting daisies!'

'What are you picking everlasting daisies for, Sav?'

'For a young woman I'm going to see in a few days, Dave.'

'Why's that, Sav?'

'Well, you know what flowers do to a woman!'

'No, I don't actually. You'll have to tell me.'

'Well, I think I'll let you find out for yourself one day, Dave.'

'So, who's this young woman, Sav?'

'Oh, I don't want to tell the camera. I'm a bit camera-shy.'

'What's your wife going to say when we mention this young woman?'

'Well, I think she knows all about her.'

'Does she?'

'She does!'

'You've got a fairly open sort of relationship, is that what you're saying?'

'We do.'

'How does that work, Sav?'

'DAVE, STOP FILMING THIS! STOP IT!'

1700　As we ended the day, we reached the 1700 kilometre mark – only 300 to go! At the meal table with our hosts, Donald and Daisy, we twisted a napkin into the shape of a three and laid it beside two round plates to form the number 300. But I was too tired to get excited about the kilometre count. The meeting exhausted me further but before closing my eyes I decided to read a page or two of Bernard. I chuckled at his account of losing his hat and even more at his description of it – *délavé, informe, digne d'un musée.* We had more in common than I realised – even our hats were 'faded, shapeless, fit for a museum'. Having lost his, he was despairing. *Impossible de continuer sans lui. Mon bien le plus cher.* Really? His most treasured possession? I laughed aloud at his melodrama.

The proverb about laughing last and laughing loud didn't cross my mind.

It soon would.

Day 70
Bad hat day

Monday 1 November

Turning the calendar page, we said goodbye to October, as we had to September, and to August before that. No more pages to turn before reaching the finish line.

We also said goodbye to Donald and Daisy. Dave drove Carnsey and me the twenty-five kilometres to the previous finishing point, where the two of us would start our walk for the day. With all my *early rises*, I should be a degree candidate for *health, wealth and wisdom*. However, as I tumbled out of the Land Cruiser, trying not to dwell on the hours of lost sleep or my aching feet, I felt anything but healthy. Or, for that matter, wealthy. And as for wise? The fact I even began this Walk was proof that I was seriously lacking in that department too.

I went through the well-oiled routine of preparing backpack, water, sunscreen, boots, food, magic bean and – of course – my hat. Wait up! My hat? A careful search through all the pockets and compartments of my backpack and every nook and cranny in the car revealed nothing. By an uncanny coincidence, like my mentor before me, I too had lost my hat. Was it some kind of bad joke? Candid camera? For all its sad, faded, misshapen appearance, my hat and I had been inseparable for two whole months, weathering 1700 kilometres together. Now, without my trusty partner, I felt naked, exposed, foolish and incomplete.

Dave, ever the instant problem-solver, from somewhere among our mess of boxes and bags, extracted the old straw hat The Bruce had kindly yielded. He flung it across to me. I refrained from instantly flinging it back. This was *not* my hat and I did *not* want to wear an ugly, old, smelly, straw garden hat.

'Do you like my hat?' Doctor Seuss asked.

'No,' I replied in no uncertain terms, 'I do not like your hat!' while common sense whispered, 'Too bad, it's all you've got.'

1710   A couple of hours later, I was already tired and sore and still sporting the dreadful straw hat – and still pouting. Carnsey was pouting too, because once more I was leading us down a Gentle Annie with the exotic name Brooklands-Pimpimbudgee Road. No, he was not a happy chappy, convinced I had set us on another dead-end and that we'd end up backtracking before the end of the day. With every passing moment of the thirteen kilometres, I began to wonder if he was right. As there was no phone coverage, we had no lifelines and our only way out *would* be to backtrack. The road became increasingly narrow and at one point was impassable even for walkers. We had to detour through a paddock. Carnsey's restrained but well-timed grievances continued at regular intervals and really got up my nose.

Two geldings in a field ran along beside us for a few minutes enjoying the welcome distraction from their monotony. I couldn't help comparing the two of *them* with the two of *us* – the smaller bay fellow kept giving pathetic little nips at the hindquarters of his bigger chestnut buddy who, ears back, responded with equally half-hearted kicks.

1723   Thankfully, my predictions proved correct and there *was* no dead-end. As we stepped out onto the Kingaroy-Cooyar Road, our relief was tangible and my planned defence against Carnsey's anticipated told-you-so accusations proved unnecessary.

However, what could have been a magnificent three-hour country hike, in cool and pleasant walking conditions, had turned out to be pretty dismal. We'd traded the enjoyment of the journey for the worry of what-might-have-been.

But now, back on track, our mood lightened considerably. When just thirty minutes later the sign for Maidenwell came into view, we were positively jovial and, with no pre-arranged hosts, we began the adventure of finding our own lunch and our own beds for the night. Quiet little Maidenwell boasts both a café *and* a pub – but not much else. So with the prospect of both food and beds we were once more masters of our fate.

The café, surprisingly, turned out to be a tasteful little restaurant, almost Mediterranean style, run by owners of an olive plantation. A section of the shop was dedicated to a display of their products – oils, soaps, and even olive oil ice-cream. Olly, the waitress, was friendly and efficient and all up it was an unexpected little haven, all to ourselves, in the middle of nowhere. It would be an ideal lunch stop for a bus tour and I amused myself imagining it being overrun with a gaggle of happy little old ladies. As I wiped up the last of my soup with the bread roll, I was glad all those little old ladies hadn't descended upon us right at that moment.

But we struck a blank at the pub regarding beds, so we crossed the road back to the café to present our problem to our new friend, Olly. She exceeded expectations by producing the key to the CWA hall next door. When I turned the key in the lock and stepped inside this big echo-filled hall, I wondered how often the door was actually opened. Unless there were a lot of inhabitants out there invisible to the naked eye, probably not very often.

With time to kill, we decided to follow the enticing signpost the few kilometres to Coomba Falls. Walking

without a backpack *and* without my trusty hat felt strange, as indeed did walking without *having* to walk. Waterways of any kind have always enticed and beguiled me and Coomba did not disappoint – the sound of rushing water over rocks growing louder as we followed the trail leading down to the waterhole. Untold years of molten silver pouring tirelessly over rock had smoothed and shaped courses among the cubistic clusters. A single wild goat watched proudly from his vantage point on high.

That night, the pub served us up a mighty roast beef meal which we devoured while glued to the television. Having been deprived of the idiot box experience for such a long time, we succumbed instantly to its spell – watching *Home and Away.*

Note to self: we both seriously need help.

Olly's magic key opened the door again and we found ourselves back in our big, freezer room – in just two days we had climbed to an altitude of 520 metres, with a corresponding drop in temperature. With only bare floorboards, there was no warm corner anywhere. The decision was quick and unanimous – to bunk down in the newly renovated shower and toilet block. It was at least insulated with lino.

Tucked in our warm sleeping bags we talked about Olly, imagining what her real name might be.

OLIVIA ?   OLWYN   OLGA ?
    OLINDA ?   ?

Whatever it was, we both agreed that Olly was a jolly good fellow.

We also agreed to find out her real name before moving on next morning.

Day 71
Sheep country

Tuesday 2 November

For the first time in seventy-one days I woke up cold.
Also, for the first time, I threw on a singlet under my
royal-blue uniform – which reminded me I still hadn't
heard anything regarding the small-size, royal-blue shirts
I'd ordered for my boys. Only nine days till they'd be
walking those last kilometres with me, and I really had
my heart set on having matching shirts for them.

I returned the key to Olly and chased down a magic bean
with a hearty breakfast. Carnsey picked up the freshly
delivered *Toowoomba Chronicle* and came face-to-face
with ... *himself*! We considered drawing Olly's attention to
the first-rate article and large size photo of our fame and
glory but decided, instead, to let her be amazed when she
discovered it for herself later.

A voice called from the kitchen,
solving the mystery of her name.
She was destined to work there –
on an olive plantation, selling olive
products. We laughed.

However, a few minutes later, as we walked off down the
road, I wasn't laughing anymore – I was shivering. My
teeth were rattling and my bare arms were alive with
goose bumps. The road was in total shade and it would
be another hour before the first rays of sunshine would
begin to thaw me out. The sun I had dreaded so much
during the first part of The Walk had now become a
welcome friend.

The morning did eventually warm up and I ended
up needing my shocker of a straw hat for protection.

Thankfully we were – once more – away on backroads with no spectators. We even hit some dirt tracks – red earth underfoot, purple weeds on both sides and blue sky overhead. We were surprised to meet a car out there, though perhaps not as surprised as the occupants were to see us. The driver was plucked right out of Australian folklore – the Jolly Swagman himself with an impressive bushy beard that reached down to his steering wheel and a weather-beaten Akubra that covered – I guessed – a balding head. We struck up an easy conversation that turned naturally to The Walk and languages.

'There are nearly seven thousand languages spoken in the world,' we told him.

In typical, dry, country fashion, Mr Swagman turned his head (along with his beard) ever so slightly towards his passenger and drawled, poker-faced but with a jolly twinkle in his eye, 'How many of those languages do you speak, Joe?'

That summed up our roadside talk for the day. We could have done with a bit more stimulating conversation or action to break the monotony.

But where there's a will there's a way.

Carnsey decided to take advantage of a full bladder to stir up a red ants' nest. With military zeal he opened fire on the enemy camp, inciting an immediate and aggressive response. As the red army retaliated, waging a united and rapid attack in the direction of the feet of the artilleryman, the latter beat an equally hasty retreat, still emptying his last rounds of ammo. It occurred to me that if Carnsey had tripped over backwards at that point, it might well have been the funniest thing to happen on The Walk. Just the thought of it kept me quietly amused for hours.

Note to self: don't include this incident in my book.

Two of these sheep are identical ...

The only other thing to break the monotony of the day was the sheep. A paddock full of them! A hundred jolly jumbucks. I'm a bit partial to sheep – both in paddocks and on my plate – which reminded me that I still owed Hélène for her succulent anniversary lamb chops.

But the appearance of sheep held greater significance – these were the first I'd seen during The Walk as, for all that time, we'd been in cattle country. The sighting of sheep meant we were approaching home.

A few kilometres later we had further evidence, when we came upon our first $\qquad$ 1763
home road sign – a sight for sore feet – *Stanthorpe 227 km*[1].

I could now count the remaining days on my fingers – ten.

---

[1] The finishing line, however, was a further 10 km south of Stanthorpe - a total of 237 km still to walk.

Day 72
Yellow socks

Wednesday 3 November

The common brown snake is the second most venomous terrestrial snake in the world. Our hosts, James and Becky, along with their little kids, had found one in their garden just the day before we arrived. With the animal still lurking somewhere outside, I consulted Mr Google and learned more than I wanted to know.

> *The venom of the common brown snake causes diarrhoea, dizziness, collapse, convulsions, renal failure, paralysis, cardiac arrest and sometimes death.*

Oh, I see – only *sometimes* death. I *do* feel relieved.

> *Notorious for its speed and aggression, when highly agitated it holds its neck high, appearing in an upright S-shape.*

I looked outside, straining to see any upright S-shapes.

> *This species tends to initiate its defence with non-fatal blows.*

Most reasonable of him really! Quite the gentleman!

But we saw no sign of Sir Brown, donned our boots, and set off. Sometime later, however, we *did* see something else that shocked us – bright fluorescent yellow socks! Farmer Fluoro had stopped his ute and was walking back to say 'G'day' to us. I stared unbelievingly at his socks. Shockers! Did the man have no pride? Then recalling the unflattering hay-hat that I was wearing, I considered it wise to steer clear of the topic of fashion statements.

G'day bloke

Dave chimed in first. 'How y' goin'?'

Farmer Fluoro was going very well thank you very much. And he cheered us with some friendly banter.

He offered us some water – but it wasn't thirsty weather.

He offered us a lift – but that joke had long since worn thin and we laughed politely.

He asked who was looking after my wife and kids while I was tramping all over the state – but I took it as a rhetorical question and changed the subject.

He told us about a Frenchman who was rollerskating from Darwin to Melbourne (more than twice as far as we were walking) – but we just rolled our eyes.

And he told us he had a Bible in seventeen languages – but I didn't believe him.

It happened to be a Gideons' New Testament which included one verse – John 3:16 – in all those languages. I didn't confess to Farmer Fluoro that I'd been given one of those little New Testaments when I was in high school and hollowed out the pages to hide my smokes!

Farmer Fluoro's son had just returned from Paris and tried out his French on me and I was impressed with his great accent.

'Do you read your Bible in French?' I asked him. A shake of the head. Nope, he reads it in his mother tongue.

Before Farmer Fluoro took his leave, we couldn't resist paying him out for his dreadful socks after all. He didn't appear too traumatised by our unkind comments and we cheerily parted company.

Back on the road, Dave read to me from his current book, *Leading with Love* by Alexander Strauch:

> *People must work closely together ... at times this is difficult. The longer we work together, the more we get to know one another's faults and annoying personality traits, which can make life frustrating.*

By this time we could read each other's minds. I broke the silence by asking the obvious question. The thing Dave found most annoying about me? - that I kept changing the schedule when it should have been set in concrete. And me? - that Dave greeted me twenty times a day. No surprises there! We said no more and walked on.

I noticed that Dave had adopted a new walking posture several times a day, each time picking up speed to put some distance between us, one arm swinging and the other pressed against his ear. When he'd return to his normal two-arm swing, even as much as an hour later, there'd be a double bounce in his step and he'd be grinning like a silly Cheshire cat. Love was getting grander and grander for young Dave.

The phone call that caused me to join Dave in the cat-smile competition was the news that my hat had been found. I was elated. It had fallen down behind my bed at Donald and Daisy's in Nanango. They'd even driven out more than fifty kilometres trying to find us in order to return it but missed us as we'd vanished up one of our Gentle Annies. They promised to send it with someone coming our way since by then we were one hundred kilometres from Nanango – a little too far to make a special hat delivery.

It was amazing to think we were that far ahead of my hat! My courage surged with the thought of only 200 kilometres to go and I repeated over and over in my mind, like the little train in the children's story: I *think* I can, I *think* I can, I *think* I can!

1800 At the evening meeting in Crows Nest, overwhelmed by the statistics of the languages still without Bibles, one lady stood up and declared with conviction, 'Well, I don't think the Lord is coming back yet then.' Addressing the young people, I also shared with conviction, about investing our lives:

'Don't be afraid to invest your life in Bible translation. Go to people who don't have His Word in their language. It's not that they have rejected the Word. They simply haven't had a chance to hear it.'

It was the most impassioned plea of any during The Walk.

'There's nothing more rewarding than to give your life to help make God's Word available for an entire language group.'

Yet, even as I was talking, I realised that when I returned to France to take up the baton in my own translation project, I would once more feel discouraged. The idea of going back was a very real struggle. It had been such a long, hard road over seventeen years – sometimes too hard to bear. Just like walking 2000 kilometres.

But I knew the worst of the 2000 kilometres was over. I was on the last segment of my long walk home. I *was* going to make it. I was *determined* to make it – with the winning combination of *my* weakness and *His* strength. One step at a time.

While I was pushing on, encouraged, believing I'd make it, Bernard, on the other hand, wasn't sure. He was tempted to throw in the *sponge* (as we say in French), to give it all up – *tenté de tout laisser tomber*. Added to other extreme hardships, he had just fallen victim to a traumatising attack by bandits, good reason to entertain dark thoughts – *remuant de noires pensées.* He was downcast and angry – *entre abattement et colère*. I was distraught. We had been walking buddies for seventy-two days. It would be sad beyond belief not to make it to the end together. I was now only 200 kilometres from the finish line – just one tenth of my Walk to go. There were only thirty of Bernard's 300 pages to go – coincidentally, also just one tenth. Once again, we were neck and neck. I was tempted to flip ahead to see what would become of my buddy.

With great difficulty, I resisted.

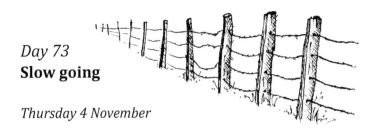

Day 73
Slow going

Thursday 4 November

The dawn shadows were still long and the air crisp when we found ourselves on the road. I watched a rosella parrot sitting on a fence post. When it suddenly disappeared into thin air, I set off to investigate. The post, as I discovered, was hollow.

'Is it possible the bird fell down there?' I peered down into the darkness. Dave's small torch illuminated the bird happily squished up, a metre down at the bottom of this narrow vertical tunnel. This was obviously Mrs Rosie's home where she was preparing for her late spring brood. How, I wondered, would the little ones ever make their way all the way up and out?

'Goodbye, Mrs Rosie,' I said. 'We've got thirty-seven kilometres to walk today.'

Later in the morning, as a result of a succession of interruptions, our average walking speed dropped from *five* kilometres an hour to less than *one*.

At 10 am a random newspaper reporter pulled up beside us, wanting to take photos and do an interview. He was disappointed to find only two of us, as Carnsey was off ahead in a quiet rest area doing a phone interview with ABC radio. After chatting for a while with Mr Reporter we suggested he come back half an hour later, and excused ourselves to get back to the business of walking.

We hadn't gone more than a few metres however, when Tracey from the previous night's audience arrived and pointed at her favourite coffee shop across the road. She was on a mission to 'bless us' which translated to 'fatten us up' and we were soon indulging in coffee and pies. A few minutes further along we had just caught up with Carnsey, in animated conversation with the ABC, when Mr Reporter returned. As soon as Carnsey finished his phone call, the three of us were subjected to another round of questions and photos. I was looking nervously at my watch when yet another car came to a stop beside Mr Reporter. It was my hat delivery. I nearly kissed the delivery man. If I'd been in France I *would* have!

I took one look at my hat and realised it had changed colour – it was a lighter grey. It dawned on me that Daisy had washed it. It also dawned on me that perhaps I should have thought of doing that myself from time to time. With the accumulated sweat of nearly two thousand kilometres washed away, no wonder it was a lighter colour.

BEFORE DAISY

AFTER DAISY

Finally back on the road, we were soon accosted by silver-haired Ruth, who'd just heard Carnsey's ABC interview and got the surprise of her life to actually see us on the road. We succumbed readily to her senior charms and lunch invitation and, within a few minutes, were tucking into a ploughman's pie and a hot chocolate.

In over two hours we'd walked no more than a few kilometres.

'These next days we're going to be hard pushed to keep up our kilometres,' Carnsey commented.

I agreed and added, patting my taut tummy, 'But we'll have no problem keeping up the kilojoules.'

Our afternoon was free of people interruptions, mainly because we diverted off the main road, got lost down a long dead-end road and ended up having to cut through private property in an attempt to get across to Goombungee Road – including a kilometre of bush bashing. Carnsey grumbled and I felt the dig.

'I reckon we stick to main roads. I don't like back roads. I like knowing where we're going.'

However, it was a bit late for that. Carnsey leapt the electric fence but I had no leap in me and stepped gingerly over it instead. Carnsey's mood took another turn for the worse when, some time later, we had to backtrack to retrieve his sunglasses that had fallen off in the leap. The increasingly long grass did nothing to brighten my mood. It wasn't actually the grass that bothered me, but the Joe Blakes that slither around in it, unseen. What's more, we knew this was the season they were particularly active.

At first the grass was only shin deep but it soon became thicker and full of thistle and milkweed. We pressed on and I found myself involuntarily lifting my knees higher with every step. Carnsey casually mentioned the brown snake that Becky had seen. I tried to ignore him, my knees jerking ever higher. Carnsey forged his way ahead through grass that was now waist-high, with me valiantly following in his slipstream, trying to convince myself that he was scaring *them* away but thinking it more likely he was just stirring them up. I imagined dozens of agitated S-shapes rising up out of the sea of grass. We lumbered on, crashing through stinging nettles, clambering over another fence, and stumbling our way through a patch of swamp and into more long grass.

'If Carnsey says another word, I'll ...!' and I imagined all manner of bodily harm I would inflict on him. Right on cue, knowing full well the effect it would have on me, he muttered nonchalantly, 'Lucky it's not snake season.'

In that instant my feet lifted off the ground, skimmed across the top of the grass and didn't touch down until we eventually approached two farmhouses.

yes, we did it to me again!

'Which farm do you prefer to trespass on?' Carnsey asked, enjoying his little game and getting me back for the countless wrong turns and dead ends I had inflicted on him. 'Do you prefer the one with the angry farmer wielding a shotgun or the one with the Doberman?'

We met neither man nor dog, however, and were glad to climb through the last fence to find ourselves on none other than Goombungee Road. We'd made it.

With every passing hour we were nearer home. Our evening meeting in Highfields attested to this, as it was alive with familiar faces. None of them, however, were as familiar or beautiful as those of the two small boys pressed against the back window, peering in at me – Hélène and the boys had arrived just as the meeting was ending. I left Dave and Carnsey to pack up while I escaped with my family to a little hide-away cottage where we'd be enjoying a couple of nights together.

Snuggling into bed, Hélène said, 'I guess you're not used to having someone else in bed with you!' I asked if she was testing me. We laughed.

No, I wasn't used to it. But I had no problem slipping back into old habits.

Day 74
TV news

Friday 5 November

I slept like the proverbial fallen tree trunk. Whatever Hélène had put in my drink knocked me out like a light.

The boys woke early and jumped into bed with us – gift time. Joseph loved his crocodile, which Hélène promptly intercepted to ensure it was sanitised before he had a chance to become too cuddly with it. Flynn loved his camouflage hat which, as it turned out, perfectly matched his favourite camouflage trousers. The hat too would go through a thorough disinfectant process. Hélène's gift was a little less of a hit. She thanked me politely and arranged her everlasting daisies in a vase.

 After breakfast, I rushed off with Dave and Carnsey to officially walk into Toowoomba where we received a rousing welcome from the Centenary Heights students and were expected for a TV interview for WIN News. Chris Logan's attire stood out in stark contrast to mine, particularly his spiffy red tie alongside my sad and saggy hat. He asked a lot of questions about the minority languages of the world in the context of globalisation. This touched a chord with me and I quickly gathered my thoughts to condense a hot topic into a few sentences:

> 'As the world races towards globalisation, languages play a big part. Only a few languages are achieving global currency at the expense of thousands of minority languages which are falling by the wayside. We might think that's normal, but that's because we come from the privileged position of a strong-currency language, English.

But for the people who speak the thousands of minority languages in our world, it's not normal at all. Their cultures, traditions and lives are being trampled on, violated and oppressed in the name of globalisation – for those people it's a disaster. We should wake up and be concerned about them.'

Chris asked if Bible translation was one way we could show concern for these minority languages and whether it had any practical effect on a minority language group. I quickly mentioned the story of *Hidden People*. In 1960, the Binumarien people of Papua New Guinea had decreased in number to only 111 and were dying out. Their despair at being so few and so vulnerable was such that the women didn't want to bring any more children into the world, resorting to primitive and dangerous practices to abort their unborn babies. A Queensland couple, Des and Jenny Oatridge, went and lived with the Binumarien people for forty years. They learned their complicated language and translated God's Holy Word. Little by little the truths of God's love for the Binumariens sank deep into their hearts, transforming the community from within. Today the Binumarien people number 500 and are taking their place, heads held high, in the ever-changing and kaleidoscopic fabric of the Papua New Guinean society.

Then it was back with my wife and boys. Hélène had a surprise for me – a packet. The shirts! The mini royal-blue Wiggles shirts for my boys had arrived. They excitedly slipped them on – perfect fit! I swelled with pride to be standing there in The Walk uniform with my little men.

Flynn said, with an ear-to-ear smile fit to burst his eleven-year-old face, 'Little Sav.' And I swelled a tad more.

We must have sold over 100 of these books at our different meetings. It was our "bestseller".

A great read!

Joseph took my hand and, looking up with melancholic eyes, said quietly, 'Now I'm looking forward more than ever to walking with you on the last day, Dad.'

If my chest had swollen any more, it would have exploded right out of my royal-blue shirt.

After a lovely afternoon with my family, I put my feet up and sat back with the *Toowoomba Chronicle* to read and relax. Suddenly my antennae went up – there had been a snake attack in Nobby. We would be walking right through that little township in just two days' time.

> *A sixty-one year old woman has died after being bitten multiple times by a brown snake at her property, on Mount Sibley Road, near Nobby.*

I mused that not all brown snakes were gentlemen after all. I closed the newspaper slowly and put it down.

Flynn and Joseph waited eagerly to see their Dad on the WIN News and we sat and watched through all the important items until smiling Samantha Heathwood finally introduced *An epic journey of biblical proportions.* That was us! My hat looked sadder than ever on TV and Chris's tie looked redder than ever. They did a sterling report.

However, I had talked, lived and breathed this Walk for so long that I failed to be impressed by *us* – and *an epic journey* seemed somewhat overstated.

Day 75
Relay race

Saturday 6 November

It was *relay race* day. Five groups of friends
brought their water bottles and joined   1837
us on the road in what turned out to be,
coincidentally, a one-after-the-other series.

First in the line-up was a retired couple who, despite
their sixty years, set a cracking pace. I'd have liked to see
them keep that up for 2000 kilometres but somehow,
looking at them striding it out, I thought they just might
have been up to it.

Several hours later they passed the baton to
none other than Mrs Royal herself. Hélène   1853
is a keen walker from way back. She might
well have been up to walking 2000 kilometres, though
I doubt she would have lasted the distance on The Bruce,
being more of a Gentle Annie walker. But then again,
who isn't? This morning was Gentle Annie territory as
we walked past some beautiful countryside, trees and
shrubs, including a gorgeous magenta bougainvillea in
full and impressive bloom. We marvelled at its long,
        arching, flower-laden branches that
                were filling the sky.

We walked past something else filling the sky and it too caused us to marvel. Those dark green road signs look deceptively small when you drive past at a hundred kilometres an hour but when you walk up to them they are huge. Dave stood on tiptoe and almost managed to reach the white lettering – *Stanthorpe 126 km*[1]. That was our *third* Stanthorpe sign and for the *third* time I felt a choke of emotion. Was it pride of achievement? Was it long-term exhaustion? Was it thankfulness to God? Probably all of the above and more.

1864

Hélène was still with us when Carnsey's sister and family arrived waving their offering of no less than nine massive bananas. Did I have a sign on me that read *Feed the monkey bananas*? They walked with us until other friends appeared, also bearing gifts of carbohydrates. A second paddock of sheep appeared on the scene too, but they didn't walk with us. They just raised their curious, woolly heads – a silent cheer squad watching us plod by.

Next came some folk who had travelled 350 kilometres from Roma with their two small children, keen to join us. By that time, however, the Gentle Annies had run out and we were back on a highway – the New England Highway. After only one hundred metres they decided that trucks were encounters of the 'too-close' kind, so they bundled their little brood back into the car and headed off.

As I counted down the last kilometres for the day, I was startled by the raucous screeching of a flock of magnificent sulphur-crested cockatoos, feeding in a paddock in the cool of the late afternoon, heads bobbing

---

[1] Plus the additional 10 km south of Stanthorpe to get to the finishing line.

up and down as they kept a watchful eye out for danger. They were large, healthy specimens with shiny, white plumage. Just before leaving France I had seen a single cockatoo in a cage in a pet shop, its feathers dull and unkempt, eyes sad, head low, crest limp – it reminded me of how I sometimes feel living in my adopted land.

What a contrast between that bird and the wild ones, free and alive. They took noisily to the wing in a burst and flurry of white. In a strange way I felt I could identify with them. In spite of the pain and the hardship of those eleven weeks on the road, I *was* free and on the wing, an Aussie in Australia, not *flying* free but *walking* free. True, many times I had felt trapped in The 2000 Walk, but surely we are all trapped in something. Maybe the secret is not to be free of what is trapping us as much as to find freedom *inside* the cage. These thoughts cushioned my steps during the last kilometre of the day.

Middle Ridge Uniting Church was bustling with activity – our biggest meeting of the whole Walk with, once again, dozens of familiar faces looking expectantly at us, among them our three *ladies*. My lady was there with Flynn and Joseph. Dave's lady made a special guest appearance all the way from Sydney. Yes, Veronica really existed and her vivacious personality and Asian eyes were already charming people, not the least of whom was, of course, Dave himself. I'm not sure he'll remember anything or anyone else from the evening, but I'm sure he will remember every word, blink, smile and chuckle that emanated from the persona of Veronica.

1874

In contrast, Carnsey's lady had alighted quietly. Settled in a back seat, Natalie was not looking so comfortable. Officially they were *off* but unofficially there was something to suggest they were at least a little bit *on*.
I guessed there was a potential relationship still waiting to happen there, but this crazy Walk hadn't really been the right potting mix for their seedling to take root, let alone blossom.

And then there was the brown paper packet.

'Hey, someone sent this for you three guys,' the man said, thrusting it at me. The packet wasn't ticking so I guessed it was safe to open.

Three pairs of dazzlingly bright, yellow fluorescent socks.

Day 76
Multi-generational

Sunday 7 November

I could now count the remaining Walk days on just *one* hand.

The wind picked up during the morning, almost blowing us along into the small farming community of Nobby and past the sign announcing Mount Sibley Road. Somewhere up that road was where Mr Brown had delivered his fatal blows. My guess, given the wind conditions, was that he was lying low for the day. I would have liked to be doing the same.

Two cars pulled over beside us in the space of a few minutes. Out of the first stepped an older sparky lady who, holding her hat down, announced we'd be staying at her place, where she lived together with her son and daughter-in-law.

'Who's the one with a bad back?' she asked, an instant ball of business. I confessed. 'Well, I have a nice firm mattress on the floor for you,' she announced to my delight. 'And a spare double bed. Pete and Jacinta have a spare queen-size bed too.' We looked at each other, silently wondering just how big this house was. It sounded more like a hotel.

The next person to come by offered us a lift. He had seen us walking, driven past and turned back.

'We're actually walking home,' I called out over the noise of the engine and wail of the wind, 'all the way to Stanthorpe.'

His startled reaction was evidence he obviously knew that was more than one hundred kilometres down the road.

'Fair dinkum!' he exclaimed. Having set him up, I smiled to myself, because now I could recount the rest of the story. 'We've actually walked all the way from Cairns.' The look was unforgettably priceless. As he drove off, Dave said in a dry voice and with a poker face, 'He doesn't watch WIN News, does he?' I laughed.

1900 Mid-afternoon the support vehicle tracked us down as we were tramping along an awesome Gentle Annie. By our calculations, and without having planned it, we were at *exactly* 1900 kilometres. I was euphoric. If there had been any lingering doubt that I would make it to the end, it had all but dissipated. My feet were giving me no more grief and these higher altitudes were providing cool walking days. The conditions were right and the finish line was in sight.

How to commemorate this countdown milestone? Sawn-off slabs of wood lying around the base of a windmill would serve my creative idea. Dave carted them back to the Land Cruiser while I just watched – my bad back being my excuse. We jacked the Land Cruiser up onto the blocks, removed three of the wheels and lined them up side by side. Two wheels made two giant zeroes and the third, end-on, formed the number one. That made: 100.

Such impressive effort required photographic evidence. Just then a car came by, which, to our surprise, was driven by the local policeman.

'It's a wonder someone didn't give me a ring to let me know something odd was happening out here,' he remarked.

I'm not sure what sort of delusion Mr Young Policeman was living under regarding the *megatropolis* status of rural Clifton, but I hadn't recalled seeing any other human being in the previous few hours. There was no-one around to be seeing anything or phoning anyone. To confirm my thoughts, I overheard a conversation between the two ladies in the car.

First lady: 'They'd have been waiting there a long time. Not many cars come along this way.'

The second lady, eyeing our wheel-less vehicle in bewilderment, mumbled a question that I didn't quite catch.

The first lady replied with a tone of disdain, 'Oh *I* don't know! Because they're *boys* I suppose!'

I refrained from making the correction: *lovely young boys*!

With Mr Young Policeman gone, we replaced the wheels and returned the blocks before finally checking into our 'hotel' for the night. I let out a slow whistle. Wow! Pastor Pete and his wife own a new, modern brick mansion where they live with their two small children and Pastor Pete's Mum. There are nine bedrooms, ten outside doors, four kitchens, four toilets, four bathrooms and five living rooms – seriously. It is known as a 'multi-generational residence', and feels more like a small village under one roof than a house. The immediate advantage for me was that I had my own bathroom.

Peeling off sweaty clothes at the end of the day was always a pleasurable experience, even prior to getting wet and clean. I particularly enjoyed removing my bright yellow fluorescent socks. Yes, I'd given in. I'd reckoned if a good sort of a bloke like Farmer Fluoro could wear them, they couldn't be all bad. So, in his honour, I wore

...and a partridge in a pear tree.

them – for just one day and on dead-quiet back roads where no-one would see me.

Lying blissfully submerged in *my* bathtub, I must have looked like an old hippo with only the eyes and nose breaking the surface of the water. In that happy position I mulled over the multi-generational residence. What a brilliant idea. A large extended family could live together under this roof, each nuclear unit independent, but still connected. In our Western world where our family units are *dis*integrating rather than *in*tegrating, this was an attractive concept.

The term 'multi-generational' is also applied in a different way to some Bible translation projects, particularly in countries difficult to access. These projects may take many decades and may require a *relay* strategy over two or even three generations. The vision and perseverance needed in these multi-generational situations are incredible. However, we have the promise in the book of Revelation that God will raise up the right people for even these difficult tasks because He is in the business of drawing people to Himself *from every nation, tribe, people and language* (Revelation 7:9). And how can they be drawn to God if they can't hear His message in a language they understand? Translating the Bible is not the idea of any individual or organisation; it is at the very heart of what God is doing in this world.

Our host, Pastor Pete, runs the little AOG church in Clifton, and did a great job inviting people from several different denominations, including Anglicans and Lutherans, to our meeting. Our dear Blackbird, sprightly senior citizen that she is, was there too, returning to her old stomping ground to encourage us and bring some of her old friends to hear us. Taking me by the hand she solemnly made a morning tea appointment, en route, for the next day.

Our presentation was in the small CWA hall, jam-packed and literally humming with the warmth and pleasure of God's people gathered together, young and old alike. The plastic chairs and blinking lights gave an informal feel, belying the rousing worship music planned for us. When Pastor Pete put on canned music, I wondered, in all honesty, where it was going. However, when he brought to life his twelve-string guitar to accompany the CD and led us in simple worship, I was deeply moved.

Skilfully keeping in time with the canned music, Pastor Pete took it up a key and we followed, raising the volume at the same time.

Bible translation is not an end in itself but rather, as the song says, it's about the Saviour's love. Jesus, the sinless one sent by God to die in place of a sinful world. He lived the life I couldn't live and died the death that I deserved. *That* is what we want to translate, into each of the remaining languages across the face of the planet. Pastor Pete continued to strum, while, as one, we raised our voices even higher.

> *Oh how marvellous, oh how wonderful, is my Saviour's love for me.*

With just a sliver of a new moon, the night was dark when we arrived back at our multi-generational residence. And that was when I found out that Pastor Pete's wife was hoping to build an extension to the house so the kids could have their own special *toy* room.

Way to go, kids!

Day 77
Map of Australia

Monday 8 November

My addiction to back roads struck again. We ventured away from the mapped roads but, after less than an hour, we were lost and I was in Carnsey's bad books – again!

The only feasible way ahead seemed to be the railway line. I was definitely not keen, having learned that following the railway meant either crunching along on uneven rocks or picking our way along unevenly spaced sleepers. Either way it made for laborious walking. What's more, Blackbird and her promised morning tea would never find us if we were on the railway line. She'd be driving around in vain looking for us on all the back roads and getting in a flap.

Carnsey had *had* enough. He wasn't about to follow my lead anymore and spat the dummy. Without a word, he lunged across the grassy paddock and made for the train line, leaving me no choice but to follow in his wake. I made a half-hearted lunge, trailing somewhat timorously behind, hoping he was scaring away any ankle biters as he blundered along. The train line proved laborious – as anticipated – and I was relieved to emerge, a couple of hours later, at some semblance of civilisation where I could put my feet back on terra firma.

The trouble was that Blackbird had no idea where we were and, to make it worse, *we* had no idea where we were either. Carnsey cast me a sideways glance as if to say, 'What now, wise guy?'

'We'll ask someone,' I said feebly, knowing full well that nobody would be able to connect us with our meals-on-wheels lady. At this point, however, out of nowhere a little grey car appeared and, with no better options, I unenthusiastically waved the driver down. My mouth was open, question ready formed on my lips, when I found myself looking into the beaming face and bright eyes of none other than Blackbird herself.

She issued a military summons, 'Follow me,' and flew off ahead down the dirt road in search of a suitable spot to spread out the spoils from her picnic basket. We followed expectantly, just as an ominous, black, shiny shadow rippled across the road ahead of us, slipped into the grass and disappeared. It was a big one!

Blackbird didn't do things by halves. We sat on the grass verge gorging ourselves on lamingtons, fruit cake and chocolate cake, washing it all down with mango nectar and apple juice. Even then we hardly made a dent in her ample reserve which could have fed an entire bus load of tourists. However this was a quiet road and not a single vehicle interrupted our feast. Neither, thankfully, did any rippling shadows.

Blackbird trundled off, satisfied with having accomplished her mission of overdosing us with carbohydrates. Now it was up to us to burn them off. With five hours of walking still ahead, that was easy.

Warwick came into view, signalling the end of our walk for the day and it was now less than an hour down the road to Stanthorpe - an hour, that is, if you're driving.

While we were still a kilometre out of town, a local friend, Greg, stopped to say 'G'day'. He knew nothing about this crazy Walk and had wondered why on earth I was walking out there. It had been encouraging to see several familiar *faces*, like Greg's, during recent days, but Warwick was my first totally familiar *place*. It already felt like home territory.

I know, they look more like haystacks :(

Familiar and fond memories buoyed me along. There was the cheese factory where, as a child, I'd come regularly with Mum to buy cheap offcuts. And Victoria Street, my favourite short cut to bypass the town centre, which I had driven up hundreds of times. I crossed the bridge over the Condamine River below Tullock Park, named after my uncle and aunt who used to live right beside it and were flooded out every time the river rose.

And just like that rising river, with every step I took, something inexplicable was rising within me – a swell of emotion without a name. Sometimes it ran like a mild electric current, thrilling me and sending shivers down my spine. Sometimes it tightened like a gentle cramp in my chest, squeezing my lungs and contracting my throat muscles.

Everything was familiar, everything was easy, everything was known, everything was mine and everything was home. The sign said *Stanthorpe 58 km*. Behind my sunglasses, salty streams flowed unchecked to drip off the corners of my mouth. The reality 1932 of what I had achieved flooded over me, overwhelmed me and engulfed me. At this point, I was home. Though we still had three more days of walking, the kilometre count was so low that mentally I'd already made it - only another fifty-eight kilometres plus the additional ten to the southern side of Stanthorpe to the finish line on Ma and Pa's farm.

Carnsey didn't speak. I had no idea what he was thinking or feeling, if anything, but I didn't want him to talk. I wanted to savour this bittersweet moment alone. My moment of victory. My achievement. My pain. My perseverance. And I wanted it all to myself. I savoured it as we made for our night's lodging in the caravan park.

We rang the bell and waited for someone to appear. I hung back, leaving Carnsey to do the talking while I ran my eyes meaninglessly over the numerous brochures and up to the map on the wall. A map of Australia. A very big map.

I stepped closer and leaned into the first map of my land I'd seen since before I began The Walk. It drew me in until I fell under its spell, disappearing into the list of now familiar names beginning with Cairns in the north, and following the black scar of The Bruce halfway down the east coast. At that moment, I was unaware of where I was, oblivious to anyone or anything around me.

Frozen in time, I held my breath, whispering to myself, 'I've done it.'

Day 78
Calm before the storm

Tuesday 9 November

Waking up in a cabin in a quiet corner of a caravan park was bliss. I was exhausted, physically and emotionally, both from the many hours walking and the innumerable intense people-hours. I was desperately in need of rest and my dream was to crawl into a hole and not see anyone or do anything for days on end. The caravan park was a tiny foretaste of that dream, a little like the calm before the storm.

After a lazy breakfast, we headed off – it was to be the last time we would walk without company. The next morning, we'd be joined by a dozen mates, and then on the following and final day, many others would swell the ranks for the last ten kilometres and cross the finish line with us – including my two boys in royal-blue. Awesome! But for the moment, I was enjoying the calm, trying not to dwell on the storm.

The calm, however, was short lived.

A car pulled up and out tumbled an enthusiastic chap – Carnsey had invited a friend and therewith went our quiet morning. In the afternoon, another car pulled up – Carnsey had invited a couple of other mates from Brisbane and therewith went our quiet afternoon. My energy levels were depleted and I had nothing to give, no interesting conversation, nothing. I walked in silence, leaving Carnsey, once again, to do the talking.

I loved the walk, though. The back road between Warwick and Dalveen was unbelievably beautiful, winding through Aussie bush and past paddocks dotted with spring-white lambs. Over a century ago, my Grandma travelled down this same road. She used to recount the story of how, as a thirteen-year-old, her father took her to Warwick in his horse-drawn sulky, for dental treatment. Given the condition of her teeth, and to avoid the possibility of having to return for further treatment, the decision was made to simply extract them all – good and bad – in one sitting. She then had to travel back in abject agony over that very road – at that time nothing more than an unpaved series of ruts – which jolted and jarred the sulky and intensified the pain. Too young to be fitted with dentures, she spent her teenage years toothless. I was walking on my Grandma's road and thinking of her, the woman who gave birth to the woman who gave birth to me. And there was a deep connection there with the country that gave us all birth.

1950

As the day drew to a close, Carnsey, Dave and I took a photo of the three of us side by side, pulling grotesque faces. It went on our blog with the title *Unscathed* and the comment: *Some would say that something as gruelling and crazy as walking 2000 km would have long-lasting traumatic effects on our general sanity. However with only 50 km left to go, we are happy to inform you that we have come through totally unscathed.* It was intended to be funny but as I look at that photo now, my face actually appears close to how I really felt.

Me   Dave   Carnsey

What did make me laugh, however, was the huge number
of overseas friends who had to look up the meaning of
the word *unscathed*.

I wasn't at all sure that I *was* coming through unscathed
though – I was feeling rather more *scathed*. Our evening
meeting was in the Baptist church, where folk had been
eagerly following The Walk, evidenced by the print-outs
from our blog that papered the walls.

I wondered whether they'd print out our grotesque faces
and pin them up too.

Some of the familiar faces in the meeting were not from
Warwick, however. Some had travelled a long way to join
us. Mr Mediterranean had flown from Townsville. Two
other chaps had flown up from Melbourne. Mark had
driven from the Sunshine Coast and nearly picked up a
hitchhiker – of the large bovine variety. Neither came
off unscathed from the one-hundred-kilometre-an-hour
encounter, but Mark was intact and, like the other guys,
was chomping at the bit to walk the last stretch.

Dave, Carnsey and I, on the other hand, were all feeling
sluggish with the end drawing nigh. I'd lost count of the
number of meetings and our reserves were low.

Day 79
Men on the road

Wednesday 10 November

Our hostess sent us off after a hearty breakfast, backpacks stocked with individualised lunches, including – would you believe it? – bananas. I checked behind my back once more for a sign.

Most of the guys had already arrived for our appointed *rendezvous* – as we say in English – amid a warm atmosphere of camaraderie and laughter. Those who had joined us were looking forward to the challenge of some serious walking. Dave, Carnsey and I, on the contrary, were looking forward to the end of almost three months of it. Hence all were in good spirits, albeit for different reasons.

Dave's Dad was the last to turn up, wearing a shocking straw hat that had definitely seen better days. Russell was with us when we crossed the 1000 kilometre mark, and would now be with us when we clocked up 2000 kilometres. We ribbed him that he had to keep walking now to the 3000 kilometre mark but his was the last laugh when he challenged the three of us to go for a victory lap!

Carnsey scratched around in the support vehicle to finally unearth the sunscreen, still in near mint condition. How fortunate we had been to walk in cool, overcast conditions almost the entire way. We scrutinised the sky, a combination of clear blue and clouds, and concluded that it would be either cool or stinking hot.

Still bouncing, Dave declared loudly, 'Whatever happens, it will be a *brilliant* day.' That's our Dave!

325

The senior citizen of the newcomers offered to drive the support vehicle, making a great show of being extremely disappointed at having to drive instead of walk. Another round of laughter, because we all knew he was lying through his false teeth.

'And what about you, Sav?'

I thought for a second and replied, 'I've had enough. I think I'll keep the driver company in the Land Cruiser for these last two days.' More peals of laughter because everyone knew I was lying through my proverbials too. After walking 1950 kilometres, feral horses couldn't keep me from completing the final fifty. Rain, hail or shine, I would be crossing that finish line, if necessary crawling with my face in the dirt.

I quoted the Taruuba proverb: *When you kill a snake, make sure you cut its head off.* All eyes looked my way waiting for an explanation. 'That means, when you do a job, don't leave it unfinished but go all the way to the bitter end.' Our driver departed, leaving us to get on with the business of cutting off the snake's head.

And as coincidence would have it, only a few minutes later Dave called out, 'Hey, it looks like there's a dead snake over here.' And sure enough, there it was, as if conjured up by some proverbial magic.

We gathered around the drain that cut under the road to collectively observe the *dead* snake. However, the red-belly black, too shiny and plump to be anything but alive, slipped effortlessly into the drain with a flick of its tail. The two youngsters of the band, Dave and Mr Mediterranean, took delight in flinging rocks at it in an attempt to flush it out while I hurriedly set up the camera ready to film as it exited the other side. It occurred to me that Black Beauty was likely not to be in the best of moods having been showered with stones, and that I was right in his line of escape. A yell exploded in my eardrums at the same time as the beast emerged, flinging itself at me like a wild thing. Stumbling, I fell heavily to the ground. It was on me, fangs piercing my neck while I screamed and thrashed my arms, desperately trying to rid myself of the evil, writhing body.

Actually, the yell was Carnsey's very bad joke, the rest, roughly what my brain conjured up in the nanosecond that followed. My heart took a few minutes to resume its normal rate. The snake never did emerge and we left it in its seclusion and continued on our merry way.

Contrary to my expectations, it was great being a larger group. The freshness of the new blood was exhilarating, coursing like a stimulant through my veins, drawing out frivolity and cheeriness I wouldn't have imagined possible. I smiled more than I had in weeks and the sound of my own frequent laughter, in contrast to the dreariness that had set in during the previous few weeks, surprised me time and time again. It took an injection of outside newness to help me see how dull we had become. Carnsey had already acknowledged it, using the word *boring* more than once, but in survival mode, I hadn't been aware of it. I was now intoxicated with the light-hearted banter and easy talk, inviting me to return to a world of fun and playfulness. I was beginning to surface from a long hibernation. Having our mates join us for these last two days was the best decision we'd made.

Five magnificent horses thundered up to the fence as we passed and, as one, turned and galloped off, flinging their tails in the air. Twice more they circled, repeating their choreographed performance. The last horses Carnsey and I had encountered were biting and kicking each other. The contrast with these five was striking, and the comparison was not lost on me.

At midday we sat in the shade of an old bridge and opened our Styrofoam lunch boxes. Between mouthfuls of salad roll and banana, the friendly repartee continued and the remainder of the walk passed quickly. The day had stayed cool. Dave was right. It *was* brilliant.

1972 Now just one day – twenty-eight kilometres – from the finish line, the three of us talked into the video camera to record our impressions for our blog. We came up with the expected and unavoidable clichés:

Then we were speechless at Carnsey's words, which were anything *but* expected:

> 'I often tell the story of perseverance. One step mightn't seem like it's really significant, but if you continue to do that for seven hours you've done more than thirty kilometres.'

So far so good, but then he lost the plot:

> 'And if you do it for eighty days, like we've just done, you get up to 960 kilometres.'

He quickly corrected himself:

> 'No, I mean 972 kilometres.'

Dave and I were dumbstruck. For months we had been talking, calculating, measuring and even arguing about kilometres and the number 2000 had been the focus of absolutely *everything* we'd been doing. And Carnsey had got the count wrong – out by a full 1000 kilometres. He saw the look on our faces, realised his mammoth mistake, laughed with embarrassment and dug his hole even deeper:

'I mean 200 kilometres.'

Out this time by 1800! We paid him out big time and took great delight in knowing that this was one story that would *never* die.

Our blog for the day got the title: *Confused Carnsey – problem with numbers.* The video was a winner - one of our most popular.

The dirt road up to our hosts' property was lined with balloons, and a banner was suspended between two gum trees: *Welcome 2000 Walkers.*

Our hosts, Don and Gloria, opened wide their home to us with those three magic words: shower, food and bed. This was no mean feat because by then our group of seven had almost doubled in number, including Carnsey's dad and brother. The all-men's affair was one of easy chat, buffoonery and loud laughter.

Mr Mediterranean and I were kept busy turning a massive pile of onions and row upon row of neatly aligned sausages while Mark gave a running commentary on our efforts.

'You can tell who the Alpha male is,' he announced, with a drawl and exaggerated importance. 'He's the one holding the biggest tongs!' Mr Mediterranean and I responded with theatrical flourish, brandishing and comparing our tongs. While mine were of the short kitchen variety, Mr Med was wielding the exaggeratedly long barbecue type so he took away the coveted title of Alpha male.

After we'd polished off the snags, we picked our way through the dark to an empty field where a heap of logs, stacked in the traditional teepee style, awaited a match. The flames soon shot a million firefly sparks into the night. Chairs were moved away from the heat and then, two hours later, nearer again as the wood was consumed and the flames licked low. The crackle of the fire and chirping of night insects became the backdrop to discussions about football, the Melbourne Cup and dozens of stories and questions about our experiences on the road.

Carnsey's Pa asked if I found it hard to believe that I was nearly to the end.

'Funnily enough, I don't really feel as excited as I thought I would. It's been so long now that I'm sort of used to it. Tomorrow will probably feel like just another day.'

Carnsey's brother nailed it. 'It's become just like a day job now.'

The laughter of Aussie blokes around a barbecue or campfire is a unique earthy music, rising and falling in bursts and waves, so different to the way the French do it. I felt embraced by the music, the fire, the stories, my country and my people, and I like to think that during those hours I recovered a smidgen more of my lost Australian-ness.

Our bedroom was a shed strewn haphazardly with a carpet of mattresses. Long after lights were out and intermittent snores passed like secret signals from one end to the other, I lay wide awake. But this time it was unrelated to caffeine. I felt neither excited nor stressed but somewhat emotion-less really. Perhaps I was simply over-tired.

The last time I checked my watch, before sleep finally overtook me, it was 4 am.

Day 80
The finish line

Thursday 11 November

The last day! After only two hours of sleep, I was running on empty. But quite frankly, I didn't care how little I had slept or how much I would be walking because, from that day on, I would be sleeping a whole lot more and walking a whole lot less.

Ready for those final twenty-eight kilometres, our little band of merry men had increased to fifteen, the youngest being an eleven-year-old lad sporting a brand-new, royal-blue shirt identical to my own. As Flynn strode off beside me, I didn't know which of us was prouder.

Two hours later, Flynn was still striding strong and talking non-stop with anyone who would listen as we arrived in the small township of Thulimbah, where first my mother, then I, had grown up. It was my home town. Every step transported me back in time. I pointed to a very old house and whispered to Flynn in French, 'That's the house where Grandma grew up.'

Ahead of us a good friend, Autumn, ran down her long driveway, waving her arms and cheering. She is so bright and full of life that I've always thought she should be called Spring.

'Hello lovelies,' she crooned, planting kisses on the cheeks of anyone in sight.

I whispered again to Flynn, indicating an old CWA hall, badly in need of a paint job, 'That's where your mother and I had our wedding luncheon.' Little did I imagine on that day, more than twenty years back, that I would be back having hoofed it all the way from Cairns.

Next, we passed my childhood home. I still haven't got used to the idea of someone else living in *my home*. I have had many *homes* since, but this was my first. The huge cactus out the front was still there and in full bloom. I pointed out to Flynn the window that used to be my room, the place I waited for the school bus, where I came off my bike, where my little dog was run over and where I planted the gum trees. Flynn may remember little of the one-minute tour but, in that minute, I recalled a thousand images, voices, people and events.

1981 At the following township, The Summit, we stopped for a drink and a pie at the local shop across the road from where one of my brothers lived.

1985 In Applethorpe, an eighty-year-old friend extracted himself from his gardening to enthusiastically shake hands with all and sundry. With a twinkle in his eye, and turning his head in the direction of the gathering clouds, he warned us, 'You might get a shower before the day is out. They're predicting storms.'

1988 As we came to the outskirts of Stanthorpe none other than my mother tumbled out of her red Toyota Corolla and came stumbling towards me. Not only was she still a good driver, but she also had some sprint left in her.

'Look, Mum,' I said, 'I'm wearing my hat.'

She laughed, gave me the once-over and declared, 'You're not looking as bad as you did on TV.' After a moist-eyed hug, Mum bundled back into the car and rushed off to finish preparing lunch for me. I was left smiling and shaking my head in amazement at the energy level of my eighty-one year old mother.

By then our group had grown to twenty. As we passed the Uniting Church, I pointed out to Flynn, whose short legs were still keeping up the pace admirably, 'This is where your mother and I were married.' To me it seemed like yesterday but, of course, to him, it was a lesson in Ancient History.

The Anglican Church opposite had posted a special sign on their maxi-noticeboard. 1990
We all lined up underneath and posed for photos while ominously overhead the dark clouds also lined up. With the cameras clicking, someone from behind commented, 'Look at those legs. Now those are real he-man calf muscles.' I decided they were talking about me, and I did begin to feel a tad he-man-ish at that point too.

Before tackling the final ten-kilometre leg to the famous finish line at Ma and Pa's farm, our group disbanded briefly in the centre of town for a lunch break. While most patronised the local cafés, I slipped away in the opposite direction to patronise my mother's cooking. It was soon evident I could have invited everyone to Mum's because she had turned on an unbelievable spread. Perhaps she thought it was a hunger strike I'd been on for eighty days.

As we re-grouped at the Presbyterian Church we began to see the results of the hard work that Hélène and her team of local coordinators had put in. A small crowd had gathered, braving the approaching rain clouds and toting multi-coloured helium balloons, overtones of our send-off in Cairns. Very fitting. Young and old, families and individuals, were milling and talking, greeting and laughing in a festive atmosphere. Though the clouds sank lower, the balloons and the spirits of all were flying high. One white balloon detached itself from its string and sailed upwards, a clearly defined dot against the darkening sky.

In the midst of it all I got to say a brief hello to Hélène, who was running around like a headless chook. Clipboard in hand, she was coordinating vehicles, permissions, warning signs and all the other behind-the-scenes logistics that had to happen for a large group to be walking on public roads. Another seventy had swelled our group to almost a hundred, among them an eight-year-old lad sporting a brand-new, royal-blue shirt identical to my own. Joseph was walking beside his Dad and we were both smiling.

1992   Two kilometres further on was another pick-up point for more walkers. The coordinators were all smiles too as our procession rounded the corner into view. Then a little further on there was another cheer squad – a dozen of my boys' mates from their adopted school for the year, Glen Aplin.

1994   They held high four cards making the number: *1994*, the number of kilometres we had walked. Was it possible? We only had six more kilometres to go! I went cold and blinked away tired tears. It was real. I was within a spit of achieving this impossible goal. I stumbled on, exhausted, peopled-out, longing for it all to be over. And along with me, ahead of me, behind me and all around me were people and balloons. I overheard scores of excited conversations while the balloons were being dragged sideways by the strong wind. Sky Blue was bouncing it out up in front with his little group of admirers, none more so, of course, than Veronica. Big Red was there, easily spotted, chatting to all and sundry, and enjoying the limelight. In contrast,

I felt depleted, dazed, each foot falling automatically in front of the other – a rhythm learned over 2000 long kilometres.

Ronnie fell in step with me and asked, 'Are you excited?'

I replied by quoting the opening line of Dickens' *A Tale of Two Cities: It was the best of times, it was the worst of times*. I explained that there had been so much pain and hardship along the way, so much frustration, not to mention the drudgery of getting up each day and constantly moving; I had used the word *relentless* a lot during The Walk. It was obvious Ronnie wasn't too impressed with my answer.

He chided me gently, explaining that memories are like a photo album. 'You can pick the ones you keep and put them in the album. Don't keep the bad ones,' he exhorted.

I felt something like *weary anger* bubble up from somewhere inside me and I retorted somewhat unkindly, 'A more honest alternative would be to just put *all* the photos in the album, because that would be more realistic of what I've been through.' I didn't feel that Ronnie was allowing me to validate my experience, my achievement, in all its complex reality, the good and bad mixed together. A dark cloud settled over me, something akin to the ever-threatening ones above and I walked in heavy silence.

I didn't notice Clayton come alongside.

'Howdy,' he said. As our eyes met he asked, 'How are you feeling?' I tried to think how I could explain it better than I had to Ronnie.

'I could give different answers,' I replied, 'depending on which *thread* I choose to talk about. There was the pain and discomfort thread that ran from beginning to end. There was also, without any doubt, the sense of God's control and leading that wound its way through the whole experience. There was joy and fun there too, and the sense of achievement and accomplishment. There was exhaustion and sleep deprivation. It was all bound up there together.'

Clayton said, 'It sounds a bit like life in general, doesn't it?' On hearing those few, simple words, I felt a great YES-wave flow over me, a sense of being validated, that the pain was okay, that it was all okay. That was my experience and it was all okay. It was even okay that I didn't feel like talking right then.

1999 Our last pick-up point was the little Severnlea Uniting Church just one kilometre from the finish line. Dozens of cars were parked untidily. Scores of people were milling around, almost all of them looking at the sky. The first of the big drops began to fall. We hesitated. Should we shelter in the church or should we walk? About fifty people were waiting to do just that – walk. Many had come from afar – from Home Hill, Cairns, and even Port Augusta in South Australia. All were watching, huddling, hesitating.

'Let's go and just get wet,' I said. And we went. All 150 of us. Like the mice of Hamelin, we moved forward, drawn in the one direction. Suddenly, like magic, carried by the wind, came the distant sound of the Pied Piper himself, invited by Hélène for the occasion. His bagpipe music wailed down the dirt road calling us on. It cried its melancholic tunes to the gum trees and fruit trees. Its highland strains warmed and cheered us all, drawing us on, while the rain fell heavier. His next tune broke in waves of emotion:

No matter how far or how wide I roam, home ...
I still call Australia home ...

And the rain kept falling.

My Mum had hoped to walk the last kilometre with me, but now, because of the rain, I knew she'd be with the waiting crowd up at the homestead, high and dry on the verandah. I felt a wave of sadness wash over me. Mum had walked the first kilometre with me in Cairns and she had her elderly heart set on walking this last one.

By then dozens of umbrellas had opened like giant mushrooms. As the umbrellas went up, the balloons slowly started sinking – as did my hat. Wet through, it sagged limply. We were a good pair, me and my hat!

We moved aside to let a car pass. It rolled up slowly beside us and stopped for the driver to let out his passenger. An unidentifiable person bundled clumsily out, completely enveloped from head to foot in a large, semi-transparent white raincoat. It was my mother! I should have known a little water wouldn't stop that indefatigable little lady. She wouldn't have missed this for anything. It was hard to tell through the rain, but I think I saw a tear in her eye.

The group slowed and stalled. Faces turned back towards me, urging me forward with Carnsey and Dave at the front of the pack. I took Mum with me as the mob separated to let us through. That's when I was reunited with my sons; I should have known they'd be at the front! Group momentum picked up again. When we rounded the bottom of the orchard, the piper came into view, standing solemnly beside the finish line and pumping out strains of Amazing Grace. Mum was right behind me, which, now I come to think of it, is where she has been my whole life.

As I walked those last metres to the tape strung across the path, the tears began. There was Hélène holding one end of the tape. The tears flowed. Dave, Carnsey and I pushed through the tape together.

It was over.

I was home.

2000

Taking Hélène in my arms, I looked over her shoulder and saw, through blurred vision, the hundreds of people crowded on the homestead verandah, spilling out onto the lawn, clapping and cheering.

A camera was aimed at me, filming the first words I would say. I didn't think I'd be able to get anything out, but the words came spontaneously, straight from the heart, without thought or premeditation:

'I'm never *ever* doing this again.'

over page ⟶

Epilogue

It's been six years since The 2000 Walk.

The day we crossed the finish line, the local Stanthorpe newspaper, *The Border Post*, published a front-page article, including a large photo of me and my boys in our royal-blue shirts. I keep a copy of that article; it's called *Walking home with dad*. One of my most treasured memories of The Walk, without a doubt, is doing it as a family. It *did* become a family affair, and we *were* in it together. All three generations.

November 11, 2010.

And now, in hindsight, I am more grateful than ever to my amazing mother, wife and boys for their support of this crazy project, expressed in different ways and at different times - thanks family! But beyond my own personal and family experience, The 2000 Walk became a very *big* affair. Many hundreds of people were involved in some way, most of them behind the scenes. Lawrence Springborg, Member of Parliament for Southern Downs, summed it up succinctly in his speech on our arrival day, 'This isn't something that has come together in just a few weeks or even months. These things take years and they take many, many people working side by side.'

And oh how I am grateful to you too, the *'many, many'* who made possible both The Walk and this book! You know who you are, and even though some of you were in different corners of the globe, we really did all work side by side.

Speaking of working side by side, my feet totally recovered within just a week or two of finishing The Walk. Dr Thong-man was right. After my eighty-day odyssey, they just needed a rest.

The thirty-three Chilean miners also recovered, and the news came out that, with grateful hearts to God, twenty-two of them became believers in Jesus. Theirs was a remarkable story with a happy end to a sixty-nine day ordeal.

My paperback walking companion, Bernard, was less fortunate. He succumbed to an amoeba attack and had to be airlifted back to France where he took a month to recover. Sadly, he fell short of his 1700 kilometre goal by only thirty-five kilometres.

As for me, I don't *really* know how many kilometres I *actually* walked. It was difficult to keep track of how much the Gentle Annies added and the short cuts knocked off. As a result some of our distance measurements were approximate. But I *did* walk all the way from Cairns to Stanthorpe.

Soon after the completion of The Walk, we three Wiggles went our separate ways. Dave and Carnsey each continued courting and, within two

G'day bloke

weeks of each other, married a year later. Carnsey stayed with his bride in Brisbane and Dave moved with his to Sydney. Our friendships have been reshaped by The Walk but, contrary to predictions prior to our adventure, we are still very much on speaking terms. I owe a lot to my fellow walkers. I would never have done it without them.

Over the intervening years, as Ronnie so rightly predicted, the photos in my grey-cells album *have* been shuffled and sorted. I thoroughly enjoy talking about The Walk and reminiscing about the great people I met and places I passed through. I focus not so much on the pain but on the pleasure, not so much on the fatigue but on the friends.

These last years I've been back in France enjoying walking alongside my friendly canal again, but often yearning to return to my homeland. My boys, now teenagers, have talked of walking across France one day and at one stage tried to lure me into their dreams and schemes.

And, you know what?

I actually think I *would* like to do something like that again!

important update over page →

Update

In the six years since The 2000 Walk, the number of languages still needing Bible translation, but with no work even started, has decreased from 2252 to fewer than 1800.

While that's encouraging, we still have a huge task ahead of us. But it is an achievable task – just like walking 2000 kilometres – one step at a time.

The 2000 Walk was a tool to promote awareness of the huge task ahead. The book you are holding in your hands is also a tool for the same purpose – and you can play a very important role in that by sharing it with others. Please lend it around, buy copies as gifts and promote it among your contacts.

www.walkinghome2000.com

Sav

walkinghome2000@gmail.com

ps.   you can find out the current translation
       needs at: www.wycliffe.net/statistics

Printed in Australia
AUOC01n1558050816
277943AU00001B/1/P